ENOUGH TO RISE

A Journey of Reclaiming Self-Worth &
Breaking the Cycle of Generational Trauma

JENN M. CHOI

For my mom and dad,

in love and in legacy.

CONTENTS

PART 3: BREAKING THE CYCLE

AUTHOR'S NOTE

THIS IS A self-help memoir about my personal journey—one of reclaiming self-worth, healing from generational trauma, and breaking free from unhealthy patterns. It is written through my lens, perspective, and emotional experience.

Relationships can be complicated, even with the people we love and admire—especially within families. But relationships can also be beautiful, transformational, and healing.

The people mentioned in this book, including those closest to me, are presented as I experienced them at particular moments in time. They are human beings with full lives beyond these pages. I recognize that their experiences and truths may differ from mine. Multiple truths can coexist at the same time. Just as light can dance with shadows—and love with pain. In some cases, names and identifying details have been changed to protect privacy. Where names remain, their inclusion is meant to honor the significance of these relationships in my life, not to define or diminish anyone else's story. So many people have changed my life for the better. I write my story with deep gratitude for them.

Though parts of my story may feel emotionally raw for others, I write from a place of love and care. My hope is that by sharing my story, I can empower others to reflect upon their own journeys as they walk toward more freedom and love.

INTRODUCTION

DEAR READER,

Life breaks us open. Sometimes gently. Sometimes with the force of a raging fire that burns down all that we once knew. And when the smoke clears, we must gather the strength to begin again, even when we feel broken and lost. Little by little, we spread our wings, wider and wider, until we can rise from the ashes like a phoenix. Until we find out who we truly are.

Maybe that's why you're here. Chances are, if you're reading this book, there's a gap between who you are and who you want to become, or where you're at and where you wish to be. Perhaps you're feeling stuck at a juncture in your life where you want to make a big-ass change, whether your current challenge is about your career, your relationships (including your relationship with yourself), your family, or some other aspect of your life that's calling for attention. But change can feel scary. And it's hard to know what you truly want, and who you truly are, beyond familial, cultural, and societal conditioning—especially if you grew up with childhood trauma as I did. Especially if there's a part of you inside that feels unworthy.

Ever since I was an awkward girl with a bowl haircut growing up in Chinatown San Francisco, I've struggled with self-worth issues. No matter how hard I strived to be the perfect daughter, I never felt good enough. There was a lot of love in my family—but also unspoken pain. Like many children of immigrants, I grew up feeling the impact of generational trauma, long before I had the words to understand it. For me, that included emotional and physical neglect and abuse. Yes, my parents loved me deeply, and I truly believe they tried their best. However, I had to face the hard truth that they also hurt me. By the age of four, I already knew how to fend for myself, locked in an apartment alone for hours, staying small to stay safe. My obedience was shaped by fear—by the threat of punishment and violent outbursts I didn't know how to predict. I wasn't allowed to cry and didn't feel free to be me. I felt unseen, unheard, and unworthy.

I buried my painful memories in my subconscious, unaware of my complex childhood trauma until decades later. Trauma is an intensely stressful experience that feels so overwhelming or scary that it changes how we think, feel, and act moving forward. As a coping mechanism, we often repress our trauma to survive. Until I was in my twenties, I believed that I lived a totally normal life with a happy childhood. That's how far I'd repressed what had happened to me. Then everything changed when both my parents fell gravely ill, just as I turned twenty-six. As I cared for two sick parents, I was finally forced to face the adult manifestations of my childhood trauma: low self-worth, anxiety, overwork, fear of abandonment, unhealthy relationship patterns, people-pleasing, perfectionism, and repeat burnout—they all showed up despite my outward-facing success. I also had to face the demons of my sexual trauma, including an assault in my twenties.

When I lost both of my beloved parents, I felt like a big part of me died too. Losing them set my whole existence ablaze. All my life, I wanted to prove that I was good enough to my Chinese immigrant parents. But with both parents gone, who would give me the validation I needed so badly? Why did I fuck up and fail to save them? Would I ever feel worthy?

I was deep in an existential crisis, feeling lost and confused about who I was.

Thankfully, as you'll come to see, my parents' lives were not in vain. Within these pages, you'll follow me as I embark on a healing journey that breaks me free. Rising from the ashes of my grief, I break free from past conditioning to reclaim my self-worth and break the cycle of trauma in taboo ways that would make my ancestors blush. I work with therapists and coaches, sit with psychedelic medicines, tap into sexuality to reclaim my body, and seek alternative healing modalities that ultimately lead to my spiritual awakening.

However, it's not until I immigrate to Berlin, Germany, and become a mother that I truly understand the love from my parents—and for myself.

When my son was born, parenthood opened a portal for me to the deepest healing. As I struggled through retriggered childhood trauma and rage episodes that threatened to destroy my marriage, I realized that my parents had experienced significant trauma in their own lives. Like me, my parents were trying to survive in a foreign land while living with their own repressed trauma from the Cultural Revolution in China and a family history of loss. I felt the weight of generational trauma—the imprints of war, revolution, migration, secrecy, and shame encoded into my DNA, passed down through generations of unresolved pain in my family.

At times I felt hopeless, almost on the brink of collapse. But I pushed forward with the strength and resilience that I'd also inherited from my parents and ancestors.

Through healing my childhood trauma, forgiving my parents, creating a loving family with my partner, and finding my true self, I break the cycle of generational trauma. I see that the validation I sought needed to come from *within me*. That I'm enough at last—as I was all along.

Maybe you're like me, someone who's struggled with self-worth too. Someone who feels a sense of void inside, despite outward-facing success ticking the boxes of what your parents, culture, or society tell you that you "should" do. Like nothing you ever do is good enough. Like parts of you are stuck or lost. Maybe you've awakened to the pain of your childhood trauma. Maybe you've just begun.

Wherever you are in your journey, I'm here to meet you and offer a space for you to self-reflect. I'm also here to give you hope. Hope that you too can heal and break free.

How This Book Will Flow

I'm writing this book as a hybrid between memoir and self-help, with about 80 percent of the content as memoir. Why? Because there's great power in vulnerable storytelling. I believe that the more I can honestly share and give you examples from my own life—which is still a work-in-progress—the more you can reflect upon your own.

Through vivid scenes, raw emotions, and personal reflections, I invite you into my story in the hope that it makes you feel more seen. My story is personal, but the themes are universal. I'm writing from the lens of a child of immigrants, which is a much-needed perspective. However, this book is really for anyone who wants to reclaim their self-worth and break the cycle of generational trauma, no matter their background. The narrative is a forward-moving story, so you can move forward with my past selves as I grow through the ups and downs of my healing journey.

Then, at the end of most chapters after the memoir piece, I include a self-help section called "Moment to Self-Reflect." In these sections, I share valuable life lessons, transformative concepts, and reflection questions. My hope is that they'll help you connect with the chapter on a personal level and explore how it might relate to your own circumstances and experiences. Lessons and concepts will continue to build upon each other throughout the book to make things easier to understand. I also reflect back on the events of the chapter from the lens of a more self-aware Jenn, who is now speaking to you from the present as an empowerment coach.

As a professional empowerment coach and Designing Your Life coach, I've seen how valuable it is to help people illuminate their own truths through self-reflection, rather than tell them what to do. Over the past five years as a certified coach, I've witnessed my amazing coaching clients improve their relationships with family, romantic partners, friends, work, money, and health—all by improving their relationship with themselves and reclaiming their self-worth. I love helping my clients uncover who they are beyond familial, cultural, and societal conditioning to design the life and work that they dream of. And I'm excited to bring elements of that to you here!

Also of important note, although I'm not a therapist, I've been in psychotherapy for many years and have worked with various incredible mental health professionals during my journey. Thus, I believe that the combination of me speaking from my personal experience as a human and guiding reflection as a trauma-informed coach is powerful. I don't aim to replace professional support, but I do aim to help illuminate areas where you might feel called to get support. You don't have to do this alone.

With all that's going on in the world, I feel the urgency of getting this book to you. It has taken many tears to write this, but I'm grateful for the process. This book has created a safe container for me to self-reflect, and I hope that it offers you a safe space to do the same.

The Power of Self-Reflection

Throughout this book, I'll invite you to self-reflect. At times, self-reflection might feel uncomfortable, especially if you weren't encouraged to think or feel for yourself growing up. Especially if you come from a family, culture, or society where you're expected to bend over backward to serve everyone else at the cost of yourself. You might also feel the urge to rush through or skip the questions because you don't have time. I understand. In our fast-paced world, many of us are busy, and taking the time to process our thoughts, feelings, and experiences can feel indulgent. But what if I told you that the answers to our greatest questions often lie within us?

Self-reflection has many benefits, including increased self-awareness, personal growth, better decision-making, more clarity about goals, reduced stress, and heightened self-compassion. That's why I encourage you to make this time and space for yourself.

You deserve it.

If you have a journal or another place to keep notes, I suggest that you write down some of your reflections. Writing is one of the most powerful ways to bring your feelings, thoughts, memories, and beliefs to light. It's an accessible, free, and beautiful way to hold space for yourself. Since concepts and lessons will build upon each other, it might be easier for you to keep all your reflection notes in a place that you can revisit later on. I've done that with my own journals. And in the future, you'll also get to look back and celebrate how far you've come!

As you're reflecting, remember that this is for you—not for anyone else. Some of the thoughts, feelings, or memories that come up might feel challenging. You might feel tempted to hold back on the truth of your experience, filter what you say, or protect others by omitting important details. But the more you give yourself permission to dig deeper, the more you can heal and design the life *you* dream of. Allowing yourself to feel the full range of emotions is a radical act of self-love. Above all, I encourage you to be gentle with yourself. To give yourself the space, care, and grace that you need.

You hold the keys to unlock your personal power. You can break free from past trauma and design the life, love, and work you dream of. This book isn't just about my story. It's also about your story, what meaning you make out of everything that's happened to you, and what future you want to create. It's a reclamation. Of yourself. And all that you're destined to become.

Perhaps, if you still have your parents, you can heal and break free while they're still alive, finding your true self, compassion, and repair before it's too late. I lament that I lost my beloved parents so early but wish that my lessons reach you in time.

We are the generation that our ancestors have been waiting for. It is time to reclaim our inherent worth and generational gifts. As we heal our individual wounds, we heal collective wounds. As we change, the world around us changes.

Thank you for choosing to embark on this journey of transformation with me. May we carry our torches through the shadows and step into the fucking brilliance of our own light.

I am worth it, as are you.

With love,
Jenn

PART 1

BREAKING DOWN

1

BEND BUT NOT BREAK

I DROVE ALONG the highway, waiting for it to split open and swallow me up whole into the earth. On the side of the rubber-marred asphalt by the bay, a tuft of green weed burst through the ground. It rebelliously defied gravity. But me? I sunk lower and lower into despair.

My palms sweat onto the steering wheel like guilt oozing from my pores. I turned on the radio to drown out my thoughts. But no matter how high I blasted the volume, no matter how catchy the song, it was futile. Visions of my dad struggling to breathe with end-stage lung disease kept invading. Anxiety about my mom's precarious health also crept in. I was terrified of losing my parents. Terrified of doing something wrong. No matter what I did, it never seemed good enough. But I had to choose what to do, even when the pressure felt like it would crush me.

I had two choices that day. Just like I had two names.

Born one ordinary February morning to my extraordinary immigrant parents, I was given two names: my English name, Jennifer, and my Chinese name, 蔡路萱, *Choi Lo Shurn*. One to assimilate as an immigrant family living in San Francisco, and one to honor our ancestral heritage. With these names, I lived a dual life. Not quite Chinese enough for my parents, nor American enough for mainstream society, I was a mishmash of both cultures. With a high nose, full lips, sharp face, tan skin, brown eyes, and black hair, even my appearance seemed mixed. In college, my classmates said I looked like Pocahontas or Eva Mendes, the Cuban American actress. And in Chinatown, shopkeepers would gasp when I opened my mouth.

"Wah, you speak our language?" they'd ask in Cantonese, one of the main Southern Chinese languages. Everyone seemed confused about who I was, including me.

Growing up, I never really questioned my names. I just took them as they were, things assigned to me because adults knew better. As a kid, you don't typically ponder such existential things like, *What does my name mean? Who am I really?* And really, in my family, you didn't question things at all. Obedience, filial piety, and external achievements were currencies for love. From a young age, I was taught that you obey your elders, no matter what. Just as generations of my ancestors did under the ancient Confucian concept of filial piety. Besides, there was no space for questions—I was too busy pleasing everyone else.

But on March 8, 2010, everything changed. I'll remember that date for the rest of my life. You know what they say: When it rains it pours. And damn, did it fucking pour.

At the time, I was twenty-six years old and working at Exelixis, a biotech company in South San Francisco that specialized in cancer medicines. I'd just celebrated three years working as an assistant research scientist and was proud to have such an impactful job. However, the days in the laboratory started to drag. Although I bonded with some amazing colleagues, my day-to-day role had little social interaction. I longed to connect with humans instead of DNA sequencing machines. On the bright side, telling hot dudes at bars that I was a cancer researcher definitely scored me points. And the salary was great, far beyond what I'd ever imagined as a kid from Chinatown with a bowl haircut. My boss, Jana, was awesome too. She was supportive, empathetic, and a great mentor.

On the surface, I'd made it. I had a stable job that afforded me an apartment with roommates, a vibrant social life where I partied with friends, and a job that my immigrant parents wouldn't be ashamed of. Yet underneath the sheen of achievement, I was always expecting the other shoe to drop, never believing that the good times could last long. Just as I never believed I was good enough, no matter how much I busted my ass off at work.

As I was driving that fateful morning in 2010, Jana called. "Jenn? Hey, I know you weren't going to come into the office today, but I really think you should. There's an urgent All Hands meeting."

Shit. I could hear the panic in her voice. This was something huge. And I knew my chill boss well. She was never one to raise an alarm unless there was a need to. For a split second, I felt like I was standing in the eye of the storm. A quiet moment where I had to choose what to do. *I could go to the office, but what about mom?* A lump grew in my throat.

As I ended the call with Jana, my hands clenched the steering wheel until my knuckles turned white. My mom had been complaining about sudden weakness, to the point of feeling faint. She had missed school for the past three days, which was uncharacteristic, as she always made it to class. Though she was already in her sixties, my mom had gone back to university to get her master's degree so that she could teach math.

I was scared that it was something serious, especially since my dad—who we called *Baba*—was already gravely ill. Sick with severe lung disease at seventy-two years old, Baba had been living in a care facility for the past three months, miles from home and hooked up to oxygen. Having one parent sick was already devastating. I did not know if I could handle any more bad news.

I had taken the day off so I could bring my mom to see a doctor at the hospital, but the call from Jana threw a wrench in my plans. *Fuck. Should I choose to be a bad daughter, or a bad employee?* I felt paralyzed but knew I needed to make a move. So, I did what I always did—consult with my mom, the ultimate boss.

Fifteen minutes later, I pulled up to our family home on Mason Street, near the border between Chinatown and Nob Hill. Cable cars climbed up and down steep hills in our neighborhood, and the bay glistened in the background, punctuating the horizon with teal water that cradled the sky. When it wasn't foggy, you could see sailboats gliding by in the distance—like something straight out of a postcard. Our block was diverse, as colorful as the buildings painted blue, yellow, and pink. There were some white residents, but many neighbors were Chinese immigrant families like ours. Laundry hung outside apartment windows to dry, the cotton garments waving like flags staking their belonging in a foreign land. I could speak about this neighborhood for hours and not even need to catch my breath. I love it that much.

But when it comes to telling you about my family home—well, that's a different story. When I think about the rent-controlled, two-bedroom apartment where my family lived for twenty years, a knot forms in my stomach. I couldn't understand how we lived in such a beautiful neighborhood but let our home decay the way it did. Like many Asian parents, mine were hoarders, avoiding waste like the plague. We accumulated old furniture picked off the street, saved every magazine, and even washed plastic sporks for reuse.

The apartment itself had such potential. We had high ceilings, crown molding, bay windows, and those long, narrow hallways typical of San Francisco apartments. My mom even bought a used piano for the living room, marginally elevating a space worn down by wear. But you can't sleep in potential. And potential doesn't smell like old musty towels mixed with mildew wafting from the bathroom. Nor does it feel like sticky peanut oil residue coating every surface in the kitchen. If you walked through the hallway, you'd also have to watch your step because at any moment a painting could fall over on you. My mom's paintings not only hung on both sides of our hallway but also stood two layers deep on the floor, leaning against the wall. Getting from the front of the home to the back felt like an obstacle course.

It pains me to talk about this home. Growing up, I felt so ashamed of how dirty it was that I never invited friends over. The stains on our burgundy carpet in the living room. The grime on our windows. Even our mop and vacuum collected dust since they sat untouched in a backroom crammed with stuff behind the kitchen. We owned a feather duster with brown chicken feathers, but my parents never used it to dust. Instead, my mom used it to hit me whenever I misbehaved as a kid. "Aiyaaa! *Nay gah say nui bao!*" she'd shout, calling me a dead bad girl in Cantonese as the thin wooden handle cracked against my flesh. I can still feel the sting of the lashings, my body recoiling in response. However, I got used to it. Corporal punishment is common in Chinese culture, at least historically. Children shiver with fear when they see a feather duster, a household item synonymous with harsh discipline. To me, this was all normal. The hitting, the forced obedience, the decay of our home.

However, what we accept as normal can still hurt. What we put up with can still push us away. I felt immense relief when I moved out at twenty-two. But I still call it home, as I think I will forever, a part of it in me everywhere I go. A part of our childhood home always lives within us. A place of dichotomy, of complicated love, of family.

We lived on the second floor of a three-story apartment building with six units. After I parked my car, I nervously walked up the stairs. My shoes clacked against the metal edges of the faded blue stairs, my fingers skimming the chipped brown paint on the handrails. When I finally reached our door, I immediately wanted to sneeze, an involuntary muscle memory from my childhood growing up allergic to the pervasive dust and mold.

Every time I put my keys in and turned the doorknob, I'd mentally brace myself for whatever I'd see on the other side. Today was no different.

As soon as I entered the apartment, my mom spoke. "Jenn, ah. You're home," she said in Cantonese.

I stepped into the doorway of my mom's bedroom at the front of the home, next to the living room. Since I was about eight years old, my mom slept by herself in a separate bedroom from my dad. I never asked why. Nor did I ever ask why my dad, my younger brother, and I were forced to sleep in the same bedroom together until I went to college at eighteen. Our bedroom was down the hallway, with a bunk bed for me and my brother Stan that made an L-shape with my dad's bed. There was no space to be me in that cramped room. No space to express myself growing up. Even after I moved out, Stan and Baba still shared a bedroom, my brother sleeping on the bottom bunk as he always did. But in all fairness, maybe my mom needed the space for her stuff. Her art and math books piled high on her dresser, with mounds of clothes toppling all over the room.

My mom lay curled up in bed, surrounded by the stacks of weeks-old Chinese newspapers she normally slept with. I hated seeing her so weak.

For days, she huffed and puffed going up the stairs. Her poop was black as coal, an ominous sign.

I walked next to her bed. "Mommy, I'm worried about you. We should go to the hospital. But there's also some big news at work. My boss seems concerned. What should I do?"

She looked up at me through her reading glasses and straightened a copy of *World Journal,* one of the largest Chinese newspapers in the United States, in her hands. "Jenn ah, obey your boss. Go to work first," she insisted in Cantonese.

I nodded obediently, exactly as a dutiful eldest child would. Whatever my mom said was it, the last word, the law of the land. She was the matriarch of our family, and I, a humble daughter. Even in my twenties, I felt like a little girl in her presence. "Okay, Mommy, I'll be back right after. But can you please get ready so we can go to the hospital when I'm done?"

"*Ho lah,*" my mom sighed, agreeing to my plea.

Before we move on, I want to clarify a few things about my cultural background.

Chinese isn't just one spoken language. Rather, it's a family of languages—or dialects, depending on who you ask—united by a shared written system. Mandarin, the official language of modern-day China, sounds very different from some regional languages. My ancestors are from the Guangdong (Canton) Province, and they spoke mainly Taishanese and Cantonese.

Although my parents spoke multiple languages, they typically spoke to me in Cantonese. Sometimes, especially in our family home or around other relatives, I'd reply in it when I knew the words. But it was a struggle for me to express myself. When it was something simple like talking about food or making plans, I'd use Cantonese. But whenever I needed to explain something complicated—like what happened at work or share my feelings—I'd use English, my main language.

There was constant code-switching in my family between languages, which is common for many immigrant families. For the flow of this book, I'll write our dialogue primarily in English moving forward, without indicating every time we code-switch. But I want to share with you a few important reflections. First, it requires an incredible amount of mental energy to code-switch, which can be a barrier in communication. Second, constantly straddling between languages can create identity confusion. And third, sadly, there was so much lost in translation between my parents and me. It's no wonder why I grew up so confused about myself.

That day in March, at twenty-six, I was as confused as ever, bracing myself for whatever would come.

On Highway 101, I cranked open the window of my beat-up burgundy 1990 Honda Accord, letting the California breeze blow in my face as I drove to work. Thirty minutes later, I pulled up to the parking lot outside our lab. I crawled out and locked my car, letting myself linger for longer than usual in front of the building. Letting myself look at the lab as I'd known it, as my safe routine, for the past few years.

Something was brewing. I could tell. Especially when I realized that some of my colleagues were assigned to different meeting rooms than the cafeteria, which is where I was headed. My pace quickening, I crossed the street to the main building where our cafeteria was. Rows of foldable chairs packed the cafeteria. People whispered. Nerves cut like knives through the air.

I took a seat, bouncing my legs in anticipation. Then our CEO finally broke the news. The moment he started talking, I already knew: We were toast. Stunned, I scanned the room, looking at everyone impacted. Damn. All of us, huh? Over two hundred people. Forty percent of the company, in total, laid off in a single day. He explained why this was necessary and shared some heartfelt words of empathy. But the words felt empty to me. Empty like my bank account if I couldn't recover fast enough. Corporate America can be so goddamn cruel.

After the announcement, I received a thick envelope from HR in another room. As I read through the details of my severance package, I felt momentary relief. Several months' worth of salary, not too bad. Kind of a jackpot even, buying me a few months off work to deal with my mom and dad's escalating health crisis.

What felt worse, though, was the blow to my ego. The blow to my already low self-worth, so intricately tied to my performance at work. I did my best and still got fired. *Was I really that useless? That dispensable?*

I didn't have time to process though. My mom was waiting for me. I rushed to my cubicle to collect my stuff. I tossed my clear laboratory glasses, a framed photo of the time my coworkers and I went bowling together, and some pens into a cardboard box. I murmured quick goodbyes to everyone, swore to connect on LinkedIn, and turned in my badge.

By noon that day, I was driving back the other direction on Highway 101 with a cardboard box in my trunk.

When I got back to the apartment on Mason Street as promised, my mom was ready to go. She wore brown cotton leggings, dyed black hair clipped into a messy bun to hide her age, and leather flats that had seen better days. At 5'3", she was an inch shorter than me but looked even smaller that day. She clung to my arm down the stairs, slid into the passenger seat, and off I drove. Straight to the emergency room of San Francisco General Hospital.

On the way to the hospital, I zoned in and out. It felt like a vivid fever dream, distorting any sense of reality. But my mom brought me back to my senses as soon as we pulled up to the hospital. I was heading toward the paid parking garage when my mom interrupted.

"Jenn ah. Wah! Look at the prices. So expensive! No. We park on the street," she ordered. Even in an emergency she wanted to save money. Typical.

"What? Are you serious? Finding a spot can take forever. We don't have time," I said.

My mom shook her head, her eyes flashing the way they usually did when she was about to hit me. "Aiya, just go! We're not parking here!"

"Fine." I complied, circling around until we finally found free street parking three blocks away.

She grabbed my arm as we got out of my car, the two of us inching our way toward the hospital. When we made it to the emergency room waiting area, it breathed a solemn air. Quiet filled the equidistant gaps between the plastic seats and the lone vending machine against the wall. By some miracle, there were only two other patients ahead of us. I had expected a packed room, maybe even someone screaming with broken bones or blood spurting from a cut finger, but it was oddly calm. We registered at the window and took our seats. Inside the stillness of our wait, I closed my eyes for a moment, imagining that a doctor would tell my mom everything was okay. *Nothing to worry about,* this fantasy doctor would say. *Just take some vitamins and sleep,* they'd advise. A girl can dream.

Just a few weeks ago, my mom was dancing in hip hop class, even at sixty-one years old. She loved moving her body, and dance classes at the community college were cheap. While many older Chinese people would've chosen tai chi as exercise instead, perhaps she found the gentle movements too slow. Tap dancing and hip hop were more suited for her intense personality. How sick could she possibly be?

Maybe this was just a false alarm? And how would we pay for all this? Sure, I had a decent severance check, but that money would burn quickly if we had to pay out of pocket. I wasn't sure what my mom's Medi-Cal insurance would cover. It's meant to cover low-income families, but you never know with American healthcare. Disease could make you destitute.

Suddenly, a woman's voice cut through the stillness. "Mrs. Choi? Please come this way."

A nurse escorted us to a small room, where we met a doctor. Tall, reassuring, and with glasses that framed his gentle eyes, he seemed like someone we could trust. So, we trusted him. Trusted him as he expressed his concern after taking my mom's blood pressure. Trusted him when, after taking a blood sample to measure iron levels, he told us that my mom had lost so much blood that she could've died. As it turns out, my mom's black stools were signs of internal bleeding. My heart pounded like a drum inside my chest.

The next thing we knew, my mom was rushed to another room further back with beds. She promptly started receiving liters of blood dripped into her thirsty veins. Even she was shocked. The smell of rubbing alcohol permeated the room as my mom let the nurse poke her with needles. I felt helpless watching my mom lay in a bed surrounded by machines monitoring her vital signs. Frozen as a nurse whisked her away for a CT scan. Once again, I felt like a bad daughter. I should've taken her to the hospital sooner. Stupid me. Stupid, unworthy me.

Numb, I wandered like a zombie through the hospital doors and across the street. Casual dining options dotted the working-class area, reflecting the international flavors of its Latino and Asian immigrant residents. Food was the last thing on my mind, but I knew I had to eat. It'd been a full day since my last meal. I stumbled into a Vietnamese sandwich shop, which I found comforting. Maybe it was the Asian lady behind the counter who looked about the same age as my mom. Or because it reminded me of one of my favorite childhood meals, a savory barbeque pork banh mi sandwich from Little Paris, a Vietnamese restaurant in Chinatown. Either way, it felt like a small moment of normalcy in all the chaos of the day. Two sandwiches later, I mustered up the courage to slink back across the street.

I pushed through the hospital doors, only to find out that things had changed yet again. My mom had moved out of emergency triage to a new room upstairs in inpatient care.

I walked into her room and gasped. "Wow, Mommy, this is an upgrade!"

Her bed was right next to the window overlooking the rolling hills of our golden city. The sun was starting to set, and warm ochre rays bounced off the windows of Victorian-style homes where families gathered for dinner.

Because of the prep for the CT scan, my mom hadn't eaten in hours. I offered her an extra sandwich from my backpack, but she insisted on eating the hospital food because she didn't want it to go to waste. In her eyes, even a single grain of rice lost would be a travesty. When I was a kid, she warned me that every grain of rice left in my bowl would be the number of pimples on my future husband's face. I licked every bowl clean.

When a nurse rolled the dinner tray in, it looked like the stuff Baba ate at the care facility. My mom scarfed down the mashed potatoes, cubed meat in gravy, and a carton of apple juice. After her last bite, I got up from my chair at the foot of her bed and moved it to the head, sitting closer to her.

"Well, at least I don't have anywhere else to go tomorrow. They fired almost half of us. But I have enough money to take some time off and figure it out. I'm okay," I said. *Just like I always have to pretend to be okay*, I thought.

My mom pursed her lips. "Ah, Jenn ah . . . you're not worried?"

"No." I laughed awkwardly, suppressing my anxiety. "I just need to be here for you and Baba."

Suddenly, a young Asian doctor with thick black hair and a chiseled face entered the room, extending his hand to my mom. For the purposes of this book, we'll call him Dr. Chan. "Hi, Mrs. Choi. I'm Dr. Chan. I'll be the oncology doctor on your case from now on."

My heart dropped to the floor. I knew what that fancy word "oncology" meant—it meant cancer. The fucking thing that I'd been researching for years in the lab. I'd seen and studied how cancer ruined other people's lives. I hated that it now terrorized my family too. As the doctor showed us the CT scan results and explained to my mom in Cantonese what they meant, my panic rose.

"Mrs. Choi, we believe that you might have stomach cancer," he revealed.

I looked over at my mom quietly as I let out a deafening scream inside my head. A few moments later, I asked him what was next.

"We need to do more tests to confirm anything. Tomorrow we'll take a biopsy. I know it's been a long day for both of you, so please try to get some rest," he said.

It was the permission both of us needed. Within the course of a mere nine hours, my entire life's priorities had shifted. Out the window, city lights flashed like a stream of stars, and the weary sun had long gone over the horizon.

After he left the room, I took my mom's hand. "I'm sorry."

"Ah? Sorry? For what? This is life. At least he spoke Cantonese. He's handsome, isn't he? Do you think he's married?"

I smiled and let out a sigh of relief. Even after the cancer bomb dropped, she was still the same mom I knew. I found reassurance in that, and with it, I let go for the night.

The next morning, I brought a container of *jook*, rice porridge, to my mom. It's what Chinese people always eat when someone is sick. Rice, the all-in-one deal—not only does it give your future spouse pimples, but it also magically heals every ailment.

My mom slurped up the *jook* in her hospital bed with vigor, her face appearing radiant again despite the circumstances. Well, at least her blood transfusion worked. My morning coffee did not. I could feel the heaviness of my eyelids, my body crying for rest. The bright natural daylight of the hospital room did wake me up a little though.

After she finished eating, I pulled out the day's edition of *World Journal* from my purse, placing it on my mom's lap in bed. I had picked up a copy on my way to the hospital, not wanting her to feel too disconnected from her routine. As she spread open the pages, I decided that it was finally time to bring up my dad.

"What do we do about Baba?" I asked.

"You can't tell him yet," my mom firmly replied. She stared me straight in the eyes, pupil to pupil like daggers.

The weight of her words felt like a giant elephant trying to balance itself on my shoulders. My mind immediately flashed to a vision of my dad, with his innocent face, in the care facility wondering when my mom would come visit as she normally did. They'd been married for almost thirty years. Ever since he got sick, she'd been by his side every day, so unless she got out soon, there was no way I could keep this secret.

"And Stan?" I nervously inquired.

Two years younger than me, my brother, Standish, still lived at home with my mom. I had called him to let him know that Mom had to stay in the hospital but didn't let him know how serious it was yet. I wanted to protect him but also felt guilty holding back the truth.

My mom stared at the furrows between my eyebrows and sighed. "Well . . . you should tell him. Who else will take care of Baba if you're stuck here with me?"

For the first time in two days, I felt a sense of relief. Now the secret would be shared between the three of us. The weight of the elephant lifted a little. Jumping into responsible eldest daughter mode, I hatched up a plan. I'd be with my mom in the hospital for most of the day while Stan took care of Baba. Then I'd drop by to visit my dad too, nonchalantly, like everything was normal. When Baba worried, we would just make up an excuse that mom was busy studying for a big math test. *Genius*, I convinced myself. *So believable!* And it was. Our white lie about my mom wouldn't be too far from the truth. At least, this was the lie that I told myself.

It was on that day, in between a secret and a lie, that I learned the true meaning of my name *Choi Lo Shurn*. As a tender afternoon glow filled the hospital room, I dozed off in the chair next to my mom's bed.

"You were born here, you know."

My mom's voice woke me from my brief slumber. Eyes half open, I turned to her. She sat upright with her thin glasses on, her usual newspaper spread across her lap.

"You were born in this hospital," she said.

I sat up too.

"That was a happy day. But long birth. So painful. A nurse helped us. Nice lady. Her name was Jennifer, and that's how you got your name—Jennifer too."

I smiled and wondered if Nurse Jennifer knew how much my parents appreciated her. Enough to name a firstborn after her. It struck me then that I never cared about the origin of my names until the moment I realized we might not have a whole lot of time left together. On one hand, I had an extremely common name for an American girl born in the 1980s. On the other hand, I hadn't ever met a single person with my name *Choi Lo Shurn*. It was a total mystery to me.

"What about my Chinese name? Where did that come from?" I asked.

My mom smiled too. "I made it up. That's why no one else has it."

I leaned in. "So, what does it mean then? Does it even have a meaning?"

"Of course! Your mom is really smart, you know. Didn't want you to have a stupid name. *Choi Lo Shurn* is the weed that grows on the side of the road."

I almost laughed out loud at this great reveal, imagining a crazy tuft of weeds blowing in the wind. "Um . . . why would you name me that?"

She looked at me with pride, as if I just came bursting out of her womb. "So you could be resilient. I had a tough life in China, you know. But I made it in America. I want you to make it too. The weed on the side of the road is tough. It bends, but it doesn't break. It just keeps growing."

I let it sink in for a moment. I let it all sink in. The layoff, the word "cancer," the lie we had to tell my dad. Suddenly, I felt within me an enormous pressure. The elephant struggling to balance on my shoulders was gone, replaced by something infinitely larger. A call to duty. A call to live up to the meaning of my name and prove my worth.

Bend but not break.

Bend but not break.

Bend but not break.

I repeated this in my head like a mantra. I drilled it into me, praying that it would relieve some of the pressure. But instead, it created more. More weight on an already traumatic day. More weight for me to carry, suffocating me with responsibility.

But I had to stay strong. I had to take care of everything, as I felt I needed to all my life. On the other side of our greatest challenges is the strength required to overcome them. Within my name, I uncovered that strength. I clung to that strength like a fistful of weed from the side of the road. I clung to it as I, at the young age of twenty-six, shoulders hunched over, tumbled into the abyss of uncertainty.

Moment to Self-Reflect

Sharing the events that kicked off my healing journey feels vulnerable. That fateful day in March when I was twenty-six years old, I wasn't sure how I'd make it through. And it was just the beginning of an intensely traumatic period of my life.

But here I am. Sharing openly with you. Because you might be at your own crossroads in life, where you have to choose what to do. Where you're wondering who you are. Where you might feel lost, stuck, or confused, but you can somehow sense that within you is the will to make it through. However, there may also be a part of you that feels unworthy—that nothing you ever do is good enough.

Self-Worth and Identity

When we don't feel worthy, it can significantly impact our sense of self. Self-worth is how much you value yourself and believe in your intrinsic worth as a person, beyond external validation or achievements. You could appear to be rocking life on the outside but still struggle with self-worth inside. When we have low self-worth, it can be difficult to uncover who we are beyond familial, cultural, and societal conditioning. As a result, it can be hard to figure out what we truly want in life and how to get there.

When I begin coaching my clients, I often invite them to reflect upon their own relationship with self-worth. I'll do the same here.

Reflection Questions:

- What is your current relationship with self-worth? In other words, do you feel inherently worthy and good enough?

- In which areas of your life do you feel worthy? In which areas of life do you feel unworthy?

2

WHEN HEROES FALL

BABA WAS MY silent superhero. Understated and humble, if he had a cape, it'd be invisible.

The first night we moved into our apartment on Mason Street when I was four years old, the urban cacophony of our new neighborhood wired me awake. The cable cars rang their bells, and the steel cables running beneath the tracks hummed. Like a little lion cub nervously learning to hunt in the night, I kept my eyes wide open, though it was already late.

My mom was asleep while Baba stayed up with me. Stan wasn't back yet. My little brother was thousands of miles away in China, where he'd been sent to be raised by my grandma when I was two years old and he was just a baby. Like many immigrant families, ours couldn't afford childcare, and we were forced to find alternative means. So it was just me and my parents when we first moved in, at least for the first few months.

I tossed and turned on a mattress in the middle of the living room floor. Amidst the city noise, I heard Baba's voice beckon my attention back inside.

"It's time for sleep," my dad whispered in his calming voice. Barely audible, yet potent.

I squinted to see his thin shadow slowly pacing around the room with his hands clasped behind his back like an ancient Chinese philosopher. He reached over to grab some cardboard moving boxes from the corner and built a makeshift bed next to me. I peered over at him, then up at the car headlights from the street that reflected off the freshly painted white ceiling, and dozed off.

This is one of my favorite memories of Baba, who showed me that love doesn't have to be shouted from rooftops if it can be shown through actions. I, on the other hand, was the opposite. I wanted him and everyone in our neighborhood to know that I loved him. When he'd leave for work through our building's clanging steel gate when I was a kid, I'd throw our window open and shout, "Bye, Daddy, I love you!"

I'd watch him glide downhill, wearing his wool gray slack pants, button-up checkered shirt, and brown jacket with a pack of Marlboro cigarettes in the left pocket. He'd look up to the window, with silver-rimmed eyeglasses floating above his bony cheekbones, and wave back at me. Then he'd keep walking, while the ring of keys on his belt loop jangled loudly until he made a right turn down Washington Street.

I declared my love in crisp American English, my identity split like our geography at the edge of Chinatown and Nob Hill. Across the street, kids like me played at the Chinese Recreation Center. Up the street, rich white people stayed at the Fairmont Hotel.

Many on our block spoke Cantonese or Taishanese, pointing to the migration history that shaped the city. The Gold Rush in the mid-1800s brought many Chinese immigrants from Guangdong Province to San Francisco and other parts of California. Thousands came for the chance at prosperity in the gold mines, kicking off many waves of migration. The first waves were mainly immigrants from Taishan, a rural region in Guangdong who spoke Taishanese, also known as Hoisanwa or Toisanwa to its speakers. This is where many of my ancestors were from. Then later waves included immigrants from Hong Kong, urban areas in Guangdong, and other provinces in China.

Fortunately, I grew up with lots of people who shared my roots. To put it into perspective for you, more than one-third of San Francisco residents are Asian, while about one-fifth of the population is of Chinese descent. And to describe my upbringing in taste, if you've ever had dim sum or wonton noodle soup, then you've tried Cantonese food.

Because I grew up surrounded by my ethnic community, I didn't feel like an outsider in the city. But I often felt like a foreigner in my own family. I twisted myself to conform to my parents' ideals imported from another land, all while drinking Coca-Cola and pledging allegiance to the flag of the United States of America. While my mom and dad expected me to be quiet, I belted out Mariah Carey songs, her cassette tapes repeating on my Sony Walkman. If you ever want me to serenade you with "Hero," or bless your holiday season with "All I Want For Christmas Is You" sung off-key, you just let me know.

I repeated my daily ritual of shouting, "I love you" to Baba just in case. Just in case something happened and Baba needed to know. The same way I needed to express how much I loved his delicious cooking. "*Wah, ho sik ah!*" I'd exclaim at nearly every meal.

"*Sik fan lah,*" Baba would announce whenever dinner was ready. Every dish was a labor of love.

As in many Asian households, food was our love language—love is shown but not spoken. Children across the world could spend their entire lives never hearing "I love you" from their Asian parents, which could clash for those of us living in the Western world where birthday cards and Valentine's Day cards all shout "I love you" in different languages. But while we may not speak love out loud, we ingest it with our mouths. A plate of cut fruit communicates, *let me nourish you.* A bowl of noodles, *let me warm you.* And when a parent asks whether you've eaten yet, they really mean, *I care for you.*

So while Baba never told me he loved me, nor spoke much at all, I felt his love through his cooking. When Baba was home, there would always be a pot or wok on the stove. He'd methodically drop pieces of ginger into hours-simmered chicken soup, mince garlic to stir fry with bok choy, and steam fish with soy sauce.

These family recipes came from multiple generations in Taishan, where my dad was born in a small village of stone houses. Though a war had ignited between China and Japan just months before, Baba emerged triumphant one October day in 1937 as the eldest son of my *Yeh Yeh* (paternal grandfather) and *Maa Maa* (paternal grandmother). With two older sisters born before him and three siblings after him in Taishan, Baba was a wise voice of reason. Quiet yet respected. Lanky yet strong. He watched his family cook many meals over their earthen stove as a kid.

Later, when he moved to bustling metropolitan Hong Kong at twelve, he further developed his palate. At first, he slept under a stairwell. He told me that he and his dad couldn't afford rent in a room with a proper bed. But as he worked hard and grew older, he made enough to afford breakfasts with shrimp dumplings, sweet coconut buns, and coffee. He didn't tell me much more about his time in Hong Kong. Nor what brought him and my Yeh Yeh there to begin with, even though Baba lived there for over twenty years. He also never told me why Yeh Yeh remarried and started a second family in Hong Kong that gave Baba four more siblings. I didn't ask why. I wouldn't find out for decades.

An unspoken rule in our home was: if no one brings it up, then you don't talk about it. Avoiding sensitive topics—especially about our pasts—is common in Chinese households. It's also common to keep big secrets, even from immediate family members. This approach intends to protect loved ones, to "save face." Saving face is important in our culture. It means preserving dignity and a good outward image while avoiding disrespect or embarrassment. This especially applies to a family or group, as Chinese culture prioritizes collectivism over individualism. You're expected to bring honor to your clan, hiding anything that might bring shame to your family. But sometimes I wonder what we lose when we try too hard to preserve our image. What we miss out on when we avoid discussion—like getting to know our fathers better.

In his mid-thirties, Baba made another big move, this time overseas to sunny California. In Cantonese, California was historically called *Gum San,* which translates to "gold mountain" in a nod to the Gold Rush. And America is called *Mei Gwok,* which translates to "beautiful country." One of his uncles, who was already in America, sponsored his immigration. In his new home, Baba—legally known as *Kong Shing Choi*—kept his routines, getting coffee and pastries for breakfast every day. I loved going with him to the Chinese bakery on Powell Street, where I'd chomp on pineapple buns and drink milk infused with a splash of his coffee. He knew everyone by name, forging bonds with other immigrants. He came from a village and built a new village thousands of miles away.

My dad was the chef of our house, especially since my mom rarely cooked. Ever since I was little, my mom was in and out of school, always busy studying for her next degree. So not only was Baba the chef, but he was also the breadwinner. He worked at Imperial Palace, a famous high-end Chinese restaurant on Grant Avenue. Except there, he wasn't the star chef. He was a busboy. Instead of masterfully creating dishes for hungry diners to enjoy, he humbly cleared away their plates.

The guests all had lives vastly different than ours. They could afford dining out. Local politicians, famous actors, and even football stars graced the tables. As a kid, I often tagged along for my dad's lunch shifts, sitting near the kitchen. As the carts rolled by, parading course after course, I'd drool. Sometimes at the end of his shift, I'd get to try tidbits of what the rich grown-ups tasted. My favorite was crab rangoon, fried wontons stuffed with Dungeness crab and gooey cream cheese. After the guests left, I would proudly watch my dad fold cloth napkins in the opulent dining rooms. The multi-colored chrysanthemums in vases reminded me of Fourth of July fireworks.

Even when Baba worked late-night shifts, he would always feed my brother and I before leaving the house. After Stan moved back to America when he was two, we spent many late afternoons sitting in front of the TV watching cartoons. Baba would carry two big bowls of boiled pork and cabbage dumplings into the living room, where my brother and I would gobble the dumplings up. It'd be many hours before my mom or Baba would come back home.

On the days that Baba didn't work at night, he cooked us elaborate family meals made with fresh vegetables and meat from the bustling markets on Stockton Street. That was the real Chinatown where the locals shopped. Grant Avenue, filled with its bazaars of plastic trinkets, embroidered silk robes, and Golden Gate Bridge sweatshirts, was for tourists.

After eating dinner, we'd gather around the TV watching NBA basketball, boxing, or horse racing—sports that seemed to bring about a rare display of excitement in my dad. And sometimes, when a Marlon Brando or John Wayne movie was on, we'd watch that too. For an immigrant that barely spoke English, he sure did love his Westerns.

Though I loved everything he cooked, Baba's crowning achievement was our annual Thanksgiving feast, with the juiciest roast turkey in the world. Normally, our oven was just a forgotten tomb to hide our collected cookware that we never used but didn't want to throw away. But every fourth Thursday in November, it would boast the one American-style meal that my dad would cook. Somehow never burnt, the turkey would lay on top of a bed of celery stalks, surrounded by russet and sweet potatoes individually wrapped in tin foil. To accompany it, a dish to preserve our original heritage—sticky rice with chopped shiitake mushrooms, dried shrimp, cured pork belly, and *lap cheong*, sweet Chinese sausage. And of course, we'd devour the entire meal with chopsticks.

Of all the holidays in America, I treasured Thanksgiving the most. To us, it meant Baba's cooking and a time to gather with gratitude. Bigger than Christmas for our family, Thanksgiving was the heart center of all holidays for us.

As a kid, I hoped that this festive autumn tradition could be frozen in time, staying forever and ever the same. But the white walls yellowed where our table leaned. And just like my favorite stuffed animal, Bear Bear, whose fur became shaggier over the years, we all grew older, most strikingly my dad.

Compared to dads of other kids my age, my dad was an older one. At forty-six years old when I was born, Baba had visible wrinkles by the time he used to pick me up from school. The other kids would ask, "Is that your grandpa?" Sure, I felt embarrassed, but I was also proud. Maybe he wasn't the kind of dad that would teach us how to play sports or lift us onto his shoulders running across the grass, but I didn't wish him to be anything other than what he was. Our gentle chef. My silent hero.

But sadly, even heroes fall. One day, when I was about eleven years old, I came home from middle school to Baba's sullen face.

"I slipped down the stairs at the restaurant," he said, shaking his head. He motioned to his tailbone. By then, he was working at another Chinese restaurant called Tommy Toy's.

A week later, the doctor told my dad that he couldn't work as a busboy anymore. In fact, Baba was forced to go on disability. Once the breadwinner, he could no longer financially support our family. It broke my heart to see my dad suffer. I hated watching him stew in shame that he never voiced, but that I could feel in his body language. What would we do now? How could we afford to eat? We'd already been living paycheck to paycheck.

This is when my mom rose up, stepping into her persona as an ox—strong as fuck. At the time of Baba's unfortunate accident, my mom was living in New York, pursuing her dream of getting a master's in fine art. She had been away from us for what felt like a year until this point. Unlike Baba, who never finished high school, my mom fought to continue her education.

In many ways, my mom and dad were polar opposites, distanced not only physically but also in mindset. I remember many nights when I could see the glow of my mom's bedroom light long after Baba, Stan, and I went to bed in our shared room down the hallway. Our bedroom window faced hers. She felt so close yet so far.

Maybe that's why I didn't think it was abnormal when my mom went to study in New York. I don't remember how she left, nor what she told us to explain that she'd be gone. That part is a blur, as many parts of my childhood were. There are huge gaps in my early memories, as if entire months or even years were deleted from the movie of my life.

It's especially hard for me to recall childhood memories with both my mom and dad. In much of my childhood, it felt like they were apart, as if at times Baba was a single dad. Sure, the four of us often ate dinner together. We even camped in Yosemite once all together, our car full of instant ramen noodles to boil over the fire. There's also that time my mom drove us on a road trip to Los Angeles.

But the gap between my parents was stark. They didn't share any hobbies, never seemed to discuss any feelings, and, to be honest, I'm not even sure what they ever discussed at all beyond family matters. As for temperament, where my mom could explode like dynamite without a warning, my dad typically stayed calm.

There was only one time that I can remember where Baba actually showed his anger. Stan was about three years old, and I was five. In our home, we had this old traditional Chinese opera mask. Painted red, black, and white with a menacing face, the mask was demonic-looking.

Thinking that it'd be fun to terrorize my brother, I grabbed it one day while we were both in the living room. I put it over my face, feeling the mask transform me into someone much more powerful.

"Rawrrr!!!" I yelled. I stretched out my arms, running toward my brother.

Stan ran down our hallway, screaming and crying, his tiny feet carrying him as fast as they could.

I chased him down. "I got you!" I hollered.

He zipped behind our bedroom door, curling into a ball.

I started laughing, as older siblings do when they think it's funny to scare their siblings. As I was still cackling, I sensed a towering presence. I turned around to see Baba standing over me.

Without saying anything, Baba yanked the mask out of my hands. Then he suddenly snapped it in half with a loud crack that echoed throughout our home.

I was stunned. Even a bit scared. I had never seen him express his anger before, nor any strong emotion. I lowered my gaze. "Sorry," I said to Stan and Baba at once.

Stan wiped his tears. Baba took the broken pieces and walked to the kitchen, dumping what was left of the mask into our trash can.

Baba hadn't uttered a word, but I felt his rage. Behind the mask of his usually stoic exterior, there was something deeper.

That's when I knew. He had a fire in him. One that silently boiled water to make soup. But one that also carried an inner strength.

As his daughter, I learned to keep my fire behind a mask too, adopting emotional suppression as a virtue. I did allow myself to express joy and gratitude though. I wanted to be seen as a good, happy girl. But I kept anger and sadness hidden, banishing them to depths within myself, deeming them invalid. Besides, if I expressed any "negative" emotions, it'd send my mom into a rage. "You dead girl!" she would yell, flying across the room to smack me with her hand. If a feather duster or other object was within reach, she'd hit me with that instead. To avoid all the drama, I just kept my emotions to myself. Especially since Baba couldn't protect me from her rage. Maybe he was also scared of her.

From the outside, you might wonder why my mom and dad stayed together. But marriages of unwavering commitment—not romantic passion—are common in Asian families. Only death, not a divorce, could do you part in traditional Chinese culture. The expectation is that you marry to create a family, and then it's your duty to honor that family no matter what. No matter the cost to your individual self, your own hopes and dreams. Family always comes first.

When my dad tumbled down the stairs, so too did my mom's dreams of finishing her master's degree. But she stepped it up to honor the family, putting our needs before hers. To save us and to "save face." Shortly after Baba's accident, she packed up her paint brushes and bought a one-way ticket back to San Francisco. No hesitation. No complaints. Shortly after, she became a professional street artist, sketching charcoal portraits of people at Fisherman's Wharf for our survival.

Though my mom made money for our family, Baba continued to manage our finances and keep the family running smoothly. He'd go to the bank, pay our bills on time, sort all our mail, and file the taxes. He also took care of our cat, Faybee, that we got when I was around twelve, feeding her canned tuna and cleaning her litter box. He was determined, in spite of his disability, to keep contributing as a stay-at-home dad. Most importantly, he continued to cook, filling our tummies. And the Thanksgiving turkey? Each year, he basted it with just as much love as the year prior.

Even as we all grew older, I couldn't bear to miss a single Thanksgiving meal cooked by my dad. Not when I went away for college, not when I started my career as a cancer research scientist, and not even when I moved out to my apartment across the city. Thanksgiving was unmissable. Until one November when it all came crashing down.

That November, when I was twenty-five, Baba's health took a sudden nose-dive. Weakened by decades of smoking cigarettes since he was a teen, his airways tightened as both lungs started to fail. When I was a kid, he'd only cough every now and then, still able to keep pace with me and Stan while walking up the hills carrying bags of groceries. But when he started wheezing, even while walking on a flat block, I suspected something was wrong.

Baba admitted himself to Chinese Hospital, the only hospital in the United States dedicated to the Chinese community, four blocks from our home. By the time I got to the hospital after hearing the news, my mom and Stan were already there. I went up the elevator to the third floor to find them, dread washing over me as I inched toward Baba's hospital room.

As I entered the hospital room, Baba greeted me with a sigh. A nurse poked his body with needles. He continued to lay there calmly, not a question, not a cry. My mom and Stan stood to the side of Baba's bed.

Once the nurse left, my mom spoke. "You could've come sooner."

"I know, Mommy, but I was at work. There was traffic too," I said.

"It's your dad. Do you even care?!" she replied.

I clenched my fist. "Ugh. Obviously. I'm here, right?"

Stan looked annoyed but stayed quiet. It was a reliable method to avoid getting caught in our crossfires.

Before my mom and I could argue any further, a female Chinese doctor with a short bob haircut and glasses walked into the room. The diagnostic tests were conclusive—loud and clear.

The doctor lowered her eyes as she passed us a brochure. "He has COPD, Chronic Obstructive Pulmonary Disease."

My mom took the brochure. Baba peered at it, staying silent. Stan and I stood equally shocked.

Like an anvil that dropped from the sky, smashing the ground in front of us, the news blew us away. It meant that he'd have long-term breathing problems and poor airflow that would get much worse with time. There was no turning back. The years of smoking couldn't be reversed. And unfortunately, by the time he landed in the hospital, it was already at Stage III—Severe. Afterward, when I Googled what that meant, I gasped for air. Severe COPD meant that his lungs only operated at 30 to 50 percent of normal lung function. Breathing now meant relying on an oxygen tank.

The fourth Thursday of November 2009 came a few days after his diagnosis. Our family kitchen was absent of its usual tantalizing aromas of turkey. No one stood over the stove cooking our usual Thanksgiving feast. I couldn't bear to be in that kitchen when Baba wasn't there. Not on that day.

In a last-ditch effort to salvage what tradition I could, I hastily threw together some mashed potatoes and roasted sweet potatoes miles away in the rented apartment I shared with two roommates in the Richmond District, on the other side of the city. We didn't even have a real kitchen, since it was an add-on unit with cheap rent above the landlord's apartment. There was a hot plate instead of a stove, and a toaster oven on top of a microwave. And forget about making the turkey. Not only would it never fit in our toaster oven, but it was a responsibility I couldn't bear. I didn't even dare to try messing with Baba's hallmark dish. I packed up the potatoes, accepted my Thanksgiving culinary failure, and hopped in my car.

I felt the heavy weight of distress driving over to the hospital. The jealousy for families feasting inside their cozy homes. My irritability, my disbelief. My deep gnawing guilt at growing further apart from Baba over the years. When I got to his hospital room, my mom and Stan were both sitting on one side of the bed.

"Jenn ah. What took you so long? It's already late!" my mom shouted.

"I hate this! Nothing I do is ever enough for you!" I yelled with tears in my eyes. "Here!" I thrust open my bag full of Tupperware with lukewarm potatoes, paper plates, and plastic forks for the four of us.

Baba watched our drama unfold. *Couldn't you two stop yelling at each other, just for a day?* he pleaded nonverbally with his innocent eyes.

Stan reinforced Baba's sentiments with the same silent plea, his gaze darting between me and my mom. The men in my family were good at staying quiet. Suppression and stoicism were the default.

We sat with our flimsy paper plates in our laps underneath the jarring fluorescent hospital light. The only one who got any turkey was my dad, served by a nurse who delivered a plate of food to our room. Though our family's kitchen was less than a five-minute walk away, it felt like a lifetime away.

I chewed quietly. Suffocating in the feeling of devastating helplessness that our favorite family holiday couldn't be saved this year. There, on the hospital bed propped up by pillows, was my silent hero blinking with his gentle eyes. The one I now longed to save.

Moment to Self-Reflect

Reflecting back, I wish that my dad talked more, that he let us know how he felt. Growing up, I didn't know much about my dad's inner world—his emotions, his hopes, his dreams, and his fears. On the surface things would look calm, but I was unsure what was hidden underneath. My dad's silence and suppression probably strived to maintain social harmony in my family, as is common in Asian cultures. However, this made me feel unsafe to express my emotions, for fear I'd be too much. So whenever something hurt me, I struggled to acknowledge it, let alone voice it.

I also find it tragic that I didn't even know my dad's life story growing up, nor any family history from his side until much later. (We'll get to that part later in the book when I discuss generational trauma). Though it's quite common in Asian culture to keep family secrets to "save face," I grieve for the missed connection that we could've had through sharing stories. Though our bond was deep, I never really got to know him. Who was he beyond what he showed? And who was I to him?

However, I'm eternally grateful for the way that he lovingly took care of me and my brother, especially as our primary caretaker in our early years. He also taught me many positive qualities that still live within me. From him I learned to be patient, kind, loyal, and nurturing. He also taught me to appreciate food as love. Every meal I have is an ode to him. Perhaps there's something you inherited from your father too.

The Relationship with Your Father

Our fathers, whether they were present or not in our youth, leave significant imprints that shape who we are. Some of us had close relationships, some of us estranged. Some of us took after our fathers, some of us vowed to never turn out the same. Whatever the dynamic, there could be great benefits in exploring our own experiences with our fathers.

There's a term called the "father wound," which describes the trauma that a person experiences when their father was emotionally or physically unavailable, absent, or abusive in their childhood. A father is traditionally supposed to protect and provide for their family. However, when we experience absence, neglect, or abuse from our fathers, it can severely impact our self-esteem, ability to trust in relationships, and mental health. In more mainstream terms, some of us have "daddy issues."

I feel extremely guilty talking about this. As if I'm being a shitty daughter for acknowledging that I have a "father wound." My dad really loved me, and I believe he did his best—which unfortunately isn't the case for everyone. But the truth is, our relationship did significantly impact my sense of self. I experienced emotional neglect. Because he suppressed his emotions and didn't protect me from my mom's rage and criticism, I thought that my own emotions such as anger or sadness were not allowed. Which to me meant that parts of myself were not allowed—and thus unworthy. My dad and I, we both hid key parts of ourselves. I didn't know who I was for many years.

Perhaps you can relate to this in some way. Perhaps you realize that your self-image or relationships carry imprints from the relationship with your father. However, part of healing and breaking the cycle is becoming aware of those imprints. Reflecting upon who our dads are can offer us clues to ourselves. I invite you to reflect upon your own relationship with your dad.

Reflection Questions:

- What strengths do you admire in your dad? What do you view as some of his weaknesses?

- What did you learn from him growing up, about who you should be and how you should act?

- In what ways did you feel cared for by your dad? In what ways do you feel he missed meeting your emotional or physical needs?

- Do you feel that your relationship with your dad impacted your sense of self and self-worth? How does that show up in your behaviors, feelings, or thoughts?

3

OUR MATRIARCH

MY MOM WAS a badass, a force of nature no one dared to stand up to. Where Baba held back, she unleashed. Whenever he fell, she rose, lifting our family back up.

When Baba walked home from the hospital a week after Thanksgiving, when I was twenty-five, hope shot through my heart like a lightning bolt. As my mom had modeled for me: Where there is hope there is survival.

Faybee, our gray tabby cat, circled around Baba's feet in an infinity shape. Infinity, forever, a line that never ends. Like hope that doesn't fade. Surely, by "progressive lung disease" the doctor meant slowly progressing . . . like a snail's pace, right?

Days later, Baba was back over the stove stirring dried goji berries into a pot of herbal chicken soup. The smell wafted over to my mom's bedroom, where she immersed herself in math books.

It almost felt normal again. Except it wasn't. Next to Baba's bed stood an aluminum oxygen tank. A few feet over, a paper bag burst with plastic pill bottles. Turn on the gas. Pop the pills. This was now part of his daily COPD routine.

Yet we clung to the belief that this was just a new normal that we'd have to get used to. A month passed and everything blended into the background. Just like Faybee camouflaging against the gray blanket cuddled by Baba's feet as he napped. Every time I drove across the city from my apartment to visit, I breathed a sigh of relief at the familiar scenes. Baba cooking or watching TV, and my mom studying math.

As Baba struggled to breathe, my mom breathed new life into her career. After she was a street artist in her late forties and early fifties, she spent her time working at childcare centers before deciding to go back to university again. While most people would balk at returning to university in their sixties, she relished in it. She was a master at reinventing herself. Despite our tumultuous relationship, my mom was my role model. She was a contrarian, a rebel, a woman overcoming the odds.

One sweltering day in July 1948, in Liuzhou, a city in Guangxi province, my mom pushed out from my grandmother's womb, ready to take her position as firstborn child. My *Po Po* (maternal grandmother), who was a nurse, and *Gung Gung* (maternal grandfather), who was an engineer, fawned over my mom. That kind of love for a daughter was revolutionary. Historically in China, sons have been preferred in a patriarchal system dating back thousands of years. But my mom was adored by her parents and by her four younger brothers, who came in succession looking up to her.

After the Chinese Communist Party, led by Mao Zedong, officially came into power in 1949, my mom's family migrated across different provinces. They moved to Wuhan in Hubei and later to Changsha in Hunan. With constant change as a kid and as the oldest of five, she had to hold it together, keep her head and hopes up high.

She had to hold her head high, even as she lived through the chaos of the Cultural Revolution in China. When she told me about that period in history, she'd recount her experience with plenty of stories. Unlike my dad, who stayed silent about his family history, my mom spoke about hers.

As a teen, she went to one of the best schools in the Hunan province. But when the Cultural Revolution began in 1966, everything changed. The political movement that swept the country disrupted her life—separating her from home and severing any hope of continuing her education. Schools were closed during that period. Her family was targeted for being landowners, business professionals, and intellectuals. What they'd built was stripped away. Po Po and Gung Gung were detained for a period, uncertain of when they'd get out.

Violence spilled into the streets. Struggle sessions—where people accused of being "class enemies" were publicly humiliated, physically abused, and in some cases, never seen again—became part of life. And as a Red Guard herself for some time, caught up in the wave of revolutionary fervor that swept the youth of the nation, my mom once held weapons. She even told me she once held a gun and a grenade—something unthinkable now, but not unusual in the turmoil of those years. Fortunately, she lived to tell the story. Others weren't so lucky.

Then later on, she was uprooted from her life in the capital of Changsha and was forced to work in the rural countryside for over eight years. In those rural farms and fields, she toiled and bled.

Her voice rose as she described parts of her past in vivid detail. "My friends and I tried to get away by hiding in crates on trains. We played cards at night. Jumped from car to car," she said. Then after a long pause, she started again. "I even tried swimming south once, to Hong Kong. Hah! Your mom is so strong. But I got stopped."

Later, I read that during those years, many people attempting to swim to Hong Kong faced strong currents, border patrols, and sharks. That many didn't make it alive.

Though she shared details openly, she didn't tell me about its emotional impact on her life. Like many Asians, she kept her feelings tightly bottled up, shoved into repressed parts of her subconscious. In many Asian cultures, emotional restraint is valued; showing composure is a sign of strength.

My mom dreamed of making it to America. The sun rose and set many times over the fields where she labored in China. Then one fateful day, when my mom was already in her early thirties after the end of the Cultural Revolution, a golden ticket fell into her hands. It was a photo of a Taishanese man with strong cheekbones, now living in California, who was looking for a wife.

The connection came through my grandma. Po Po was originally from Taishan, from a different village than my dad's side of the family. When Baba's family back in Taishan reached out to her through mutual connections, Po Po agreed to offer her daughter for marriage. My mom was already in her thirties, and my dad in his forties, so they were considered late to marriage for Chinese standards. Waiting any longer would bring shame to both families. When Po Po showed my dad's photo to my mom, she said, "At least he's not fat," and agreed to marry him.

Baba was considered a sought-after bachelor in Taishan. Not only was he handsome, but he also lived in America and could offer a chance for a better future to whoever married him. In fact, he had a list of potential brides to choose from. Yet out of everyone, he chose my mom. There was no long courtship, no dates, no fuss. Shortly after, Baba boarded a flight from San Francisco to marry his bride. On a joyous day in 1981, my parents celebrated their arranged marriage in my dad's village in Taishan. My mom glowed with a collared shirt, pale blazer, and red flower headpiece in her wavy permed hair. My dad smiled proudly in his slim gray suit and silver tie. Both of them held umbrellas, shielding themselves from the sun, their pasts, and the world around them.

After marrying my dad, my mom achieved her dream of moving to the land of opportunity. In America, she was a new woman with a new name—Juli Chen Choi. It was the English phonetic translation of her Chinese name, along with Baba's family name: Choi. Like many immigrants from non-Western cultures, she had to choose something that could be pronounced and written in English, but she also wanted to keep her original Chinese name. That's why it's Juli and not Julie. She didn't forget the "e." Just as she never forgot where she came from, no matter how eager she was to move on from her past.

In America, my mom thirsted for knowledge, aching to reclaim her scholarly aspirations from her stolen youth. She learned English, marking up an entire dictionary with hundreds of notes scrawled in pencil. Thankfully, even for immigrant families like ours, she still had a chance to learn in the American system. They don't call it the land of opportunity for nothing.

Before she left China, she started to study engineering through a state-sponsored education program, learning through television and books. After she made it to America, she enrolled in the computer science program at San Francisco State University. This seemed to make sense to her then. She could get a secure job and support her family with two small children.

But that job never came. Her degree collected dust. She realized that she didn't want to sit in front of a computer all day. She had always been creative and crafty. One Halloween when I was a kid, she made papier-mâché masks for us that were worthy of a Venetian Ball. She'd also sewn me a beautiful lace dress for school portraits in elementary school. So it was natural for her at forty years old to fall in love with fine art. First, in a sketching class with charcoal, and then in a passionate affair with oil paint at San Francisco State University. That's where my mom earned her second bachelor's degree, this time in fine art.

Some days, the smell of turpentine would bleed over into our meals. She'd sit in our back room behind the kitchen as I poked at the mounds of oil paint on the smooth wooden mixing board. My mom painted still lifes of gardenias, oranges, and glass vases with both precision and unbridled freedom. Wielding a brush, she traveled back to the Renaissance and Baroque periods. As she tore through the fabric of time with her art, she also bucked tradition and assumptions of what a Chinese immigrant could do in America.

When it came to painting people, many of them were nudes. Young, old, black, white. Breasts, balls, muscles, and rolls of fat all hung on our hallway walls. She painted them in all their naked glory. By the age of ten, I had seen more pussies in paint and cocks in charcoal than I could count. And in case you're wondering, no, I don't think she thought about whether this was appropriate for me and Stan. Or even Baba. To my mom, it was probably just art.

My mom fantasized about having her own art gallery exhibition in Carmel, a seaside town full of galleries down Highway 1. But she wanted more formal training, so she pursued a master's in fine art in New York. Next thing we knew, when I was ten or eleven, she flew three thousand miles away to live in a basement in Queens.

Looking back, it did seem abrupt. But I don't remember feeling sad. If anything, I felt relieved that we didn't have to live under my mom's bouts of explosive rage. Her rage was violent and unpredictable, making me question my reality. One moment she'd be a saint, and the next she'd be a banshee. I'd look in her eyes and watch her pupils dilate during the switch, her uncanny gaze fixated on me as she'd chase me down our hallway, screaming.

When my mom was gone in New York, Stan and I got a break from the feather duster. I did not miss the way the feather duster stung as punishment when I supposedly did something wrong. The bigger the punishment, the higher the number of lashings. Once, when I was around six years old, I tried calling the cops on my mom. But when I picked up the phone, she taunted me. "Go ahead. Let them take me away. Who will you be without Mommy?"

I put down the phone fast. Another time when I was nine, my white friend told me that for punishment her mom made her copy an entire page from the dictionary, writing each definition by hand. The next time my mom got mad at me, I negotiated the dictionary punishment. I appealed to her love for academics, explaining to her that it would not only punish me but also make me smarter. "Ho lah," my mom said, accepting the bargain. But half a page in, my hand started to cramp, and I begged for her to hit me instead.

However, it wasn't just corporal punishment. Sometimes a stick, feather duster, or hand would come out of nowhere, beating me for seemingly no reason at all. It's true what they say about artists being mad. Our home was less chaotic without her.

Other than the absence of the rage and hitting, no one berated me while my mom was in New York. Baba showed us tenderness whenever he was home, and so did Po Po and one of my uncles, who helped raise me and Stan when my mom was gone. They never made me feel bad about myself. I wish I could say the same about my mom.

Throughout my life, I put up with her constant criticisms, especially about my body. If I gained even one pound, she'd say, "Aiya, you're getting fat." When I walked alongside her, she might say, "Aiya, why are your feet so crooked?" If I got a tan, she'd say, "You look like a peasant. In China, the girls have white skin." And every time I slouched, she'd say, "Don't be a hunchback. You look like an old lady." The criticism also extended to my capabilities. If I got a "B" in school, I'd hear, "Aiya, why not A?"

As a kid, I felt I could do nothing right. That really messed up my self-esteem. It was confusing because I really loved my mom, and, despite the outbursts, she did show many signs of love. It was like living with Dr. Jekyll and Mr. Hyde—someone with two completely different sides. One day she'd tell me to come sit in her lap, embracing me with both arms. The next she'd call me stupid. To make sure I was on her good side, I'd do anything to please her. In many ways, I looked up to her, impressed by the way she dared to dream.

When Baba fell down the stairs at the restaurant and couldn't work anymore, my mom flew back to us, her dreams cut short. Once something to feed her passion, art became her way to feed us. Watching her artist friends sketch tourists at Fisherman's Wharf, she boldly thought, *I could do that too! I can draw anything!* With both determination and desperation, she marched into City Hall to apply for a self-employment permit. Weeks later, she set up shop.

At twelve years old, in my white canvas Payless tennis shoes, I'd help set up her stand. We'd roll the shaky wooden display out of a rented storage space by the Cannery and into our spot on the sidewalk. We'd carefully open the two wooden boards like a giant portfolio, revealing striking portraits hung in between. In a mini gallery on wheels, the famous faces of Clint Eastwood, Elizabeth Taylor, Cindy Crawford, and Leonardo DiCaprio all debuted as charcoal and pastel portraits at my mom's stand.

Many days and nights, the display stand would rattle with the mighty force of the wind. Just a block from the waterfront, the gusts blew in over the San Francisco Bay and through the streets. In restaurants, tourists devoured bowls of piping hot clam chowder and warm sourdough bread. On the sidewalk, my mom shivered in secondhand jackets, waiting for a potential customer to stop and make her feel less invisible.

For the first customer of the day, my mom offered an opening special of only ten bucks for a charcoal sketch of their face. That way, at least there'd be a butt in the seat to attract more customers. Then the price for a black-and-white portrait would go up to twenty dollars. If she got real lucky and someone wanted full color, it'd start at fifty.

When business was slow, she'd call me at home to come sit as a model. "Jenn ah. Mommy ah. No people today. Be a good daughter and come now," she'd plead from the payphone. Annoyed, I'd take the 30 Stockton bus from Chinatown to the Wharf and sit in the foggy cold, feeling pressured through filial piety. I'd only be relieved of my duty when a customer took my place.

For years, these portraits put food on our table. One summer, she flew all the way to Edinburgh, Scotland, for a chance to make more than she could at home. For several weeks, she sketched at the Fringe Festival, an annual arts and culture festival that brought thousands of performers and spectators from all over the world. Her bet paid off. Discreetly sandwiched in between the pages of old books, several months' worth of rent arrived by mail to Baba. I have no idea why she didn't just carry that cash back. Maybe she feared losing it? Cash in books does sound pretty dramatic. But drama was her style.

My mom approached life with this dogged determination, this maniacal drive to prove that she could do whatever she wanted. A chameleon, a shapeshifter, a woman proving her worth. One minute an artist, the next a math teacher as an encore career.

I wished that she could see my worth too and allow me to be me. But sadly, whenever I colored outside the lines—her lines—she scolded me. Berated me. Questioned me. It didn't make sense. She could break the mold, but I had to fit into her rigid and unrealistic expectations of me.

When I was a little girl, I watched the movie *Top Gun* with Baba in his English-learning class. We sat in an elementary school, which was used for adult English-learning classes for immigrants on the weekends. Sometimes I'd tag along. For cultural immersion, the teacher would play American movies. I thought it was so cool! When I saw Tom Cruise make loops in his fighter jet, I decided that I wanted to be a pilot one day too. But when I got home and excitedly told my mom, she said, "Impossible. Not ladylike." Boom. Pilot dream shot down.

Later, when I applied to UC Davis, I wanted to pick a major that would support a career in marketing. But my mom put her foot down. "No. That's for unmarried women who gossip at the office. Pick biology. Safe. Smart." Then in my freshman year of college when I told her I wanted to become a veterinarian and save cats like Faybee, she frowned. "Why not doctor?" And in my senior year of college when I dreamed of becoming a writer one day, I didn't dare tell her.

It wasn't until I got my job as a researcher at Exelixis after graduation that she finally stopped criticizing my choices. For the first time in my life, I earned a decent salary, and along with it, respect from my mom. She confirmed my belief formed at an early age: *Love is conditional. It isn't freely given but earned.*

To earn her love, I also bought a house I never wanted. It's complicated—just like my relationship with my mom. Let me explain. First, let's start with culture. For Chinese people, owning a house is a big deal. Even if you were still clipping coupons and washing plastic disposable utensils for reuse, a house was a way to measure your worth. It also symbolizes security, legacy, and pride.

Then let's get to my family. When I was sixteen years old, my parents somehow borrowed enough money from relatives and got bank loans to buy an investment property in the city of Pinole. About twenty miles from San Francisco, the house had multiple bedrooms and even a huge backyard. However, we couldn't afford to live in it. That, or my parents didn't want to leave Chinatown. So instead, we rented it out to a low-income family who was able to pay rent through Section 8 government housing assistance. My mom's logic was if the government pays for it, then at least we could rely on regular income. She was right. The rental income helped us pay for our property mortgage and some of our bills. Our investment also grew in value over time. So we held onto it.

Fast forward to 2008 when I was twenty-four. During the global financial crisis, foreclosed homes were on sale. When my mom spotted a listing for a foreclosed home in the city of Richmond for only $125,000—60 percent off from its previous price—she jumped at the opportunity. Chinese people love a good bargain. Located in a suburb across the Bay Bridge thirty minutes from San Francisco, the house in her view was too good to pass up. But here's the catch—she wanted me to sign for it. At the time, I had a stable income at Exelixis, so I looked good enough on paper—at least for the bank to approve a mortgage loan. But I didn't want to own a home. *Who the hell knows where I'd live in the future? Why the hell should I buy a house I don't want? Isn't one investment property for our family already enough? And can we even afford this?*

I tried to refuse, but my mom laid that Asian guilt on thick.

"Jenn ah, this is for us. This is an investment for our family. I've sacrificed so much for you and Stan. Why can't you do this for me? Aiyaaa!" she pleaded.

Damn. She was pulling the sacrifice card again. Desperate to earn her love, I complied and signed with the bank. We spent months renovating the house by ourselves because we were too cheap to hire a contractor to fix it up. Sometimes my mom's brother, whom we called *Wa Kau Fu*, would tell us what we needed to do over the phone, since he was a skilled general contractor living in Texas. For the purposes of this book, I'll call him Uncle Wa. My mom also convinced Uncle Wa to fly over and help for a bit. We painted all the walls, installed new kitchen cupboards, and redid all the floors. Stan and I both had blisters from the manual labor.

But it wasn't my house, even though my name was on the title deed. It wasn't my house, even though I had to pay the mortgage each month out of my salary. And it certainly wasn't my home, as we let another immigrant family rent it out. Though the rental income helped cover part of the mortgage and my family's bills, I hated the whole situation. My mom wanted it as a long-term investment, but it made no sense to me. Someone else lived in that renovated house, while my mom, Baba, and Stan lived in the old apartment where I grew up. And me? I shared a flat with two other roommates as if I were still living in college dorms. It was maddening.

Thankfully, I had my job, which made me feel some stability amidst my chaotic family dynamics. As a scientist, I was a good girl doing important research to save lives. But I had no idea then that the lives I'd so desperately fight to save were my mom and dad's.

One afternoon when I was twenty-five and pipetting DNA into a plastic tube in the lab, I got a call from my mom. It was February, only a few months after Baba's diagnosis. "Baba can't breathe. He's back in the hospital. A new one. St. Francis. Hurry, come!"

The next part is a hazy blur. Traumatic news really fucks up your memory. I don't remember how many days he spent in the hospital. But I know it was so long that they had to send him off to a long-term care facility for further care.

Every day, we visited my dad at the facility on Grove Street. He had a sweet roommate named Mel, who put up with our incessant noise. Mom, Stan, and I sat on the other side of a thin curtain, clamoring over Baba. By then his lungs were failing fast, but we were all in denial, smothering our worries with hope.

"Are you eating? Want some more *jook*? What's your oxygen level? What did they tell you today?" my mom would ask.

"What are the visiting hours? How long will he be here? What does he need to get better again? When can he go home?" we'd all wonder.

That damn deceptive hope. Beautiful and cruel. Like the love from a mom who loves you fiercely but also tells you that you'll never be enough.

Moment to Self-Reflect

Every time I come back to this chapter, I cannot help but cry. The love and admiration I feel for my mother, paired with the pain she inflicted upon me, is profound. It is a deep soul connection, and a deep soul wound. It is both easy and difficult to write about her.

Reflecting back, I can see why I believed for a long time that love was complicated. I had a complicated relationship with my mom. On one hand, she sacrificed for our family and showed us unbreakable love. On the other hand, she criticized me and hit me. I was afraid of her unpredictable, violent outbursts, so I hid my emotions for decades because I didn't want to upset her. But I lost myself along the way. Growing up, I didn't even know that I was allowed to have an identity outside of the one defined by my family—it was all so intertwined.

Yet despite our difficult relationship, when I think of my mom, I feel immense gratitude. She showed me how strong a woman could be, instilling the same strength in me. I also inherited her drive, passion for learning, sense of adventure, boundless creativity, appreciation for beauty, and love for art. My writing is an homage to the beauty that she helped me see in the world. I owe the birth of this book to my birth through her.

Maybe there are aspects of your own mom that you see in yourself too.

The Relationship with Your Mother

Our mothers are our earliest imprints. We grow in their bellies, rely on them for survival after coming out from the womb, and look to them for love. Some of our mothers were present and nurturing; some were absent or unpredictable. Some of us worship our mothers; some of us fear them.

Just as there can be a "father wound," a "mother wound" can also exist. It results from neglectful, abusive, or absent parenting from a mother. We often rely on our mothers for comfort and security. When our emotional and physical needs aren't met, we can struggle with self-worth, people-pleasing behaviors, mental health issues, and dysfunctional relationship patterns.

It has taken me a long time to admit what my mother did to me. I still feel that, when I speak my truth, I'm betraying her. However, there was indeed neglect and abuse. My feelings and needs were unheard, and she was absent at points of my life. She continued to hit me not only in childhood, but also when I was an adult. That's abuse. As a result, I started to believe that the world was unsafe. When I reflect back on what she shared with me regarding her upbringing, I can't help but think that her violent episodes made sense. How the fuck is someone supposed to remain peaceful when they've held guns and grenades?

On top of the physical abuse, there was also verbal abuse. Her criticisms made me feel small and unworthy. I tried hard to conform so that I could be the perfect, obedient daughter in her eyes, proving myself to her and everyone else. But no matter what I did, I never felt good enough. I also formed the belief: *Love is conditional. It isn't freely given but earned.* Me being forced to buy a house may seem like such a first-world problem, but it was a prime example of our complex dynamics. I could not stand up to my mom, even when I wanted to say no. I wanted to earn her love so bad.

Maybe you're getting misty-eyed too as you think about your own relationship with your mom. Maybe it's happy tears, maybe it's not. Or perhaps it's a mix of different emotions. Exploring the impact our moms had on us is key to our journey of self-discovery and self-worth.

Reflection Questions:

- What strengths do you admire in your mom? What do you view as some of her weaknesses?

- What did you learn from her growing up, about who you should be and how you should act?

- In what ways did you feel cared for by your mom? In what ways do you feel she missed meeting your emotional or physical needs?

- Do you feel that your relationship with your mom impacted your sense of self and self-worth? How does that show up in your behaviors, feelings, or thoughts?

4

HOME ALONE

I'M FOUR YEARS old, sitting on the carpet alone, wondering when my parents will ever come home. If they'll come home.

The carpet is khaki, the pale hue of a desert, a barren landscape where I don't see anyone for what feels like days. Baba's at work and Mommy's at school—a typical day for me with no childcare because my parents can't afford it living in San Francisco. Sometimes I'd be dropped off at a family friend's apartment up the street so she could babysit me. But not today. This all feels normal to me by now.

It's the first home I know, the one before we moved to Mason Street. It overlooks Polk Street, at the corner where it intersects Washington in Russian Hill, a quaint residential neighborhood west of Chinatown. If you've ever visited Lombard Street, famously known as the crookedest street in the world, then you've been in this neighborhood. Pick the right hill to stand on, and you can see views of the bay spanning from the Golden Gate Bridge to the Bay Bridge. Have the right salary, and you could be living large in a historic hilltop mansion. Not us, of course. We, like many other low-income residents in the neighborhood, live in cramped apartment buildings with many units. Ours has twenty-four.

Outside our building, the 19 Polk bus zips by. Patrons sip their cappuccinos at the bustling cafés, shoppers browse in boutiques, and rowdy crowds fill the bars at night. I wish it were as lively inside our home. Inside it's quiet. Inside it's lonely. We're in a one-bedroom unit with a living room as you enter, a small kitchen to the right, a bathroom to the left, and a bedroom next to the living room. Potted plants by the window keep me company. Our alarm clock with the glow-in-the-dark numbers ticks.

I pull at the lint on my pink sweatsuit. I glance at the sofa with no one sitting on it. I stare at a square tin of Ching Kee egg cookie rolls on a wooden shelf. It's a piece of Hong Kong in our home—a taste of Baba's life from before. As in many immigrant families, imported snacks are edible tokens of our roots. They bring familiar comfort and remind us that we belong. Dried squid, rice crackers, and Haw Flakes—candy shaped into pink discs made from hawthorn berries—sit stowed away in a kitchen cupboard I'm too short to reach. My stomach growls.

I'm tempted to pry open the metal Ching Kee lid and sneak a sweet cookie out. But I hold back, afraid to act upon my impulse without explicit permission. I can hear my mom's voice in my head. "Jenn ah, *joh gwai nui ah*," she would say, reminding me to be an obedient girl in Cantonese. So I wait, turning my head away from the cookie tin so it doesn't taunt me anymore. I wait, subconsciously turning my heart away from any emotion because feeling my feelings would collapse my world.

Not knowing when my parents would come back becomes one of the greatest wounds of my life. But at four years old, I subconsciously repress any feelings of helplessness, panic, sadness, or anger in order to survive. Just as my parents did when they sent my brother away.

Born chunky and round like a little Buddha, with big, beady eyes, my little brother completed our family in 1986. While I got Jennifer—a basic name for a 1980s child, my brother got Standish—distinguished and rare. He'd be the only Standish, later shortened to Stan, that I'd ever know.

I'd love to say that I was the best *Ze Ze* (older sister) from the start. That I felt an immediate bond. That I was as happy as I looked in our family photos about a baby joining the family. But I'd be bullshitting you. According to my mom's retelling years later, I was one of those jealous siblings, yanking my

Dai Dai (younger brother) off the sofa when my parents weren't looking. Hey, can you blame me? I was only two.

Like many immigrant parents, mine struggled to raise young children on their own. They were far from their homeland, separated from their families, low on money, and held back by the language barrier. On top of that, my mom tragically lost her dad—my Gung Gung—to colon cancer in China mere months before Stan's birth. My mom never spoke about her grief to us, but I can imagine that it hurt. Baba had already lost his dad—my Yeh Yeh—too. And although his mom—my Maa Maa—was still alive, she was still back in Taishan.

Baba did have a younger brother in San Francisco who we called *Sei Suk*, which translates to Uncle Four. He had moved to San Francisco a decade after Baba. We'd go visit him sometimes, but Uncle Four was busy working and raising three kids of his own with his wife, who we called *Sei Sum*—which translates to Auntie Four.

In case you're wondering why we called our uncle and aunt that instead of their names, let me start by saying that Chinese kinship terms are extremely complicated. In English for example, you simply use the general terms "aunt," "uncle," "grandma," or "grandpa." But in Chinese, you distinguish between your mother's side of the family and your father's side of the family with different terms for each relative. Then you have different terms to indicate whether they are older or younger, sometimes using numbers. I'll save you (and me) the headache from a long explanation of kinship terms, but I needed to explain this part for now.

It's one of the many reasons why it was hard for me to grow up between cultures. So much was lost in translation. How the heck was I supposed to know who I was when I didn't even know the real names of my relatives? The kinship terms also imply a hierarchy. Obeying anyone older is key.

At our home on Polk Street, pressure mounted for my mom and dad, who needed to go to school and work. But who would take care of me and Stan? Certainly not the American system. The lack of accessible or low-cost childcare for young children in the country is inhumane. So my parents sent my brother away to live with my grandma in China.

When Stan was just a few months old, my mom dropped him off with Po Po for an indefinite period. Po Po had moved in with my Uncle Bo in Shenzhen, a metropolis linking Mainland China to Hong Kong. Po Po and Stan were the perfect match—a widow with hope to love again, and a baby boy who needed the love.

Do I think it was hard for my parents to send Stan away to live with my relatives abroad? Probably, even though it's a common practice for Chinese immigrants in America. But even if it's common, separation can still hurt—at least I could imagine so for my parents.

On my end, as a toddler, I likely felt relief that I had my parents all to myself again. But as the time passed, I felt increasingly lonely and wanted someone to play with. Every so often, I'd ask my parents when my brother would come home.

"Aiya, don't be so impatient. When things are ready," they'd reply. But 'ready' felt like an eternity.

Thankfully, at our home on Polk Street, I had a children's map of the United States to play with. I'd sit on the floor, pulling a plastic magnifying glass across the cardboard map, revealing cartoon symbols of each state. A juicy orange for Florida. A prickly cactus for Arizona. I'd get lost in this map, forgetting my hunger while Baba was at the restaurant working and Mommy was at the university studying. Me and my map, we became best buddies—it was there for me when no one else was.

As a kid, you don't know what the term *abandonment* is, but one can feel the absence. The loneliness. The belief that you're not worthy enough to make people you love stay. At least, this is the subconscious belief I formed by the time I was four. *I am not worthy enough to make people stay.*

Other memories of living on Polk Street are few and far between. However, I do remember that once I fell off my wooden highchair in the kitchen as it crashed backward toward the refrigerator behind me. Luckily, Baba was there, soothing me. But what if I fell when nobody else was around? What would happen to me? I made sure to be extra careful when alone at home after that. Sit like a good little girl on the living room floor. *The world is unsafe. I have to stay small to stay safe*, I learned to believe. This belief would live inside me, diminishing my self-worth for years.

It wasn't until we moved to Mason Street, when I was four, that my dreams of having someone to play with came true. I can remember the lead-up to my brother's arrival, my parents promising me that it'd be any day soon.

One day it felt different. Baba rushed around the apartment moving things. My mom had been gone for days because she went back to China to bring Stan back to America. When there was a commotion downstairs that evening, I ran to our apartment door, peering through the white privacy curtain and glass pane. I could hear footsteps coming up the stairwell.

When my mom opened the door, she announced the arrival of my brother and Po Po. Stan blinked at us, as if trying to figure out if he had just woken up or was falling into a dream. It must've been so confusing for him at just two years old. I don't remember my parents' reactions. I don't remember greeting Po Po. I just remember the joy bursting from my heart. *He's here! He's here! I'd never be alone again*, I thought.

In some ways, it was true. After a few weeks, my brother and I became inseparable. Our two-year separation didn't estrange us—it made me appreciate him even more. We splashed in the bath together. We squealed with joy in the tire swing at the playground, my mom pushing us high. And we even went on car trips to Brentwood, another town in the Bay Area, to pick fruit in the orchards. In those early years, my mom was the one who would take us on outdoor adventures while Baba was the caretaker at home. In that regard, my mom and dad complemented each other. Each of them doing what they could to provide for our family.

As a bonus, not only did I get my brother back, but I gained a grandma too. Po Po immigrated to America when she brought Stan back, so there was even more love around us. Po Po lived in the bedroom with me and

Stan for a bit; this was back when Baba and my mom were still sleeping in the same bedroom together.

Though Po Po was already in her sixties, her cheeks glowed, her short, black, permed hair shined, and her walking pace was as fast as mine. Po Po was strong, but she spoke softly. She loved my brother as if he were her own child. I was also the benefactor of her warmth and care. I remember how she'd take us to the McDonald's on Grant Avenue regularly, how the Happy Meal french fries tasted when we dipped them into our vanilla ice cream. Po Po joined us for all our Thanksgiving feasts and birthdays too.

There's a photo of my brother and me from my fifth birthday, where we lean in to blow out candles on my cake together, our cheeks puffed out in unison. Surrounding the sponge cake covered with whipped cream are multiple plates overflowing with cherries, peaches, strawberries, and even artichokes. It is abundant as fuck. Baba didn't make much money as a busboy, but that era felt rich in food. In the photo, our home still looks clean in the background, before it would later fall into disarray. The sheer lace curtains still look fresh without holes in them yet. The wooden arms on the chairs behind us look shiny and scratchless. There's even a silver vase with roses in it. It was a golden era.

There are happy memories like these, where we're surrounded by relatives we love. A few years after Po Po's immigration, Uncle Wa and Uncle Ha—my mom's younger brothers—immigrated from China to San Francisco too. Uncle Wa would sometimes help look after me and Stan as well. Eventually, my Uncle Bo—my mom's youngest brother—moved too. This is how entire immigrant families end up moving to the United States. One member pioneers the immigration, and the legacy grows from there. There was a similar story on Baba's side of the family, where two of his brothers—whom we called Uncle Four and Uncle Six—moved to the United States with their families as well.

We had joyous times with lots of relatives around. There were many Christmases spent with uncles, aunties, and cousins. Multiple Chinese New Year feasts receiving red envelopes with cash from our extended family. And those precious Thanksgivings devouring Baba's roast turkey shared with an ever-growing table. These kinds of memories are part of why I remembered my early childhood as happy for many years, even as I became an adult. I have to remind myself that there were so many good times amidst the bad.

———

I wish I could say that it was all sunshine and roses after my brother's return. But something changed. In need of money and her own space, Po Po got a job at the On Lok Senior Center in Chinatown taking care of other elders. She also moved to her own apartment fifteen minutes away. Our home felt emptier without her. My mom was busy at school and Baba was at work. Our apartment became messier, stains and dust accumulating in every room. When Stan and I weren't in class at Sherman Elementary, or in the after-school program at Yerba Buena childcare center, we were often left at home alone. It was me and Stan watching cartoons, our eyes glued to the TV for hours. Me making ramen noodles for us when we got hungry.

As we grew older, I took my big sister role very seriously, taking my brother with me to elementary school every day. When I was nine and Stan was seven, we'd walk three blocks down to the 45 Lyon bus stop on Stockton Street, sometimes accompanied by Baba, but sometimes alone. Many times, it was just me and Stan taking the twenty-minute public bus ride from Chinatown to Cow Hollow. It became totally normal for me to watch over my brother. I felt like an adult at an early age.

I still felt like a kid, though, when our mom would chase us down the hallway, screaming in fury as she hit us. At least Stan and I had each other. In 1994, when I was ten, a white American teen named Michael Fay made the global news headlines. He was arrested in Singapore for allegedly stealing road signs and vandalizing cars, and as punishment from the Singaporean government, he'd receive lashes from a cane. He later shared that he was hit so badly that he bled. Watching the news on TV confirmed a belief for me: *If something painful happens to me, I must've done something wrong and deserved it.*

My brother and I accepted the hitting, never fighting back. However, the pain lived inside me, needing a place to go. I regret to admit that at some point in our childhood, I started pinching Stan so hard that my nails left a mark on his arm. I also blackmailed him when he broke an antique camera that my mom got from the flea market, forcing him to follow whatever orders I gave him. He didn't fight back. Back then, I didn't think about the consequences of hurting him, even when his eyes welled with tears. I just knew I felt relief when I could let my own frustration out, asserting my power as an older sister.

I'm embarrassed that I treated Stan that way, especially when I loved him so much. He was my partner in crime. My little buddy. My bro.

Siblings get you when no one else can. They've witnessed your joy. Your life milestones. They've laughed with you, doubling over until your stomach hurts and you can't breathe because your inside jokes are so funny. They also know your pain. They've seen your tears and maybe even cried them with you.

My brother understood me in ways my parents never could. He understood the struggle of trying to fit in as an American with Western ideals while also living up to the expectations of our immigrant parents. We even spoke a different language to each other than with our parents, embracing English as a way to communicate more fluidly than in Cantonese.

Stan also understood me in ways that I thought other classmates couldn't. Their lives seemed so perfect. But of course, as a kid you have no idea what happens in other people's homes. I just knew that in our home, Stan and I shared secrets. Secrets of getting hit. Secrets of being left alone at home. Secrets of being so poor that we received government food stamps and the shame that came with it.

In elementary school, I qualified for the free lunch program, but I didn't want to let my friends know, so I'd bring my own lunch. Some days it was a bologna sandwich with ketchup. On other days, when there wasn't anything left in our fridge, I'd bring an orange in a paper bag, pretending to not be hungry. To keep up the façade and make the same reused bag look full every day, I'd hide a hairbrush inside. I see it so vividly now, the turquoise plastic handle, the black bristles. I feel the weight of it, a light tool for beauty in contrast to the heaviness of my shame.

I'd bury the painful parts of my childhood deep in my subconscious, carrying them with me unknowingly for years, choosing to remember the happy memories instead. But our past hurts can shape our future if we let them. If we let them fester in our hearts like an ulcer in the stomach that turns into cancer.

Moment to Self-Reflect

Before we dive into reflection, I need to be honest with you. This was one of the most difficult chapters for me to write. The loud-ass voice inside me said, *No one cares, Jenn. Your childhood was fine. Probably normal for a child of immigrants. Other people had it much worse. Look at the children going through war. War, Jenn! Bombs and homelessness and death. Why are you bringing up the bad parts? Why are you complaining? Your parents did their best. You're so fucking privileged. You're so ungrateful. Just move on from your past. Just let it go.*

Yup. Those were my incessant inner thoughts while writing this. And thoughts you might even have about your own childhood, which is why I'm sharing all this transparently with you. Perhaps you're like me, thinking that a lot of stuff you experienced was normal. That other people have it worse so you invalidate your own experience. Or you could be someone who went through such a tough childhood that you just never want to look back because it feels like too much.

I get it.

But the thing is, our past trauma lives within us if we don't acknowledge it, feel it, and heal it. It acts out in our adult life, making us feel unworthy. It shows up in people-pleasing behaviors, limiting beliefs, and patterns that strain relationships at home and at work. It also separates us from our true, authentic selves, which makes us feel lost, disconnected, or numb.

Childhood and Limiting Beliefs

When I work with my coaching clients on their limiting beliefs, I often ask about their childhood, and I'll do the same here. A limiting belief is a deeply held conviction that holds you back from achieving your goals. It's a psychological barrier that influences your actions and impacts how you perceive yourself, others, or the world. Many people aren't aware of their limiting beliefs, but these subconscious beliefs could negatively affect our quality of life.

More often than not, our limiting beliefs stem from our childhood. That's why it's important for us to examine where our beliefs might come from. To move forward toward our goals and look to the future, sometimes we have to move backward into our past so that we can understand what to do in the present.

For many years, I recounted that I had a happy childhood. And in many ways I did. But the truth was I also repressed a lot of painful memories, thoughts, and feelings. The pain from my early abandonment wound has haunted me for years.

Reflecting back to my childhood, I can see that I experienced physical neglect, a form of trauma. Physical neglect is when a child's basic needs, such as shelter or food, are not met, or the child isn't adequately supervised or kept safe. When my parents left me alone at home for extended periods at age four, and likely even earlier than that, I felt abandoned. It resulted in the limiting belief: *I am not worthy enough to make people stay.* This, in combination with my mom hitting me, led to another limiting belief: *The world is unsafe. I have to stay small to stay safe.*

Regarding the physical abuse, I also formed the belief: *If something painful happens to me, I must've done something wrong and deserved it.* If you've experienced something similar, you have my deepest empathy. Studies have shown time and again how damaging it is to someone's psyche to be hit by a parent.

It's no wonder, then, that I took it out on my brother when we were kids, pinching him and blackmailing him. I still feel guilty about that and have apologized to him since. When I was a child, I felt powerless under my parents. I unconsciously needed to assert power over someone else. This is how it happens in many families: When someone experiences wounding, they perpetuate that pain by taking it out on other family members. Or in some cases, bullying others outside the family. It is a cycle of pain that we must break.

Reflecting upon my childhood hasn't been easy, but it's been fundamental in my healing. I've also unearthed beautiful memories to feel grateful for—even amidst the trauma—so I hope that it's the same for you.

Reflection Questions:

- What was your childhood home like? (Describe the surroundings, what it was like inside, the overall mood of the home, and how you feel about it). If there were multiple homes, then reflect upon each.

- What were some of your favorite memories as a child?

- What were some of the most difficult experiences you had as a child?

- Do you have any siblings? If yes, what was your relationship like with each of them as children? If you didn't have siblings, how do you feel about that?

As we reflect back on our childhood, the origins of some of our limiting beliefs could become clearer to us. When we become conscious of our limiting beliefs and how they show up in our lives, we can start to shift them or let go of them altogether, which we'll learn how to do later in the book. But for now, identifying your limiting beliefs is a big step.

Reflection Exercise: Getting to Know Your Limiting Beliefs

- Turn to a fresh page in your journal or wherever you're keeping notes. It's better to start with a blank page because you'll make a list which you'll revisit throughout the book.

- Make a list of limiting beliefs that you have about yourself, your life, or the world.

  - It could help to think about areas of your life in which you feel stuck or unfulfilled (relationships, family, career, finances, health, home, etc.). Then examine which beliefs come up that hold you back.
  - Helpful structures:

    - I am _____.
    - I'm not _____ enough.
    - If _____, then _____.
    - The world is _____.

5

NUMBING THE PAIN

BY THE TIME I was a preteen with braces in middle school, I learned how to escape from pain. I'd run down our long hallway when my mom would chase me, my plastic jelly sandals clapping against the vinyl flooring. I'd zone out when she hit me, pretending that I didn't feel the stings radiate across my body. And when she called me stupid or fat, I'd drown out her voice as if I were listening to an old tape recording of her criticism and could just turn the volume down.

I felt invincible—running from pain, numbing it, tuning it out.

It seemed like the only reasonable way to deal with an impossible situation. If I fought back and yelled at my mom, her rage would escalate. So I chose to see the good side, practically worshipping her. Her embrace made me forget that the same arms that hugged me also hit me. And the way she fought for our family's survival redeemed her in my eyes. My love for her was hardcore. So I dismissed my pain with that hardcore toughness, just as she harnessed that toughness to emerge from immense hardship alive.

My inner strength became my rebellion. I was proud of my ability to *yun*. In Cantonese, the word *yun* means "to bear, to endure with unrelenting strength." It's a concept we Chinese people pride ourselves on. No matter what happens in life—no matter how difficult or painful—you're expected to grit your teeth and power through. You remain resilient. You put up with shit. You hold it in. You don't complain. You don't ask for help. You just *yun*.

I witnessed my parents *yun* all my life. Baba didn't complain when he worked long hours at the restaurant. He didn't talk about his pain after he fell down the stairs and couldn't work anymore. My mom powered through many cold days at Fisherman's Wharf as a street artist, hustling to put food on our table. Whatever physical, emotional, or psychological challenges they faced, they endured with unrelenting strength. They didn't talk about it. They didn't share their feelings. They didn't ask for help. They *yun*-ed. And they expected the same of me.

The thing is, they didn't explicitly tell me to endure everything, hold it in, and never ask for help. But it was implicit. First of all, they modeled it for me. If you witness something over and over again as a child, it becomes learned behavior. Second, it felt like I had no right to complain. It seemed like no matter what I experienced, it was nothing compared to the hardships they experienced growing up in China or the struggles they faced as immigrants in America.

Additionally, as the eldest child, there was pressure on me to hold it together in ways Stan didn't have to. There's even a term called "Eldest Daughter Syndrome," which describes the high expectations placed on the eldest daughter to caretake younger siblings, be a role model, and bear responsibility. Where Stan could mess up and be forgiven, I'd be punished.

So I learned to *yun*.

Once in middle school, I went ice skating with my best friends Lily and Alice at an indoor rink. Unfortunately, I never learned how to skate, and my limbs flailed on the ice as I tried. Suddenly, I twisted my ankle and tumbled, my body sliding across the ice like a penguin. When my friends asked if I needed help, I waved them away, blushing from the embarrassment as I hobbled over to a bench. Later, when I went home, I hid my swollen purple ankle from my parents, hoping that if I *yun*-ed enough, my ankle would heal itself. It did. Kinda. But to this day, my left ankle is still bigger than the other.

It felt easier to ignore pain than to feel it. Even when I reached puberty.

I don't remember when I got my first period. Maybe around thirteen years old? There was no celebration to commemorate my entry into teenhood.

No talk of the birds and the bees. Speaking about sex was taboo in Chinese culture. However, my mom did share that it was a natural part of becoming a woman and that I'd be losing lots of blood. "Jenn ah, you're losing blood. Hurry, drink *dong quai*," my mom would say to me when my period was heavy. She'd boil me the dried herbal medicine in a ceramic pot over our stove, a common practice in Chinese culture. *Dong quai*, also known as female ginseng, is believed to nourish the blood, improve circulation, and regulate menstruation. But I didn't notice the benefits amidst the bitter taste of the medicine.

Whatever I learned about sex or dating at the time came from sexual education class at Marina Middle School or by watching TV. Teachers stressed using protection to avoid pregnancy and STDs. Shows like *Baywatch*, *Beverly Hills 90210*, and *Saved by The Bell* taught me that I needed to look a certain way to attract guys. The beautiful girls I saw on TV wore heavy makeup, had perfect bouncy hair, and walked confidently in their voluptuous bodies. They commanded attention from boys. In contrast, I stayed scrawny, flat-chested, and stringy-haired—far from the busty lifeguards running in slow motion on *Baywatch*. There was no way I could compare. I felt ugly and undatable. From what I could tell, puberty didn't change my body, except for the monthly bleeding.

However, what puberty did change was my relationship with Stan and Baba. Once so close with Stan as kids, I drew away from my brother, preferring the sisterhood I found in my female friends instead, especially Lily. A child of Chinese Vietnamese immigrants, Lily was my best friend since we were eleven years old. Our friendship started with a mutual friend ditching us and then a spontaneous merry-go-round adventure at Golden Gate Park to salvage the day. Within six hours, we knew we'd be BFFs. As we entered teenhood, we wore our Gap anorak jackets, CK One perfume, and Motorola pagers at the mall. We'd send each other "143 637," which meant "I love you always and forever" in pager code. I had found my sister from another mister.

As for my relationship with Baba, I was no longer daddy's little girl. I had outgrown that innocent era of my life, and it seemed harder to relate to him. Other than the occasional times when we'd still watch NBA basketball together on TV or eat dinner together as a family, there wasn't much to talk about. I also started idolizing my mom more after she took over the financial responsibilities in our home. My silent hero had fallen from the pedestal I put him on as a little girl.

Cramped in the same bedroom together with Stan and Baba, I felt suffocated. I wanted my privacy as a blossoming teenage girl, but the only one in our family who got their own space was my mom. I was jealous of my friends who had their own bedrooms. Lying awake in my bunk bed at night, I'd fantasize about ways to escape or be rescued from my home. Preferably by a cute boy.

One day when I was fifteen years old, I was on the 30 Stockton bus after high school, minding my own business with my head down, as usual.

Suddenly, a cute guy who looked Korean, with a Tommy Hilfiger jacket, stood over my seat. "Can I get your number?" he asked. No introduction.

I looked at his spikey bleached hair. His angular face. And I froze. *What? Was he seriously talking to me?* I couldn't believe my luck. It was the first time a cute guy ever paid attention to me. Even after I got my metal dental braces off, I still believed I was an ugly duckling who was unworthy of male attention.

"Hey, can I get your number?" he asked again, handing me a piece of paper and a pen.

"Uhh . . . okay," I said, scribbling down my phone number as my heart raced. I handed the paper back, shaking.

He shared his name and jumped off the bus at the next stop. For the purposes of this book, we'll call him Sam.

I was unsure of what to make of the exchange. *Was he joking? Pulling a prank? Would he ever call?*

A few days later, my Nokia cell phone rang. Sam officially asked me out. The rest goes really fast. He was seventeen and seemed more experienced than me, so I willingly followed his lead. I don't even remember our first date, but it feels like from the moment we started dating, we lived in his bedroom.

There's this stereotype of Asian tiger moms who breathe down their children's necks. But in my case, I got lots of freedom to roam as a teen. I don't think that my parents had the capacity to watch my every move. Who has time for that when you're busy struggling to survive? So I was able to spend lots of time at Sam's.

I was totally smitten with him and fell hard, trading my virginity for his love within weeks. Or what I thought was love. We tried to be safe, but unfortunately, a few months into dating, I missed my period. When I took a pregnancy test, it showed positive. Shocked and ashamed, I shared the news with Sam. We agreed that I'd get an abortion. I could not imagine raising a child while I still felt, in some ways, like a child myself.

This next part is hazy for me. It's taken me a few decades to be able to process it. I do know that I went to my pediatrician because I was just fifteen years old. She then referred me to some other doctor at another clinic. I have no idea why, but I had to keep the fetus for another month so I could get a vacuum aspiration abortion instead of one with a pill. I did not question them. Just as I never questioned my mom and dad.

I kept the pregnancy a secret from my parents, too ashamed to ask for help. I wore jean overalls to hide my baby bump at Lowell, where Lily and I both went to high school. I did not tell anyone—not even Lily—choosing to *yun* it alone. Sam didn't come to the abortion appointment with me. I don't remember asking him. I don't remember him volunteering to come.

On the day of the appointment, I recall no feelings. I carried a Hello Kitty purse that held a cell phone that never called my parents for help. I walked into my appointment in some clinic downtown, the lady doctor instructed me to get naked, and I lay down on a table. A medical instrument entered my body, and two beating hearts inside me became only one. I was so emotionally numb that I couldn't even shed a tear. I walked out like a robot. I don't remember what happened afterward.

Sam broke up with me a few weeks later. I don't remember the reason he gave me. As I mentioned before, my memory is fuzzy here. It feels like I completely blacked out at parts. I do remember that immediately after the breakup, I walked in the rain, bawling because I'd failed my first relationship.

But I still couldn't feel anything at all for the baby that could've been. When I told my mom and Baba about the breakup, they said something along the lines of, "That's the way it is sometimes. Let's have some dinner, and you'll feel better." I swallowed my grief with chicken and rice.

A few weeks later, my pediatrician hinted at telling my parents, but I'm not sure if she ever did. We never spoke about it at home. We never spoke about anything emotional at home. Looking back, I must've deadened my feelings to cope with the trauma. I must've *yun*-ed it.

What saved me afterward was partying and my hella tight community of friends. Though I grew up with many Latino, Black, and white friends, I'd say my core social group for most of my youth was Asian American. We shared similar cultural experiences, found belonging in each other and, in the case of my Cantonese friends, spoke the same mother tongue. Though I felt insecure about myself growing up, in truth, I was quite extroverted and popular. I was voted Class Clown in middle school, attended many sleepovers, and even delivered our eighth-grade graduation speech. By the time I got to high school at Lowell, I'd amassed a ton of friends.

The grandest adventure of all was raving, the pinnacle of my teenhood. It was an epic, love-filled, drug-fueled era of my life. I went to my first illegal rave in some warehouse, popping an ecstasy pill that a friend's boyfriend gave us. Ecstasy, also known as MDMA, is a synthetic drug that can make people feel heightened empathy, euphoria, and surges of energy. One pill and I was hooked. I closed my eyes, became one with the trance music, and felt infinite love for everyone around me. It filled a void in me I didn't realize I had. With Ecstasy, love felt unconditional. I didn't need to prove myself to anyone, nor offer up my body in exchange for love.

When I turned sixteen, I got a fake ID, which got me into legal raves in the city. I told my parents that I was sleeping over at friends' houses, and they believed me. In concert venues, like Bill Graham Civic Auditorium and Maritime Hall, I raved with thousands of partygoers. We exchanged bracelets made of colorful beads, threw neon glow sticks in the air, and worshiped DJs like Paul Oakenfold, Tiësto, Alice Deejay, and ATB. One night, I dressed as an angel and danced on the marble steps of City Hall, rolling high on Ecstasy. To rave where politicians worked felt like a big fuck you to the system through "PLUR," which stood for the rave culture principles of peace, love, unity, and respect. Dancing felt like a revolution. On the dance floor, I couldn't feel pain. Only love.

But even the raving wasn't enough to feed my teenage rebellion. I also started smoking weed. One of our friends had access to marijuana and blessed our friend group with it. We'd hit the bong or pass a joint to unwind after school. I laughed so hard that I couldn't breathe and ate everything in sight when I had the munchies. A toasted Eggo waffle with syrup and butter while high tasted like pure bliss.

I also drank alcohol. The first time I drank vodka, I danced with reckless abandon at a friend's house party. But within hours, I vomited into a toilet, praying to the porcelain gods, horrified at the projectile reaction to something that people could buy at the supermarket. Surprisingly, I felt better by the next morning, and I was looking forward to the next chance to go at it again. Alcohol made me feel superhuman. When I was seventeen, I'd get into nightclubs with my fake ID, chugging Smirnoff Ice, partying late into the night with my friends.

All of this was illegal. The Ecstasy pills. The weed. The underage drinking. But I didn't give a shit. While high or drunk, I didn't need to be an obedient girl. I didn't need to think about my responsibilities. The taboo substances made me feel free.

From my teens to my twenties, drugs and alcohol helped me *yun*. To be clear, I wasn't an addict. It's not like I relied on them every day. And in some periods with lower stress and forced focus on school or work, I did maintain long stretches of sobriety without weed or ecstasy. However, I continued to rely on alcohol for regular escape.

It's no wonder, then, that when Baba was diagnosed with COPD in my mid-twenties, I partied to escape from reality. You could find me in stilettos, a bodycon dress, and fake eyelashes four times a week in downtown San Francisco clubs or bars. Slide, Vessel, Ruby Skye, and Redwood Room became my second homes. I'd wait in line with my friends, smile at the bouncers and promoters who all knew me, and enter a world where I could drink my night away. The dark dance floors, disco lights, DJs spinning at the booth, and makeout sessions with random guys made me feel like a celebrity.

Party Jenn, also known by my nickname "Meow," was my alter ego. Meow was glamorous, wild, and free. She didn't have to be an eldest daughter. She didn't have a sick dad wrecked by lung disease. Alcohol became a familiar numbing agent. Cranberry vodkas, a coping tool. Nights blended in repetition as I partied my pain away.

But when the mornings came . . . fuck. Some days I'd wake up with my dress still on, one hand stuck in a potato chip bag, my head pounding. If any of my other roommates were up first, using the only bathroom we had in our Richmond District apartment, I'd use it as an excuse to stay longer in bed. I'd stare at the bird decal stickers on the wall, fantasize about curling up in the papasan chair in the corner of my room, or wish I could just sit at my desk at the foot of my bed mindlessly surfing online. But eventually the pressure of needing to go to work would get to me. I'd drag myself out of bed and brush the alcohol smell from my breath.

I'd rush to work at Exelixis and, after I finished at the lab, drive to Baba's care facility to fulfill my daily obligation. Most days, my mom and Stan would beat me to the facility, their names written higher up on the visitor sign-in sheet. We still hung onto the hope that Baba would come home soon. When it was all of us together as a family, it felt okay, sometimes even strangely normal. My mom would open containers of food she'd brought, and we'd gather around Baba in chairs, eating while peppering him with questions about his health.

But if I was alone with Baba, an awkwardness would fill the air. I wish I could say that I was present. But I stayed numb. Days dragged on as I visited Baba at the care facility, sitting in a chair next to his bed. Visiting him felt like a checklist exercise. Something to tick off on a "be a good daughter" to-do list. I felt guilty about my detachment but didn't know how to connect better.

Whenever any feelings of being a shitty daughter showed up, I'd immediately search for a club promoter's Facebook event on my phone and feel instant relief, looking ahead to the next party. To break the silence, I'd ask Baba a few generic questions like, "What did you eat today?" or "Anything happen?" He'd reply in short wheezing sentences. Despite the circumstances, he seemed calm, quiet, not wanting to cause a stir. He had to *yun* too.

My mom would come to the care facility twice each day. Once before her math class at San Francisco State University, and once again around six in the evening with food. I was envious of her loyalty. She asked Baba detailed questions and anticipated his needs. My mom was consistently there, propping up our family with her strength. She was a machine. No warm, fuzzy vibes, but a well-oiled piston that kept going. Again, we fell back into an accepted routine.

But routines can easily be broken, like dreams that shatter when the people you love become gravely ill.

When my mom went to the emergency room in March 2010, it took us by horrifying surprise. Our matriarch, a mere mortal. How could it be? And how would we manage to go on? I could not see a life where my mom wasn't our fearless leader. Nor see myself being able to carry our family through. But I clung to what she told me in the hospital after we heard the word "cancer". I clung to it like a lifeline after I lost my job and had to dive into my interim role as Chief Operations Officer of the Choi household overnight.

Choi Lo Shurn. The weed on the side of the road. I could bend but not break. Even when I felt like a big truck ran me over, I wasn't allowed to break.

On the second night that my mom was in the hospital, I lay awake in my bedroom, tossing and turning. Before I went to bed, I texted Lily, seeking counsel from my best friend of over fifteen years. "I dunno what the hell to do if it's really cancer." Then after scrolling on my phone for what felt like hours, I eventually dozed off.

The next morning, Lily's voice greeted me on the phone. "Guess what? My mom made your mom soup. I'm gonna walk over and go with you to the hospital."

My cheeks flushed red with shame, the feeling I'd get whenever someone would offer help. "Aww, that's so sweet, Lil. But . . . are you sure? I don't wanna burden you. Don't you have to go to work?" I blurted.

"I don't have to go into the office yet. Don't worry. I'll be over in thirty," she said before hanging up.

Filled with a mix of relief and shame, I dragged my feet over the edge of my bed and stumbled to my closet. Though my apartment felt cramped with no living room, my bedroom closet had ample space. It was the kind you could walk into, and I utilized every inch of it, stuffing it with shelves, a hanging shoe rack, and hangers filled with clothes.

Standing in the middle of my closet, I pondered what to wear. Black reminded me of a funeral. White in Chinese culture also signified death. Then from the mélange of monochrome, a green, long-sleeve shirt popped out. *Nothing screams alive like green, right?* I snatched the shirt and pulled it over my head, praying that it'd bring a change of luck.

My phone rang. "I'm heeeere!" Lily announced.

I grabbed my purse, closed my door, and flew down three flights of stairs. When I opened the front door and stepped outside, Lily wrapped me in a hug. Glowing with her shiny, long, bleached blond hair and wearing a camo print jacket, she looked like both an angel and a soldier. I needed both with me that day.

Lily held a plastic bag. "Here," she said, lifting it up toward me. "It's ginkgo and tofu soup. My mom says it's good for healing."

"Lil, wow. You really didn't have to do this. Thank you," I said, taking the bag. I brought my gaze down to the sidewalk. It was just soup, but it brought me so much shame. The fact that someone did anything for me at all was embarrassing. I had prided myself on being independent for so long. I wanted to shrink my problems and myself away.

"That's what friends are for, okay? Please let me help you. So you can concentrate on helping your mom and dad," she pleaded.

I allowed what she said to sink in. In my head, I saw a set of dominoes lined up behind one another. If we could prevent one of them from toppling over, we could save the rest.

After spending my life going at it alone, always helping others but refusing help myself, I finally surrendered. For so long, I thought that help was weak, that it was shameful, but I couldn't make it anymore on my own. My soul was weary, frayed like the bottoms of my brown leather moccasins, and I couldn't fight off help any longer. I drove Lily in my car in resignation, but also in renewed strength.

When we got to my mom's hospital room at San Francisco General, my mom lit up when she saw Lily's familiar face. "Lily ah, how are you? And your family? Thank you for this soup. Gingko is nice for the body," my mom gushed.

I sat at my mom's feet on the hospital bed as Lily pulled up a chair. We spent an hour chatting, my mom eating the soup directly from the thermos Lily had brought. It was as if we were out having a normal lunch on a normal day. Except that my mom was in a hospital gown.

"Hi . . . sorry for the interruption," a man's voice said.

I looked up and saw Dr. Chan, his face just as gentle as it'd been in the days before.

"I have some news to share," he said.

Lily squeezed my hand and let go, taking Dr. Chan's arrival as her cue to leave us. "Bye, Auntie Juli. Call me later, Jenn," she whispered before disappearing down the hall.

My heart started racing. The fear of potentially hearing that my mom only had a few months to live gripped my tense body. From my understanding of stomach cancer, it has a poor prognosis, especially at later stages.

Dr. Chan stood over my mom. "So . . . we looked at your biopsy and blood samples. It doesn't look like stomach cancer."

"What?!" I heard a voice ask before recognizing it as my own. "What is it then?"

"Results show that it's lymphoma, a blood cancer." Dr. Chan pulled out a folder with a stack of printed images.

Shit. Still cancer. I clenched my jaw.

"You see here?" He motioned to light-colored areas on a scan of my mom's stomach. "These are ulcers. That's why you lost so much blood. They were bleeding for a while before you came to us," he explained to my mom.

My body tensed again. I had so many questions. *What does that mean then? How bad is it? How long does she have?* But paralyzed, I became mute.

Dr. Chan proceeded. "To be specific, it looks like Gastric MALT lymphoma, which is a slow-growing, low-grade type of cancer that begins in the stomach. I'm going to discuss a treatment plan with my team and then share more, okay? Any questions?"

I couldn't believe what I was hearing. Slow-growing. Low-grade. That was damn good news on the spectrum of the big C.

"When can I get out of the hospital?" my mom asked.

"Soon, actually. Maybe Sunday," Dr. Chan said. "I'll be back tomorrow. Take care, Mrs. Choi."

My mom smiled at me, her eyes twinkling at the news.

Thank you, God! Thank you, Universe! Though it was devastating that she was diagnosed with cancer, at least it sounded like a treatable case. For a moment, I allowed myself a bit of relief.

But as always, my anxiety came rearing its ugly head. It's what I do. I overthink. I felt useless. I knew about cancer from a molecular standpoint, but not in a real-world clinical way. *How, then, would I be able to translate the medical speak into words that could save my mom?*

My mom's voice broke my train of thought. "I checked again. I didn't see a wedding ring on his finger."

I laughed. "Maybe he just doesn't wear it for work," I replied. I nipped my mom's matchmaking ambitions in the bud. "Anyway, how do you feel?"

"I want to go visit a big field of flowers when I get out," my mom proclaimed. She'd always loved flowers. Admiring them, picking them, painting them.

I grinned. "Okay, Mommy. Let's do that," I said.

I imagined us walking in a never-ending field of flowers. I could smell the sweet scent of lavender fields in Van Gogh's paintings. I remembered the time we admired the tall sunflowers near Davis when I was in college.

In that moment, despite hearing the cancer diagnosis, I felt alive again.

Flowers just keep growing. Like weed on the side of the road. They show us that life persists in defiant beauty.

I stroked my left arm gently with my right, encased in my bright green shirt. See? Alive. Filled with chlorophyll like the stems of flowers in all the flower fields around the world.

I allowed myself, just for a second, to feel a tiny bit of happiness. And I finally allowed myself to accept that I didn't have to walk through the fields or *yun* through my struggles alone.

Moment to Self-Reflect

I have to admit, parts of this chapter were extremely painful to recall. For many years, when I looked back at my adolescence and my twenties, I thought of those periods fondly. I had wild fun and made loads of friends. But I've come to learn that there was so much pain buried underneath. Pain that I had to *yun*. Maybe you've had to *yun* too.

Reflecting back, I can imagine that I was voted Class Clown in middle school because humor offered me a way to hide the hurt that I'd been experiencing at home. As I shared in the previous chapter, my early childhood trauma created the limiting belief: *If something painful happens to me, I must've done something wrong and deserved it.* So I took all the pain—hiding it, repressing it, laughing it away.

The most painful experience of my teenage years was my abortion, a trauma that I'd repressed for decades. For years, I numbed my guilt and grief about it, believing that it didn't impact me much. Furthermore, the experience—in combination with my mom hitting me—formed a new limiting belief about my body: *My body is shameful. It's not safe to be in my body.* And when my ex broke up with me, it reinforced my childhood limiting belief: *I am not worthy enough to make people stay.*

Limiting Beliefs from Adolescence to Adulthood

As you might have noticed through my story, limiting beliefs that originate from our childhood can have compounding effects as we grow older. New limiting beliefs can also form as we encounter more challenges. Before we move on, let's look at our limiting beliefs again.

Reflection Exercise: Limiting Beliefs Beyond Childhood - Adolescence to Adulthood

- In Chapter 4, I encouraged you to write down any limiting beliefs that you formed during childhood. Write down those limiting beliefs again.

  - For each limiting belief stemming from childhood, how was each reinforced through experiences as an adolescent? (Ages 10-19) What about as an adult?

- What new limiting beliefs were shaped by your experiences as an adolescent or an adult? Write down those beliefs and their origin stories.

  - For example, "I believe that _____. I believe this because when I was _____ years old, _____."
  - In my case, it was: "I believe that my body is shameful. It's not safe to be in my body. I believe this because when I was fifteen years old, I got a secret abortion, no one was there for me, and I thought it was all my fault."

Numbing Pain and Dissociation

When my childhood pain continued into my teenage years, it snowballed into something that I was forced to *yun*. To cope, I escaped from the pain by numbing, partying, doing drugs, and drinking. So when my parents became ill, it felt natural for me to get into the same pattern of *yun*-ing. I'm not saying that this was a healthy solution—especially when heavy substance use can lead to unhealthy outcomes for many—but I did what I could at the time. Unfortunately, my numbing led to me not being present with my dad in the care facility, and parts of my youth were blacked out. For many years, I felt guilty and ashamed about how I coped with the pain. However, I've since learned that I dissociated.

Dissociation is a process where a person disconnects from their feelings, thoughts, memories, or sense of self, often as a response to trauma. It's a defense mechanism that helps people cope with overwhelming stress by allowing them to detach from the immediate reality, numbing the emotional experience. In other words, dissociation helps us survive. It's a concept that can offer us grace when we think about the ways in which we've had to cope.

Reflection Questions:

- Do you allow yourself to feel physical pain? What about emotional pain?
- When you think of pain, what narratives, beliefs, or stories come up for you?
- When did you have to "yun" or dissociate in your life to cope?

Learning to Receive Help

Although I did rely on unhealthy ways of coping, I did eventually receive help from my best friend. Learning to receive help has been essential on my journey, even if it wasn't easy to accept at first due to my upbringing. Perhaps this resonates for you. Many of us who struggle with self-worth may think it's weak or a burden to ask for or get help from others—even when, ironically, we may love helping others. The thing is, we cannot survive on our own. We need one another.

Reflection Questions:

- How do you feel when someone offers you help?

- In what instances could receiving help be seen as strong or empowering?

- Which friends in your network can you go to for loving support? What about family members?

6

MANIC DISTRACTIONS

THE MORNING AFTER my mom's official cancer diagnosis, the doctor presented us with a plan of therapeutic attack. I say attack because, at this point, everything felt like a battle to me. I, the eldest daughter warrior, was responsible for keeping two sick parents alive.

Dr. Chan stood next to my mom's hospital bed as I wrung my hands in the chair next to her. "We'll start with antibiotics. In your case of lymphoma, there's a bacteria called H. Pylori present. Think of it as bad guys in your gut," he explained.

I imagined the antibiotics karate chopping the evil bacteria. *Hi-yah, you little fuckers!* the antibiotics yelled in my head.

"We'll use antibiotics in combination with something called a proton pump inhibitor. Together, it'll hopefully get rid of the stomach ulcers," he further explained.

My jaw dropped open. I had been fully prepared for a treatment that was more invasive. "Wait . . . so she doesn't need chemotherapy? Or surgery or something?" I asked.

He turned to me. "No, not at this stage. It's still early, and this combo is usually effective. Of course, we'll have to continue to monitor her cancer. Because if it progresses, we might have to do radiation therapy."

I looked over at my mom with glee, though I'm not sure she understood what all this meant yet.

My mom nodded slowly. "Can I go home tomorrow then?"

"You can even leave today. Your iron levels look good again. You'll just need to pick up your prescription in the pharmacy downstairs. Sound okay?" he inquired.

My mom's eyes widened. "That's great! I can visit my husband again. Thank you!" she exclaimed.

Dr. Chan smiled. "Take care, Mrs. Choi." Then he turned around and left.

"Do you understand what he said?" I asked my mom.

"No chemo. I'm okay," she replied.

I put my hands on my hips, hoping that my stance would make her take me seriously. When it came to medicine, sometimes it was like talking to a child. "No, Mommy. Your cancer isn't as bad as others, but you're not okay yet. You have to take the medicines. If you don't, things can get much worse. Can you do that? Promise?"

"Okay, okay. But no chemo," she stated firmly.

Alright, I thought. At least it was a start.

My mom didn't trust Western medicine and believed only traditional Chinese medicine was legit. It takes a holistic approach, using herbs, acupuncture, and qigong to balance the body's energy to prevent and treat illness. Western medicine, by contrast, diagnoses and treats specific diseases through targeted fixes like pharmaceuticals or surgery.

I'm not sure why my mom had such an aversion to Western medicine, especially since Po Po had been trained as a nurse in it. Whenever Stan and I got sick as kids, Po Po had to sneak us aspirin and cough syrup behind my mom's back. In contrast, my mom doubled down on Chinese medicine. Once, to try to cure my brother's asthma, my mom boiled some dried snake parts and forced him to drink the brew. However, the most extreme thing my mom ever did was drink her own pee. When I was a kid, she said there was something bad in her body and that drinking pee could cure it. I remember seeing the aluminum bowl in the bathroom to collect urine. But I didn't understand what she was trying to get rid of. Did she already have some kind of tumor then? We wouldn't know, anyway, since I don't think she ever got it properly checked.

Like many immigrants in America, my mom didn't like going to the doctor. Maybe it was the language barrier. Maybe it was the fear of high medical costs. Or the cultural gap. Whatever the reason for the avoidance of doctors, it's ironic because so many immigrant parents want their children to either become a doctor or marry one. If you don't know whether to laugh or cry from the constant contradictions we must live with in our families, I feel you. It's a cosmic joke.

We waited in my mom's hospital room after Dr. Chan's visit, excited for her possible release. Finally, in the afternoon, a nurse came and discharged my mom. After we picked up my mom's prescription in the pharmacy, we headed over to see Baba.

"So you gonna tell him?" I asked my mom on the drive over in my car.

"Not yet," she replied.

When we arrived at the care facility, Baba looked so innocent propped up in bed. Still untainted by our cancer secret.

"How was your test?" he asked my mom.

For a few seconds, I was caught off guard. *How did he know about the blood tests? Did Stan tell him what happened? Damnit! And why?* Stan was sitting in a chair next to my dad. I shot my brother a venomous stare. But then I remembered our lie. Oh yeah, the math test. The one my mom was supposedly studying for in her absence from Baba.

"Very hard. But I did good," my mom said with a poker face.

Baba blinked, seemingly relieved to hear.

My chest tightened. I hated living in a lie.

What I hated more than withholding the truth from my dad was the uncertainty of everything. I'd just lost my job and, along with it, any remaining sense of self-worth. I didn't know how long I could survive on my severance check and unemployment. I didn't know what would happen to Baba. And getting my mom to take her prescription was like herding cats.

My life was in freefall, spiraling out of control. I felt powerless.

So when my friend Christina suggested that I join a fundraising competition for the Leukemia & Lymphoma Society in the spring of 2010, I agreed. Christina was a powerhouse with a heart as big as her voice, and she was great at motivating people, including me. When my mom was diagnosed with cancer, I thought that I could help cure her lymphoma through volunteering. Besides, what else did I have to do? Sometimes we need something to channel our energy into so we can feel some form of control amidst utter chaos.

A few weeks later, I joined the "Arts 4 Cure" team of the Man & Woman of the Year Campaign for the local LLS chapter in San Francisco. It was a spirited ten-week fundraising contest where candidates raised money for blood cancer research and patient support. Our candidate and team lead was Yuliya, an ambitious woman who loved arts and spirituality.

Each week, our team of about seventeen volunteers would gather in the swanky high-rise Financial District office of our team's campaign manager. We'd assemble around a huge conference table, hash out fundraising strategies, and scarf down slices of pizza. The towering office buildings that surrounded us encouraged us to reach for the sky.

We not only reached for the sky but also reached out to our personal and professional connections. Luckily for us, several notable venture capitalists agreed to donate their time to meet with the highest bidders of our online auction. Apparently, these VCs were big shots in Silicon Valley who funded millions of dollars for startups. I felt dumb for not knowing who they were.

To make up for my perceived lack, I worked triple hard to prove myself, obsessively pouring my time and energy into the fundraising campaign. I genuinely believed that I could save blood cancer patients like my mom with my sweat and tears.

Our team's big event was the Celebrity Gala, a fancy black-tie benefit where drinks would flow and pocketbooks would open. Our event flier promised a "High Profile Guest List of Bay Area Celebrities & Socialites" at the Bentley Reserve, a historic building. And it was true. Several famous singers, tech CEOs, athletes, and even a former mayor signed up to be at our live celebrity auction. Leading up to the big event, on the outside things seemed so put together—so perfect, so posh. But behind the scenes, as vendor coordinator of our big gala, I was falling apart. Trying to scramble together a charity event, negotiate with decor and food vendors, and deal with an array of strong team personalities sent me over the edge.

One day when I was driving to a campaign team meeting, I stopped at a red light. Out of nowhere, I heard a huge bang, and my car lurched forward, jumping into the intersection. Stunned, I looked in my rearview mirror to see that a Muni bus had crashed into me. Fortunately, I wasn't hurt, but when I got out to check, my bumper had a huge dent. I exchanged insurance details with the bus driver, and then I sped off like a maniac to run to my meeting. A normal person might've taken a moment to calm their nerves. Or perhaps perceive the accident as a sign to take the day off. But no. Like a machine, I pushed on. Just like my mom had modeled for me.

By the day of the gala, I looked like a skeleton. I hadn't slept well in weeks, and I'd lost weight from the stress. I covered it up well though. I put concealer over the dark bags under my eyes, applied bright cherry lipstick, slipped into a black dress, and stomped in my stilettos like a boss. I might've felt like crap, but I looked like a million bucks—which I needed to in order to match the caliber of the event. The Bentley Reserve was a former federal reserve bank, with a converted ballroom that screamed money with its three-story columns, marble interior, and chandeliers. I couldn't look like a fool in front of 150 guests in gowns and suits. But I kept sweating, anxious about the event.

I waited for my date to the Celebrity Gala, eager for his arrival. For privacy, I'll refer to him as Marco—an Italian American I'd first met at a bar. He had a model's face, green eyes, curly brown hair, and was almost six feet tall. We'd gone on a few dates by the time of the gala, so I thought it'd be fun to invite him.

When Marco arrived at the front entrance of the gala, he looked striking in his black suit. I ran into his arms, excited by the familiar embrace. For a moment, as we walked through the crowd and to the bar in the back of the ballroom, I felt more relaxed. Sadly, that moment was fleeting. I wish I could say that I was fully present with him, that he whisked me away on the dance floor and we laughed all night. But no. The relentless chatter in my mind wouldn't stop. *Did we have enough appetizers to go around? Was the bar stocked? What's up with the acoustics?*

When another girl flirted with Marco, I had zero energy left to deal with it and simply walked away as they talked. I headed straight for the bar, chugged cranberry vodkas, and counted down the minutes until I could finally leave. The celebrity auction, singing performance, and speeches thanking the guests were all a blur.

At the end of the night, swaying left to right in an intoxicated stupor, I bumped into Marco outside.

"Jenn! Where have you been? I've been looking for you the past hour," he said with an earnest tone that surprised me.

"Around. Taking care of stuff. Call you when things settle," I said. *Hmm. Maybe this guy was more into me than I thought?* But I didn't have time to think about that. I was too tired. I gingerly stepped down the stairs to the street like a newborn baby deer and waved my arms frantically to hail a cab before anyone else could witness me disappear.

The following week, while I was in Cabo for a friend's wedding, I checked my phone and saw a message from Marco. My heart fluttered unexpectedly, realizing that I was really into him. However, I wanted to play it cool. Besides, I was still deep in the fundraising mindset and had no capacity to think about it further until the campaign was over.

Two weeks later, I was at the Fairmont Hotel for the Leukemia & Lymphoma Society Grand Finale of the fundraising competition. It was the night when we'd find out which team raised the most money. Once again, I found myself in another ballroom with chandeliers. Over one hundred guests—mostly made up of campaign teams and supportive family and friends—sat around circular tables with fancy linens. I sat with our team, shooting nervous looks at Christina as we dined.

It did feel odd that I was in a hotel ballroom when just two blocks down, on Mason Street, my mom was in her bed, cancer cells invading her body. It was three months after her initial diagnosis, and the cancer was still present. But fortunately, she'd had a positive CT scan at the hospital where the doctor announced that the ulcers had shrunk. Feeling relief that her condition had improved, she finally told Baba about her lymphoma. He didn't seem surprised. I guess deep down he knew that something was off. At least they could face their illnesses together. No more cancer secrets, no more lies.

For me, fundraising was very much about willing my mom's cancer away. I needed our team to win to feel more useful. But as the night progressed, my stomach started to churn. Between our online VC auction and the Celebrity Gala, our team had raised over $50,000 for charity—an incredible sum. But would that be enough to win?

When the emcee walked onto the stage to announce the winners, I twisted my napkin in my hands. When she announced that our team had won third place, everyone in the ballroom cheered. I should've cheered too. After all, every dollar raised would support the fight against cancer. And our campaign team did our best. But I was not happy. Tears welling in my eyes, I guzzled a glass of wine and looked around my table, meeting my team members' shocked faces.

As the other winners were announced, as the dessert rolled out, and as the event turned into a dance party, I couldn't help but hear the voice in my head.

Nothing you do is ever good enough. You've failed your mom.

Moment to Self-Reflect

I feel physically tired when I think back on this period of my life. It was so manic. My parents' illnesses and my layoff became too much for me to handle, and I coped with it by chasing things to do. Not only did I *yun* and numb my pain, but I also distracted myself from it. Staying excessively busy through the fundraising campaign gave me a false sense of control.

Staying Busy as a Trauma Response

There's nothing wrong with staying busy—we have to get shit done to survive in this world. Bills don't pay themselves, right? However, it's important to note when our need to stay busy could be a trauma response and when it leads to even more dissociation in our lives. If we didn't grow up in environments where we felt safe to feel, process, and express our emotions, then we may detach from those emotions, numbing and distracting ourselves to avoid them.

On top of that, we may have grown up in homes where staying constantly busy was modeled for us. I watched my parents self-sacrifice and work a lot, so it felt natural for me to do the same when they got sick. Perhaps you adopted this as learned behavior as well.

Reflection Questions:

- When have you found yourself constantly doing more in order to avoid facing difficult situations or emotions?

- In what ways did "doing more" help you feel better? In what ways did "doing more" make you feel worse?

- Growing up, did you see this pattern in your own family, culture, or community?

7

SCHOOL PRESSURES

REELING FROM MY perceived failure from the fundraising campaign, my eyes focused like two red laser beams on my next obsession: taking the GMAT.

For anyone who's not familiar with it, GMAT stands for Graduate Management Admission Test; it's a standardized test that's required to get into business school.

But wait, hold up ... business school? After working as a research scientist?

Yup. That's what I thought I wanted next—at least in my lostness. The layoff and my parents' illnesses made me feel like a boat adrift at sea. I knew that I didn't want to go back to working in a lab. But I also didn't know what kind of job I wanted next. Or who I really was. I believed that going to business school would help me find my way again.

In my mid-twenties, I was blessed with multiple awesome friend groups. One group in particular seemed to all have MBAs, Master of Business Administration degrees, from top business schools like Harvard and Stanford. A group of both women and men, they all appeared to be kicking ass in their careers. I had met them through my close childhood friend Rene, whose mom knew my mom from Hunan. Some of them managed large teams at tech companies while others worked at investment banks or private equity firms. I envied them. They could afford luxury brands and dined at Michelin-starred restaurants. During the day, they worked their asses off. At night, they ordered bottle service while we danced at clubs.

Yet amidst all their success, my friends stayed humble and kind. They always made me feel welcome, inviting me out even though I made pennies compared to them. I looked up to them. Many of them grew up in lower-income or middle-class families as I did, and some of them were also children of immigrants like me. If they could make it from modest origins, then perhaps I could too?

I aspired to be like my friends. They seemed to have a clear direction in life and looked happy, at least from what I could see. If I could ace the GMAT and get into business school, maybe I could achieve what they'd achieved too.

Then I could prove my worth.

In my mind, the GMAT wouldn't just help me earn a greater income. Eventually, it'd also help me earn the love of my mom. As I learned as a child: *Love is conditional. It isn't freely given but earned.*

Academic achievements had long been a currency for love in our home. This is true for many children of immigrants. Our parents pressured us to perform in school, expecting perfect grades even when the pressure felt unsustainable. And we wanted to please them, eager to prove to them that their sacrifices to raise us were not in vain. If you were ever punished for anything less than an "A" on your report card, or you measured your worth by your grades, then you know what I mean.

As a kid, I excelled in class, tested as a gifted student, and loved reading books. For hours, I'd immerse myself in the collection of great literary classics that my mom amassed for us from the sale section of Waldenbooks at the mall. My favorite book as a kid was *The Adventures of Sherlock Holmes* by Sir Arthur Conan Doyle. Through Holmes's detective cases, I could escape, teleporting from my family home in San Francisco to the brick houses in London. I inherited my mom's passion for academics and felt proud of myself when I tested into Lowell, one of the best high schools in the nation.

However, after my secret abortion, things started to unravel at school as I *yun*'ed my pain. By my senior year of high school, I smoked so much pot that I was high almost every day. I wasn't just mentally checked out—I cut class, too.

Unlike my wunderkind classmates who got into Ivy League universities, I had an average GPA. However, I miraculously got into UC Davis, the only university that accepted me. But when I had a string of D's in my senior year at Lowell, I almost had my university admission revoked. When I told my mom about the deep shit I was in, she advised me to beg all my teachers for a second chance. In tears, I pleaded for a chance to improve my grades by redoing some of my tests. Thankfully, my teachers agreed. My mom tutored me in math. I studied physics as if my life depended on it. And fortunately, I was able to pass the tests.

When I got to UC Davis, I spent most of freshman year drunk or high. With a D in Calculus, I was put on academic probation, in jeopardy of getting kicked out if I didn't shape up. Not wanting to get in trouble with my mom, I used the same tactic she'd taught me in high school: beg for a second chance. I begged a university psychologist to write me a note so I could redo Calculus the next quarter. Bawling with crocodile tears, I told her that I struggled with being so far from home. It was bullshit because the truth was being away from home gave me the freedom to party all I wanted, but I put on a good show. Thankfully, she wrote me a note.

From there, a miracle happened. My academics completely turned around, and I became obsessed with getting good grades again. But I must admit that the motivation wasn't intrinsic at first. It was to prove my worth to a guy. In the later part of freshman year, I met a hot engineering student who was incredibly nerdy. Wanting to impress him, I too hung out at the twenty-four-hour study room at the library, pulling all-nighters to cram for exams. While our relationship didn't get very far, my academic progress did. High on my addiction to prove my worth through good grades, I graduated magna cum laude with a Bachelor of Science in biology. And I'm proud as hell to say this—all while working as a waitress and lab intern almost the entire time I was in college to pay for my own tuition.

Doing is what I was used to. Staying busy, working hard, studying like a maniac. *Yun*-ing my pain.

That's why jumping into the GMAT felt natural for me.

In April 2010, a month after the layoff, I enrolled in a GMAT course, which took place inside a downtown mall. Every Wednesday, other business school hopefuls and I would dutifully march into class. At the front of the room, our instructor would cover the essentials on a whiteboard. By the end of the three hours, my brain would be fried. But at least it kept me busy.

My days started to look the same after a while. Dragging myself out of bed, I'd check my phone to make sure everyone in my family was still alive, grab my backpack full of books, and drive to my favorite café.

The café wasn't trendy by any means, with outdated ceiling lights and old wooden tables, but it offered what few others could. It was close to Baba's care facility and was affordable. My unemployment checks were a measly $400 per week, and though I still had a bit of my severance check left, my funds wouldn't last for much longer.

I'd be in the zone for hours on end studying, working through GMAT practice problems. Occasionally, with flashcards in hand, I'd fantasize about sipping sake from the sushi bar next door. Happy hour often beckoned me, but I stayed disciplined until it was time to go. Until my cell phone alarm screamed at me, reminding me to go see Baba.

Baba's care facility was just four blocks away. If he was napping when I was there, I'd continue studying at the chair next to his bed. Some days, it was just me and him. On other days, my mom was there too. My mom with her math books, me with my GMAT books. We shared a special talent for focus. Or was it mania? There's a fine line between the two.

Mania. Focus. Whatever we want to call it. It helped me detach from the pain within my family, especially when my dad had a big scare. I'd been studying for the GMAT at the café when a nurse from the care facility called me one afternoon.

"Hi, are you the daughter of Kong Shing Choi? We just called an ambulance for him because he's not doing well," the nurse said.

I left a half-eaten bagel on the table, shoved my books in my backpack, and drove right over to the care facility. By the time I got there, Baba was already lying on a stretcher, getting loaded into an ambulance by a young paramedic.

"Would you like to ride with us to the hospital, ma'am?" he asked.

I looked at my dad strapped into an oxygen mask. I thought about climbing in next to him. But I couldn't do it. I couldn't get in. Getting in an ambulance made the whole thing feel too real, and I had to separate myself from that. Reality was too fucking unfathomable.

"Baba, I'll see you there. I'm taking my car," I said to my dad as the paramedic closed the doors and carted him off.

St. Mary's Hospital was on Stanyan Street in the same neighborhood as the care facility. Five minutes later, I arrived. By this time, with two sick parents, driving around to various hospitals around the city felt routine. I knew where to park and on which floors their snack vending machines were located.

Baba was in a room on one of the higher floors with a nice view of the city. Because of his dangerously low oxygen levels, the doctors hooked him up to a CPAP machine, which forced oxygen into his lungs and kept his airways from collapsing. It looked like scuba diving equipment. Luckily for us, within hours, his condition stabilized. I don't remember how many days he stayed in St. Mary's after. It's a bit of a blur.

I do remember that one day at St. Mary's, a social worker pulled my mom, me, and Stan into the hallway outside Baba's room.

"Have you considered his last wishes?" she asked in a hushed voice. Then she passed us end-of-life brochures.

We were appalled. It was completely out of the question for us that Baba would need hospice care. We were that deep in denial. Or hope. I smiled politely and said, "No, we haven't yet. But thank you."

As soon as she left, we threw the brochures away.

The thing is, Baba was still fighting. He still wanted to live. Shockingly, days after the social worker approached us, Baba got better. Our silent hero fought like a decorated soldier. His tenacity blew us all away. The doctors removed him from the CPAP, and Baba was escorted in an ambulance back to the care facility.

There, it went back to business as usual. Weeks dragged on again without incident. We put the St. Mary's episode behind us, considering it just a scare.

I marched forward with the GMAT, burying myself in the books. However, another distraction had popped up, competing with the GMAT but making me feel giddy again: Marco.

—————

After the fundraising campaign ended, Marco and I reconnected. Although he lived in Hayward, about forty minutes from San Francisco, we managed to meet almost every week. From bars to walks at the beach, we found a sense of home in each other. I had my doubts though. *Why would this handsome guy want me? He could have his pick of so many girls.*

Though I was apprehensive, Marco was hard to resist. We'd bond over how it felt to grow up between cultures, geek out about philosophy, and obsess over intellectual pursuits. But what impressed me most was that he was a true romantic, sending me poems that swept me away. The big gestures of passion, the endless showers of compliments. I felt like a goddess.

As we built our trust in each other, we moved into a relationship. I can remember the day I fell for him. We were at a French restaurant. Somewhere between the duck breast and the crème brûlée, I felt my protective guard drop away. I knew I loved him. As he wrapped his arms around me, I felt safely held for the first time in a long time.

However, not long after we fell in love, he had to travel for work, sometimes being gone for weeks at a time. While I longed for him during his absence, at least it gave me the chance to focus on the GMAT, snuggling up to my books instead of his chest.

—————

Unfortunately, despite all my manic studying, it didn't seem enough. When the GMAT course ended, I still felt unprepared. However, since everyone else from my course seemed to be booking their test date, I went ahead and pulled the trigger.

The night before my big test in July, insomnia got the best of me. Still awake at three in the morning, I thrashed around, burying my face in my pillow as if I could smother my anxious thoughts out. *Fuck. Why did I drink coffee in the evening? Why did I stare at problems in the practice tests an hour before bed? Such an idiot.* I tried to detach from these thoughts, but they pulled me in like riptides. Finally, just before dawn, they released their grip.

When my alarm rang at nine in the morning, the bags under my eyes sagged. My shoulders sagged. My spirit sagged. But I had to put on my game face.

I drove over to the testing center and parked my car. When it was almost time for my appointment at eleven, I took a deep breath and marched to the testing area, waiting until I was called. When it was my turn, I entered the sterile gray testing room. In front of me, there was a computer screen in my partitioned booth. Next to me, an erasable note board with a marker to sketch out problems. Judgment time had come.

The test started with analytical writing, a comfortable warm-up for me. Writing was one of my favorite hobbies, and I was confident in this section. *Not bad,* I thought. *Not bad at all.* The Integrated Reasoning section was also manageable. I could look at data in tables, see graphs, and decipher them. After all, I was a scientist.

But then, just as I was getting comfortable, a difficult math problem popped up in the Quantitative Reasoning section. Bam! As if someone had performed a lobotomy on me, my mind went completely blank. Meanwhile, the clock winded down. *Shit, shit, shit!* I spent the rest of the time in the math section teetering between two opposing states: on the brink of an anxiety attack, or in some kind of rapturous trance, praying that somehow, I was guessing the answers right. When the section ended, I felt a sense of dread.

After taking an allotted fifteen-minute break to collect myself from the epic fuckup of the previous section, I plowed forward. Last up: Verbal Reasoning. Reading was another one of my hobbies, so verbal should've been a breeze.

But unfortunately, the words jumbled together, looking like alphabet soup. Before I knew it, I ran out of time.

At the end of the nearly four hours of timed torture, my unofficial score flashed onscreen. It was a total disaster. I had to make a decision. Should I send my scores onward or cancel them?

I felt the heaviness crush me, along with my own harsh thoughts. *You suck, Jenn. You bombed the test. Better cancel now.* I hit the button and obeyed. No one would get my scores. But I felt so stupid. What Asian is so bad at math? Feeling like a total disgrace, I shrank past the front desk and drove as fast as I could back home.

Back in my apartment, I hid under my covers in bed. I was so embarrassed that I couldn't even face seeing my parents that day. When my mom called me to ask where I was, I told her that I was getting sick. Which wasn't far from the truth, since I spent the rest of the day recovering in bed from the horror of the GMAT. Marco was traveling, and I couldn't get ahold of him, which drove me deeper into the dark hole of my bed.

I allowed myself a small break of a few days but decided to sign up for the GMAT again. I was determined to prove my worth. Once again, I buried myself in books.

On the day of the second test, three weeks after my first, I finally felt more prepared. I stormed into the testing center like a gladiator in the Roman Coliseum, ready to fight. Four hours later, I survived. When my unofficial score popped up on the screen, I felt a mix of relief and disappointment. On one hand, I didn't bomb it like last time. On the other hand, my scores still weren't that great. I stared at my top five business school selections on the screen. To make it into any one of them would be a dream. But were my scores enough? Would they ever be? I stalled for a few minutes, then finally pressed the button to send in my scores. It was out of my hands now.

That night, I went out with friends to celebrate my freedom from the GMAT. Margaritas, beers, and shots flowed as we scarfed down tacos at a Marina District bar. Suddenly, I felt a tingle on my lower lip. Not one of salt and lime from the tequila shots, but a hot tingle I hadn't felt before. I ignored it, though, not wanting it to take away from the celebratory vibe of the night. When I got home, I collapsed into bed, completely wiped out from the day.

The next morning, the sores on my lip had formed a little cauliflower cluster. After Googling, I found out they were cold sores and that they could surface due to stress. I guess my body was trying to tell me something. In the past five months, I had gone through a lot, from hospitals and care facilities to ballrooms and testing rooms. Stress would be an understatement. Hell would be more apt. Perhaps it was finally time to take a break?

But that break never came. One day later, I got a frantic call from my mom. "Come to Chinese Hospital! Baba is in the ICU!"

A deafening buzz banged my eardrums and knees buckling beneath me, I sank to the ground.

We can try to run away from reality. We can distract ourselves all we want. But we can't hide from what's coming. Even if we desperately need a break before we break apart.

Moment to Self-Reflect

When I look back at myself at twenty-six years old, I feel a mix of pride and grief. Pride because I managed to survive through an intensely traumatic time. But grief because I had to endure so much. To add salt to my wounds, I contributed to my own stress by taking the GMAT amidst all the chaos in my family. However, it was how I knew how to cope back then. Lost, I needed to prove my worth through achieving. It made me feel more in control.

External Achievements and Relationship with Self-Worth

For those of us who struggle with low self-worth, external achievements can feel like a way to prove ourselves. External achievements are accomplishments that are validated by others. They're often measured by what society values—things like degrees, job performance, promotions, awards, competitions, or public recognition.

As I learned as a child: *Love is conditional. It isn't freely given but earned.* I believed that I needed to obey, conform, and rely on external achievements to be loved. So I became a "high achiever," someone who constantly sets high expectations and goals in life. School, in particular, is a sore subject for many children of immigrants like me. It's as if our parents' love and our worth depended on our academic achievements. That's why I wanted to do well on the GMAT and apply to business school. I saw my friends with MBAs as more worthy than me; they had the external validation I craved. Without the ability to look inward yet, I looked to the outside for validation.

As a high achiever, I thought that I could prove my worth to my parents, society, friends, and romantic partners through my achievements. But no matter what I did, it never felt good enough. Sure, being a high achiever could bring success, opportunities, money, and recognition. But it can also cause self-neglect, stress, pressure, fear of failure, disconnection from your true self, and the feeling that no matter what, it'll never be enough.

Reflection Questions:

- Have there been times when you looked to external achievements to feel more worthy? Who were you trying to prove your worth to, and why?

- Think back on your earlier life. Where could any of your beliefs or narratives about external achievements come from?

- In what ways has chasing external achievements helped you get to where you are?

- In what ways has chasing external achievements held you back from other things like your health, relationships, or happiness?

8

THE LAST BREATH

IN MY FANTASY, Baba's homecoming from the care facility to Chinatown was going to be a big celebratory event. We'd congratulate him on healing from his lung disease, cook a big feast as a family, and even deep clean the apartment so that he'd have a comfy place to return to. It'd be just like old times. Faybee would snuggle up to him. We'd go to the bakery and eat pineapple buns. Then we'd watch basketball on TV together, just as Baba loved to do.

But in reality, he came in an ambulance, directly to the Chinese Hospital Intensive Care Unit. At least he could communicate more easily. Everyone spoke Cantonese at the hospital. There were no language or cultural barriers here.

Outside on Jackson Street, little old ladies in bucket hats strolled by with their pink plastic bags full of groceries. Inside the hospital, my mom, Stan, and I reunited with Baba, each of us holding back our tears. Even—and especially—in a dire situation, we had to remain collectively strong. Bend but not break.

Since Chinese Hospital was a small community hospital, there were only a few patient beds in the ICU. Baba occupied one of them. In between the beds, there were metal cabinets, each with multiple sockets to plug machines into, and various buttons. Next to Baba's bed, there was a monitor that showed his vital signs in red and green lines blipping across the screen. It looked like something from a sci-fi movie. Like man versus machine.

What reminded us of humanity was the kind doctor assigned to Baba. She was pleasant every time we saw her, and Baba seemed to trust her. So we trusted her too.

After a few days in the ICU hooked up to the CPAP machine to help him breathe, Baba seemed to be doing fine overall. Fine meaning stable. Fine meaning no scary crashes in oxygen levels. Plus, he could still talk a little through the CPAP, not that he usually said much anyway.

I marveled at Baba's continued strength. Despite his gaunt body with bones poking out, he possessed some kind of uncanny ability to hang onto life despite the odds. I don't know how he did it. I can imagine he suffered a lot. But he fought for every breath without complaint. Whenever we visited, Baba perked up in bed, signaling to us that yes, he was still there to make it through.

I started to think that he was invincible. I convinced myself that "stable condition" meant that he could recover and return home to our family's apartment. After all, he'd survived the past nine months.

Full of naive belief, I allowed myself to fantasize about traveling again. JetBlue had a special promotion that beckoned my name. For only $800, I could fly around the world. I could see myself in New York at a Broadway theater show. I could imagine eating a croissant in Paris, a place I'd loved since studying abroad in France my senior year of college. Maybe Marco could join me too.

One day at the hospital, while Baba was taking a nap, I sat across from my mom and shared my fantasy.

"Mommy, there's a special for an around-the-world flight ticket for only $800. I could hop around to different cities. Isn't that cool? I'm thinking of doing that now that I'm done with the GMAT," I said.

My mom almost jumped out of her chair. "Why would you even mention that?! What kind of daughter are you?! Baba is sick! Shame on you! So selfish!"

I looked down at the floor. "I'm sorry. I meant when he was better again."

My heart sank deep into an ocean of my shame like the Titanic on its ill-fated maiden voyage. The iceberg we hit was all of this. All of this shit my family had to go through and didn't deserve. I felt like I was drowning.

For so many months, each time I saw a call from my mom or Stan on my phone, I would dread the worst. Thoughts raced every single time I looked at my phone. *What happened now? Who's in the hospital? When do I finally get to live my life again and take it off pause?*

Sitting with my mom and dad at the hospital now, I could feel the cold sores on my lip oozing, as if my anxiety were bubbling to the surface of my face. I dabbed the sores with a napkin, wiping away the pus. I wished I could wipe everything away in my life and start all over again with a blank slate.

I'd keep Marco though. His love kept me sane.

By then, Marco and I were in a serious relationship. Through all the past few months' hardships, he stuck by me, unfazed by my parents' illnesses and my manic ways. It was natural, then, that I'd finally introduce him to my mom and dad.

The ICU wasn't the most romantic setting, but what else could we do? In an ideal scenario, we'd eat dim sum together at a restaurant. But we had to work with what we had.

When Sunday came, Marco and I drove together to the hospital. As we entered the automatic sliding doors, I grabbed his hand. Then we stepped into the elevator and went upstairs to the ICU, where my parents' eyes met ours.

Marco walked over to my mom, extending his hand. "Hello, Mrs. Choi, nice to finally meet you."

My mom received his hand in hers, seemingly impressed by his gentlemanly greeting. "Hi, Marco. Thank you for coming."

Then without missing a beat, Marco looked directly at Baba with intent. "Hello, Mr. Choi. Nice to meet you too. I'll take good care of your daughter."

As to why he blurted out this promise so early in the meeting, I have no idea. But at least he said it with conviction.

Laying there with a CPAP machine strapped around his head and a thick, accordion-like plastic tube coming from his mouth, Baba nodded and looked into Marco's eyes as if to say, *thank you.*

After a bit of chitchat between my mom and Marco, he had to go back to Hayward to take care of an errand. "Bye, Mr. and Mrs. Choi. I look forward to seeing you again."

Baba nodded to Marco. My mom gave him another handshake. I took my boyfriend's hand and walked him out.

When I got back to the ICU, I braced for my mom and dad's reactions. I knew that my parents were apprehensive that my boyfriend was not Chinese. Like many immigrant parents, they wanted their daughter to eventually marry into the same culture.

But my mom said, "Nice guy. Good that he's smart!"

Not bad for a start. After an hour, it was my turn to leave too.

"I'm going to Hayward for a few days," I revealed to both of them as I tightened my shoulders and prepared for backlash.

I thought that my mom would be the one to ask why and object. But I was surprised to hear my dad's soft voice break through the silence.

He looked at my mom and I and said, "It's best that you both don't go."

My mom and I shot glances at each other. We were both shocked to hear a plea come from someone who was usually so reserved, who barely ever voiced his needs.

"Mommy will still be here. It's just me going," I explained.

"It's best that you don't go," he repeated again.

Perplexed, I shrugged it off. *What's the big deal? Why would this time be any different?*

"Baba, don't worry. I won't be far. Less than an hour drive away," I said, practically running toward the door.

Any longer and the guilt of leaving him would cement me to the floor.

———

I drove to Hayward, desperate to escape for a few days. Later that afternoon, I found myself sitting at a park next to Marco. Finally, a peaceful respite from it all. A time to detach and lean on someone else's shoulder instead of having to carry all the weight. I melted into him.

Three nights later, I met up with one of my best friends, Michelle, who lived in Newark, a city in the East Bay. Sassy, fun, Vietnamese American, and always laughing, she was a true light in my life

Turning down a narrow suburban street in Newark, I picked Michelle up from her house in my car.

As soon as I pulled up, she screamed with glee. "Hi, Jenn!!!" With hoop earrings, highlighted hair, and a megawatt smile, she jumped into my passenger seat.

"Hiiii!!!" I shouted back like a teenager at a concert.

When we arrived for dinner at Claim Jumper, a popular restaurant, and sat down at a booth, you couldn't shut us up. We were two girls chatting with barely any breaths in between, laughing over spinach artichoke dip. It truly felt like a vacation. I almost forgot that my dad was in the ICU.

I was in the middle of telling a story when, suddenly, I felt a buzz come from my purse. *Maybe Marco*, I thought. I reached into my purse. But when the caller ID showed up, it was a number I didn't know with a 415 San Francisco area code.

"Hello, this is Jenn," I announced to the unknown receiver on the other side of the line.

"Jennifer, this is the nurse calling from Chinese Hospital. I think you'd better come now," a woman said.

Shit, shit, shit. I shot a glance at Michelle, who looked concerned.

"How's my dad? Is this something that can wait a few more hours?" I asked, unsure if this was yet another false alarm.

"If I were you, I'd come as soon as possible," the nurse reiterated.

My body bore the weight of her words, each fiber of my being tensing. "Okay, I'm not in San Francisco but will drive back now," I replied.

As I hung up, I entered a state of shock. Our waiter came by and set down our dinner orders. I stared at him and the chicken pasta. Then I stared at Michelle. I sat paralyzed.

Finally, when I was able to speak, I said, "Ummm, sorry. But could I please take this to go?"

Michelle looked at the waiter and gestured to her untouched plate of meatloaf and mashed potatoes. "Can you please pack mine up too?"

He nodded, looking confused but agreeing to our requests. He came back a few minutes later with a plastic bag carrying our leftovers in aluminum containers.

Michelle's eyes moistened. "I'm so sorry, let's get you back there. It might be a long night, so please take this food to your family," she said, handing me her portion.

Bless her. After working for years as a pediatric nurse, she knew what care in critical circumstances felt like. And she knew that food was love.

Less than ten minutes later, I was driving on the freeway with chicken pasta and Michelle's donated portion of meatloaf, still piping hot, in my passenger seat.

I couldn't reach my mom or Stan by phone. Part of me feared that the worst had already happened, that the nurse was going gentle on me over the phone as a part of the protocol.

I called Marco from the road. "I don't know how bad it is. I don't know anything. I don't even know if he's still alive."

I don't remember what he said. Shaking, I headed back to San Francisco. It felt like the longest drive of my life.

—

About an hour later, I parked my car in the alley near Chinese Hospital. Clutching the bag of leftovers, I walked down the narrow alley as the soft glow of street lamps lit the way to the hospital entrance. The familiar march from the lobby to the elevators to the ICU doors felt like an eternity. When I finally got to the room, I breathed a sigh of relief at Baba's vital signs on the monitor. *He was still alive!*

But then I shrank back in horror as I got closer to Baba's hospital bed. There was a tube going down his throat now, and a feeding tube poked out from his stomach. My mom looked weary, hairs sticking up out of her bun. Stan could barely lift his eyes from the floor.

"What's happening with Baba?" I asked with a tremble in my voice, half-pleading for some kind of hopeful news.

"Jenn ah. The doctor says his organs are failing," my mom shared solemnly.

I couldn't believe what I was hearing. I glanced at Stan, desperately seeking another bystander to confirm the news.

He looked up from the floor and squeezed out, "Yeah."

I took a seat next to my mom and Stan beside Baba's bed, collapsing into the chair. Together we waited. My tears soaked my shirt.

After an hour, a nurse walked over to us to deliver further news. "I'm sorry, but as the immediate family, you have to make a decision. The doctor thinks we should start increasing the morphine to reduce his suffering, which means he might go within some hours. Maybe a few, maybe twelve, it's hard to say when."

What the fuck?! What the fuck are we supposed to do now?! I looked at Baba, now an unconscious warrior losing a long fight.

My mom made the decision. "Okay," she said in a tone mixed with both dignity and resignation.

The nurse nodded. While I stared at Baba's skeletal, machine-sustained body in disbelief, she administered more morphine and removed his tubes. My mom, Stan, and I sat to the left of Baba. We quietly ate the leftovers I'd brought, now cold and congealed in a gelatinous mass. At least there were mashed potatoes, one of our Thanksgiving favorites.

We waited without saying anything. Believing that we could hold time still with our silence.

At around seven in the morning, my brother's voice pierced through the silence as he lifted his heavy, drooping eyelids with force. He had been at the hospital all day and night. "I gotta go home to sleep for maybe an hour or two. I'll have my phone on ring."

Neither my mom nor I protested. Slumping in our chairs, we understood deep in our bones how he felt. Plus, it would probably take a lot longer. Baba was a fighter. We waited with him as he fought to stay with us. Stan left to take his nap.

As I sat in my chair, I recalled Baba's last words to me a few days ago. "It's best that you don't go," he had said to me and my mom.

I repeated it over and over again like a broken record. *It's best that you don't go. It's best that you don't go.* I looked at Baba's calm face and begged silently to him. *It's best that you don't go. Please don't go yet.*

But that hope, that beautiful hope. It swirls around you like a mist, making you feel invincible, untouchable, until the cruel, ruthless reality creeps in.

Around eight in the morning, as if the machines were instructed by a conductor at a symphony, they suddenly started their opus. Except it wasn't music. It was a terrible cacophony of beeping, of alarms, of the violent ding ding ding of a bell coinciding with rapidly changing numbers on the monitor screen.

My mom and I sprang up from our chairs and bolted to Baba's side as the nurse rushed over too.

"It's time," the nurse said softly.

The noise. The noise of the machines filled the room incessantly, like some kind of psychological torture experiment.

I fished my phone out of my purse and called Stan, who picked up within a few rings. "Come now!" I screamed.

Then I turned to Baba and took one of his limp hands in my hand as my mom grabbed the other. "Bye, Daddy, I love you," I said quietly through my scalding tears.

I flashed back to my childhood memory of him waving back at me in his silver-rimmed glasses and gray wool slacks as he walked down Mason Street to go to work.

I looked at Baba's face, breathed in a few deep breaths syncing with his chest, and watched him take his very last breath.

By the time Stan burst through the ICU doors, breathless too, our silent hero was gone.

And a part of me died with him.

9

EARTHQUAKE

DEATH IS LIKE an earthquake. No matter how prepared you think you are, it will still knock you off your feet. It rips up entire city blocks around you, tearing homes and families apart. It doesn't discriminate. It does not choose who to take and who to keep.

When death took my father, I crumbled in the aftermath, at times wishing it had taken me too. I had survived earthquakes before. But I didn't expect the aftershocks.

Growing up in San Francisco, I'd experienced several earthquakes, the biggest one named Loma Prieta in 1989. I was in the back room of our family home with Stan when I was five and he was three. Suddenly, the earth shook turbulently beneath us, causing us to stumble off balance. I quivered with fear as I looked at my brother, and then I scanned the room for Baba. *Where is he? Is this the end?*

I grasped our wooden bookshelf for stability. And then I remembered that the doorway was the safest spot. In kindergarten, I had learned about the dangers of earthquakes as the teacher explained what to do. Several times in class, we had rehearsed emergency drills. The alarm would sound. Our teacher would yell, "Duck and cover!" Then all us kids would quickly duck under our desks, curling into balls, covering the back of our heads with our arms. I had been trained to escape from death at an early age. Just like I learned how to escape from pain.

As I started to run toward the doorway separating the back room and kitchen, Baba ran into the kitchen from the hallway. Together with Stan, we cowered in our doorway. A porcelain vase crashed to the floor from the bookshelf. We held our breaths, bracing for more impact. But within fifteen seconds it was over. Fortunately, our family and apartment building escaped unharmed. My mom had been out when the earthquake hit and rejoined us safely at home within an hour. When frantic family and friends called to check in on us, we couldn't understand why they were so concerned. We didn't know the magnitude of the destruction. At least not yet.

That evening, we gathered with our neighbors at Huntington Park up the hill from our apartment. In an earthquake, you need to go to an open spot away from buildings, in case aftershocks hit and cause further wreckage. Huntington Park, with its green grass, children's playground, and gorgeous water fountains, felt like a safe haven. As news reports came in over radio and TV stations, the world heard of the Bay Area's plight. As it turns out, the earthquake was much worse than it initially appeared. At a devastating 6.9 magnitude, it destroyed multiple buildings in the Marina District, collapsed a section of the Nimitz Freeway in Oakland, and took down a section of the Bay Bridge. Later, it'd be revealed that 63 people had died, almost 4,000 were injured, and the overall damage cost 6 billion dollars.

But as a kid, I was totally oblivious. I couldn't comprehend the danger nor the destruction. Huntington Park was one of my favorite childhood gems, located between the Fairmont Hotel and the majestic Grace Cathedral. Stan and I spent many afternoons gleefully sliding down the slide and running across the park where rich neighbors who lived uphill would walk their perfectly coiffed dogs. When shocked neighbors lit candles at the park the night of the earthquake, Stan and I started singing "Happy Birthday" jubilantly as we stood in our oversized hand-me-down jackets. After all, that's what we knew candles were good for. We got lost in our birthday song—in that oblivious moment amidst a terrible disaster.

Ah, to be that innocent again. To be shielded from the pain of the world even when it starts to fall apart before your eyes.

When Baba died in August 2010, I was twenty-six years old, and the life I'd built to run from pain began to show its sinister cracks. But first, my trauma responses kicked in to protect me, turning me and my mom into machines.

An hour after Baba took his last breath, my mom, Stan, and I proceeded with mechanical action as if everything was just a matter of fact. I texted Marco the news, and then I went straight back to focusing on my family's survival. Adrenaline pumped through our veins as we thought about our next steps. *What would Baba do?* we asked ourselves, still in a state of shock in the Chinese Hospital lobby. He was the one who usually took care of the administrative tasks in our family. And as much as I hate to admit this, there are a ton of administrative tasks after you lose someone you love.

"Jenn ah. Let's go tell the funeral home," my mom proposed.

I peered through the glass doors of the hospital lobby. It was bright outside, with people bustling about. The exterior shelves of the produce market across the street were freshly piled with mounds of oranges, daikon radish, and bok choy. It felt so strange to witness life move on outside. Didn't they know that I'd just lost my father?

I glanced at the time on my phone. "Yeah, it's past nine. I guess the one on Green Street must be open by now."

"You guys go without me. I can't miss class," Stan said. He had just started a new semester at San Francisco State University and couldn't lose his spot in class.

We didn't comfort each other. We didn't even allow ourselves to grieve. I don't think we had the capacity to do either.

As Stan walked away, my mom and I marched to Green Street Mortuary. There was only one funeral home in the Chinatown and North Beach area, and we'd been there multiple times before. They specialized in honoring Chinese funeral traditions, and many of the staff spoke Cantonese and Taishanese. As such, it was a popular choice for memorial services for immigrant families like ours. Whenever a relative died, we found ourselves there, bowing three times in front of their casket to say goodbye. We'd already said goodbye to my great-uncle Maynard. Then his wife. And most tragically, one of Baba's younger brothers, our beloved Uncle Six, who died in 2001. At least they'd be reunited now.

My mom and I walked through the heavy wooden doors of the building, up the brown-carpeted stairs, and turned right in the hallway toward the staff's offices.

A woman with permed hair looked up from her desk. "May I help you?"

"My husband died this morning," my mom confessed.

The woman motioned to two seats in front of her. "I'm sorry. Please sit down."

I took a seat, thinking how bizarre it seemed to conduct a business transaction so soon after my father's death. But at least it gave my family something to focus on—a distraction from the impending grief. Thirty minutes later, after a flurry of paperwork, we headed downstairs to select a coffin. Cherrywood. Traditional. And within our meager budget. Baba didn't have a life insurance policy, but we did have some savings.

After we finished at the mortuary, my mom and I tackled the next order of business: notify our community association in Chinatown. In the 1800s, during major waves of Chinese immigration to North America, associations formed to support immigrants. Within Chinatowns in cities like San Francisco, New York, Vancouver, and Toronto, you can still find these associations, which provide communal support, social services, cultural preservation, and even funeral arrangements for its members. Community was their origin story. Community was what my family needed most now.

My mom and I walked to Waverly Place, an alley with restaurants, Chinese associations, and a discount shop with imported goods on the corner. Stan had finished his one class of the day and joined us on Waverly too. Sadly, I couldn't read the Chinese characters on the buildings. I'd never really learned how to read or write despite going to evening Chinese classes during middle school. As a kid growing up in America, I didn't see the point of it, preferring to ditch class and play with my friends instead. But with Baba gone, feelings of shame and guilt suddenly washed over me for not learning. With his passing, it felt like part of my heritage had died too. I felt like a shitty daughter for failing to keep our mother tongue alive. Sure, I spoke

Cantonese, but even my verbal comprehension started to fade as I moved away from my family home. It's not easy to be a child of immigrants—there's grief even in our loss of language.

Thankfully, my mom recognized the entrance to the association and rang the doorbell. Someone buzzed us through the heavy gate. As we went up the stairs, I could hear people playing mahjong, a game that's hundreds of years old. Thick white tiles with symbols clacked fast and furious under wrinkled hands. I had never seen these people in my life, yet we shared a deep bond.

One of the elders greeted us in Cantonese. "What can I do for you?" he asked.

"My husband died. Kong Shing Choi. He was a member here," my mom said.

The old man let out a sympathetic sigh and reached for a pen and a small notepad. "When is the funeral?"

"Ten in the morning this Sunday on Green," said my mom.

With a solemn nod, the man assured us that he would pass the message along through an obituary placed in the local Chinese newspapers. Anyone who knew Baba would be invited to join the funeral. I was impressed. What was this hidden side of Chinatown I never saw, up the stairwells of little alleyways?

Before I had a chance to ponder longer, my mom led the way across the alley to our next stop: The Ning Yung Benevolent Cemetery Association where we'd purchase the burial plot. It was another nondescript location without fanfare. Once again, my mom seemed to know what to do. Like some kind of pre-programmed response. No tears. Just action.

A woman with short black hair greeted us at the top of the stairs. Before we even sat down, my mom blurted out, "My husband died. Can we buy a plot for him?"

The woman gestured to a table in the old administrative office. My mom, Stan, and I sat down at the table across from her. Twenty minutes later, after yet another round of paperwork, we got our plot. Not just for Baba, but for my mom too. She signed the papers for a plot in the Hoy Sun Ning Yung Cemetery, a popular Chinese cemetery in the town of Colma next to San

Francisco. It'd be enough space to hold their cremated remains, just as my parents wanted. My mom also went ahead and ordered a granite headstone, which would have space for both their names and pictures.

"Why wait? Prices will only increase," my mom reasoned.

I shifted in my seat. She was right. We could save money on the plot and headstone if we bundled everything together. But it made me anxious to think that we could lose her too.

I was terrified that I'd fail to save her, just as I'd failed to save Baba.

The next few days were a catatonic blur. Marco came over to my apartment to comfort me the night after Baba died. I felt like a small child in his arms—vulnerable and fragile. The day after, I hibernated in bed by myself, unable to do anything else. I wanted to disappear.

Finally, on the Saturday before the funeral, I was ready to come out of my shell. A handful of my closest friends, including Michelle and Christina, appeared like angels at my apartment door. They brought me Flamin' Hot Cheetos and Haribo gummy bears—my favorite snacks. We could barely fit in my bedroom, with some of them squeezed on my carpet as I sat up in bed. I don't know how it was possible given the situation, but my friends were able to crack jokes that brought me comic relief. Tears from laughter replaced tears from sadness. In the presence of my chosen community, I almost forgot that Baba was dead. Friends and lovers can be like heart medicine, rehabilitating our spirits after loss.

The morning of the funeral, I braved reality again, emerging to face the outside world. I put on black stockings and a black dress with puffed sleeves. I drove to the mortuary and parked my car, still in a state of shock.

I wish I could say that I remember vivid details from the funeral. That I could recall the faces of all who came to pay respects. Or what I said when it was my turn to give a speech at the front of the chapel before Baba's open casket, looking at his face one last time. But the truth is, I can't. I just went through the motions. I *yun*-ed.

I do remember afterward, though, when our relatives, Marco, and my childhood best friends, Lily and Alice, joined us for my family's funeral lunch. It was at the restaurant Lychee Garden around the corner from the mortuary. In Chinese culture, it's common to have a "mourning meal" where we remember our lost loved ones and help the spirit of the deceased transition to the afterlife. With religious influences from Buddhism and Taoism, many Chinese people believe that the spirits of our loved ones continue to exist on the other side, guiding those of us still living—sometimes even believed to do so across cycles of reincarnation. I wondered if Baba was pleased on the other side. Could he see us celebrating his life as we sat at round dining tables eating chow mein, ginger and scallion chicken, and barbecued pork? Could he see how much he was loved?

I sat at a table with Marco, Lily, Alice, Stan, and a few of our cousins. As the waiters cleared our plates, Lily asked, "What would make you feel better after this? Wanna do anything?"

I felt relieved to not have to be alone. "Yeah. Let's go to Ocean Beach!"

That afternoon, me, Lily, and Marco sat on our jackets in the sand at Ocean Beach, watching the waves caress the shore for miles. This was my happy place. Wind in my hair, flanked by my best friend and my boyfriend, I inhaled a salty breath of peace as we waited for the sunset. As the sun finally dipped into the water on the horizon, I thought to myself, *Damn, I'm handling this extremely well.*

I held it together even in the following days. As I recall—even though it's still somewhat of a blur—the funeral, cremation, and burial all happened on different days due to scheduling availability of the various venues. Death, unfortunately, is a busy business.

A couple of days after the funeral, my family accompanied Baba's coffin to the crematory, where my father's remains would turn to ash. Growing up in Chinatown, I had seen caravans of cars leave Green Street Mortuary. Police cars would stop traffic as family members cried in the cars following the hearse. But now I was no longer a bystander in the street. I was driving my car with my mom and brother in it, following my dad's hearse from San Francisco to Colma. At the crematory, I watched Baba's coffin go into the building. As I said goodbye to his body, I felt a mix of relief and longing. Relief that he no longer had to suffer and longing to bring him back to life.

Less than a week later, we buried Baba's ashes in an urn at the Hoy Sun Ning Yung Cemetery, where he'd be laid to rest on the same hill as his younger brother. As my mom, Stan, and I stood over the burial plot, I only allowed myself a few tears. Bend but not break.

But even machines eventually break down.

10

AFTERSHOCKS

A FEW WEEKS after Baba's death, the aftershocks of the loss finally hit me. Rumbling, roaring, they broke open the ground beneath me, unearthing a bubbling mess of grief.

One night, I dreamed of Baba standing in the kitchen of our family home again, chopping green onions on our round wooden cutting board. He looked so healthy, with glowing skin and filled-in cheeks that reflected the dusk light through the windows. I wanted to stand in this moment forever with him, never leaving his side. But when I woke up, reality hit. I remembered his skeletal body ravaged by lung disease, and I curled up into a ball, wailing, screaming my anguish into the void.

I wish the grief of losing a parent upon no one, yet it inevitably comes for most of us. A vengeful monster of depression, guilt, and regret ripped my insides to pieces. I questioned myself, questioning my entire existence as Baba's daughter. *Why didn't I talk to him more at the care facility? Why didn't I try to rebuild our childhood bond? Why didn't I stay longer when he told us not to go the last days he was alive? Fuck! Why did I so royally fuck up?* And the loudest, most resounding question of all: *Why wasn't I worthy enough to make him stay?*

All the sins of my past came to haunt me with agonizing fury. Like when I was seven years old and found the entire stash of Hello Kitty gifts that Baba had hid from me. I don't know where he got them or how we afforded them, but he had hidden a stash to give to me on special occasions like my birthday. One day, I found a cardboard box with a cotton comforter neatly folded at the top. I reached my hands in, pulled the comforter out of the box, and dug out all the Hello Kitty stationary and stickers underneath. When Baba came home, I saw the deflated look on his face at my ruined surprise.

And then there was the time when I was ten years old, hiding behind a doorway, watching him pull money out from a dictionary in our back room. The next day, I began a monthslong stealth operation of taking a twenty-dollar bill here and there from the envelope wedged between the pages of the dictionary. We were so poor, yet I had no conscience stealing from my own family. And for what? More candy from the corner store? What a shameless thief.

These thoughts of how I'd disappointed my father terrorized me. Convinced that I was the world's shittiest daughter, I entered a dark downward spiral, struggling to dig myself out of the earthquake's debris. However, through the darkness of my descent, I felt thankful to at least have my mom, brother, friends, and boyfriend. But romances can collapse too.

In the first few months of our relationship, Marco and I rarely fought. But the growing distance between us, with our busy schedules, did strain our relationship. Sometimes we'd have periods of intense can't-get-enough-of-you love. And at other times, I couldn't get ahold of him. I tried to avoid conflict by keeping my feelings of sadness or frustration within the relationship to myself. After all, it was a method that worked within my family. But despite the mounting tension, I genuinely believed that if I did everything I could to please him, we'd make it through. Anything for the man I believed to be my soulmate.

One night, a month after Baba died, I was in my bedroom when I got a phone call from Marco that completely caught me off guard. He broke up with me, seemingly out of nowhere, citing cultural differences.

I took a long pause to make sense of what he'd said. But I couldn't understand. I was so shocked and heartbroken that I didn't even know how to respond.

After we hung up, I thought about us. I did not know that our cultural differences had bothered him that much. How many things had gone unsaid between us? His family might have expected him to be with an Italian girl, just as mine hoped that my boyfriend would be Chinese. Yet our immigrant parents seemed to accept our interracial romance—something that's often not the case in traditional immigrant families. So I was confused.

When I told my mom the next day, she responded with similar confusion. "Jenn ah, who breaks up with someone so soon after their dad dies?"

I wondered the same. The breakup did feel extra devastating given the circumstances. I wallowed in my heartbreak, soaking my pillowcase with tears every night. It was just as I'd believed since I was a child. *I am not worthy enough to make people stay.* I couldn't make Baba stay. I couldn't make any boyfriends stay.

I guess you'd expect me to try to move on from this relationship. But there was something that kept pulling me to Marco, even after we broke up. Love is wild, ain't it?

He called me a few days later to tell me that he missed me. He confessed that he still loved me, that maybe one day we could be together again. My heart fluttered. I told him I loved him too. Sure, I was still confused about the breakup, but I was too scared to bring it up. Once again, I shoved my feelings down, as I'd been used to in my family.

In the week after our breakup, we began to write to each other again. We talked about how our lives were probably too complicated, with too many ambitions like my desire to pursue an MBA, that made us unavailable for each other. But I also wrote that I'd be ready for him at a future date.

That October, I traveled to Rome and London, turning to travel to soothe my grieving heart. After Baba's death, I needed to get away from San Francisco, which reminded me of loss at every turn. However, the whole time I was on vacation, I thought of Marco.

When I got back from traveling, just a month after our first breakup, Marco and I reunited, high on rekindled love. Only to break up again. And only to get back into the cycle of professing our undying love. We were like fire together, sometimes burning bright, sometimes burning ourselves down.

It'd be the beginning of a long, intense, tumultuous pattern of breaking up and making up between us.

I won't get into further details, especially since there are always multiple sides to every story. But there are a few things you should know at this point. One: I believed that this on-off, push-pull dynamic was totally normal in a relationship. And two: I never felt truly worthy in any relationship.

The thing is, whether my relationship was on again or off again, or even when I was surrounded by friends, I still felt alone after Baba died. The grief of losing my dad became unbearable.

After trying to keep it together for so long, I finally broke down.

One day after Christmas, four months after Baba died, I slammed into the bottom of the pit. For the first time in my once-vibrant life, I lost the will to live. To be clear, I didn't want to harm myself; I couldn't live with the shame and guilt I'd feel—even as a spirit on the other side—if I left my family. But I did not want to live anymore. It felt as if a force stole my soul and left an empty shell. I cried uncontrollably. The entire world faded to black. I could see no way forward to being happy ever again. Everything sucked. I sucked.

Yet somehow in my void, one tiny part of my brain urged me to get help. This I had learned from Lily when my mom was first diagnosed with cancer. Sitting in my bedroom, I reached for my phone. I thought of my friend Jeff, who I knew had overcome significant difficulties in his own life with incredible strength. In Chinese culture, there's a stigma around mental health, so I felt uncomfortable reaching out for help. But Jeff felt like a safe resource to me, so I texted him.

"I dunno what to do. I've lost my motivation to live. I won't do anything stupid. But I dunno," I texted.

Within minutes my phone rang. "Jenn! I'm in Vegas, but I'm here for you. What's going on?"

I felt relieved that he'd responded so quickly. "I feel hopeless," I revealed.

Jeff jumped into action without judgment. "You've got this. Here's what I would do that's helped me before. Take out a piece of paper. Write down all your negative thoughts. Then for each one, list the opposite. Find the positive. Prove that the negative thought is not true. Our brains are tricky. Sneaky bastards. They trick us into thinking that things are worse than they are. Can you do that?"

I picked up the notebook on my desk. "I think so?"

"Great! There's a book too . . . called *Feeling Good* by David Burns that I'd recommend. It goes over this in more detail," Jeff added.

"Thank you. Have fun in Vegas!" I said.

After we hung up, I picked up my pen. Empowered by my friend's advice, I let it all out. The terrible thoughts that haunted me. The fear of speaking them out loud. Beneath each negative thought, I wrote the opposite of those statements. Under the thought, '*I am a shitty daughter*,' I wrote, 'I am a good daughter.' Under the thought, '*I failed to save Baba*,' I wrote, 'I did my best for Baba.' I didn't expect it, but I already felt lighter by the time I got to the bottom of the page.

Suddenly as I was writing, a lucid vision popped into my head, breaking through the darkness. I could see myself surrounded by snow and remembered how much I loved being in Tahoe. High in the Sierra Mountains, just a few hours northeast of San Francisco, Lake Tahoe was one of my favorite places to go. I had learned how to snowboard in college and continued to do it a few times a year after I graduated. I popped open my laptop and checked for upcoming ski bus trips, a service I'd booked before. As if the Universe had extended an olive branch to me, there were still seats available for the bus going to Tahoe in two days. I booked my spot immediately.

The morning of the trip, I joined fellow snow enthusiasts on a packed bus heading to winter wonderland. Four hours later, we reached Northstar Ski Resort. With my baby blue jacket, cream snow pants, and white snowboarding boots, I got off the bus and retrieved my snowboard from the luggage compartment, ready to be one with nature.

As I ascended up the gondola toward the white-powdered mountain, I could already feel my mood lighten. I sat down at the top of the mountain, allowing the ground to cradle me. Allowing myself to be held by the earth. Peering below, I saw the majesty of a blue lake beneath me. Pine trees with snowflakes enveloped me.

My snowboard was white, with a silhouette of a bird on the tip. Staring at that little shadow of a bird, I felt inspired to fly again. I popped up on my snowboard and glided like an eagle down the slope. I felt free again. Alive. As I heard the whoosh of the fresh snow underneath me, I announced to myself, "It's still a beautiful life."

Like the changing seasons, earthquakes don't last forever. And with that impulse to keep going, I found my way back to solid ground again. Shaken but not swallowed up.

Moment to Self-Reflect

The past few chapters of my life felt heavy. I lost my dad. I lost a boyfriend. And then I lost the will to live. I broke down. But . . . I'm still here with you. I survived. If you're going through a dark time, please hang in there. As a friend once reminded me, "It's always darkest before dawn." You've got this, even when it feels impossible.

When I lost Baba, I beat myself up for a long time, feeling like a shitty daughter for not being more present in his last year alive. But now I can see that I was just trying to survive through numbing my pain, dissociating, and chasing external achievements. If nature had intended that one person's illness or death would stop further life in others, there would be no survival of our species. Trauma responses protect. However, it is profoundly sad that by numbing my pain, I also numbed love.

Feeling Your Feelings

Many of us detach from painful emotions, especially if it's learned behavior. We run away from our difficult feelings but miss out on experiencing the full breadth and depth of our emotions.

I had to learn this the hard way, through the grief of losing my father. At first I was numb, but then I went the opposite extreme and became completely overwhelmed by my grief. But maybe there's a gentler path for you?

Sometimes we fear our emotions might overwhelm us, so we avoid feeling them. But perhaps there's a middle ground. For example, I wish I could've allowed myself to cry and feel sadness when my dad was still alive, while also reflecting upon the happy memories we shared.

Reflection Questions:

- Think of a few times when you detached from your emotions. In detaching, what other emotions or experiences might you have missed out on?

- For each instance that you thought of, what feels like a healthy middle ground for feeling your feelings?

Relationship Limiting Beliefs and Dynamics

Emotional detachment isn't the only pattern I inherited from my family. My relationship beliefs also mirrored aspects of my own relationship with my parents. After losing my dad, losing my boyfriend further reduced my sense of self-worth. Two of my childhood and teenage limiting beliefs were reaffirmed by the breakup and subsequent make-up-and-break-up cycle. *I am not worthy enough to make people stay.* And: *Love is conditional. It isn't freely given but earned.* I believed that I had to suppress my feelings and avoid conflict in order to be loved.

Furthermore, I could see that the intense on-off, push-pull dynamic of some of my past romantic relationships felt familiar to me because I had that kind of relationship with my mom. Sometimes she'd be loving and nurturing, and at other times, she'd be unavailable. And if I'm totally honest, I was also unavailable in relationships at times too, digging into work to keep myself busy and protect myself from truly opening up to love.

What we learn as a survival tactic within our families can often be what we think works in romantic relationships. However, this can lead to unhealthy behaviors that get in the way of receiving the love we deserve. I invite you to reflect upon your own relationships.

Reflection Questions:

- Make a list of your most significant romantic relationships and breakups. What limiting beliefs stemmed from, or were reinforced by, those relationships and breakups?

- In what ways have your romantic relationship dynamics been similar to your family dynamics? In what ways have they been different?

Breakups can be hard. Losing people we love can be hard. Sometimes that can make us feel depressed. In my case, I've come to learn that after Baba died, I likely had situational depression. It's a type of stress-related depression that can occur after someone experiences a traumatic event or series of events. It differs from clinical depression in that it's specifically linked to an external event and is usually temporary. I recognize that this is a serious and sensitive mental health topic that's beyond the scope of this book. But I do want to say that if you're struggling, I encourage you to reach out to a mental health professional for support.

Your life is worth it.

If you're looking for helpful reading, I can recommend psychiatrist Dr. David Burns' book *Feeling Good: The New Mood Therapy*. He shares how we can become more aware of the influences of our thoughts on our feelings and moods.

Rewriting Your Limiting Beliefs

Rewriting our negative thoughts and limiting beliefs can truly change our moods and lives. After rewriting my negative thoughts, I felt much lighter. While it wasn't some kind of overnight cure, it did start to help me shift my mindset, enough to give me hope to continue.

The good news about beliefs is that we can change them. They are largely shaped by the stories we tell ourselves. Imagine how your life could transform if you told yourself kinder stories.

Reflection Exercise: Rewrite Your Limiting Beliefs

- Turn to a blank page in your journal. Write down all your limiting beliefs in a list, leaving a few empty lines under each one for the next step. If you need to, refer to your notes from the limiting beliefs exercises we did in previous chapters.

- Underneath each limiting belief, rewrite them into a statement that's more positive and empowering but that still feels authentic to you.

  - For example, I rewrote "I'm a shitty daughter" into "I'm a good daughter." That felt authentic to me, even if it was hard for me at the time to fully believe it.
  - For "I am not worthy enough to make people stay," I could rewrite it into "I am worthy enough to be loved."

PART 2

BREAKING FREE

11

BEGIN AGAIN

WHO AM I, after I've been forever changed by loss? How the hell do I begin again?

In the year after my dad's passing, I asked myself many existential questions—questions that I'd never asked before I stood at the door of death. One of grief's greatest gifts is the forced reevaluation of our lives. In our sorrow, we seek meaning. In our pain, we seek purpose.

I didn't know the answers yet. Moving toward my new future without my dad felt overwhelming. There were days when I dragged myself out of bed only to find myself wanting to crawl right back in. But I knew I had to start, little by little. Step by step.

Thankfully, my mom's cancer still seemed to be slow-growing, and the ulcers in her stomach remained small. For her Gastric MALT lymphoma, the doctors would just have to monitor her every six months to make sure that the cancer didn't get worse. Perhaps time would be on our side. After all, nearly 90 percent of patients with her type of low-grade lymphoma were still alive five years after diagnosis. She was still in Year One.

I finally felt like I could breathe again with my family back on steady ground. My mom went back to San Francisco State University where she studied to become a math teacher, supported by student loans. Stan seemed to hold it together too, studying graphic design at the same university. He still lived with my mom, and it gave me peace to know that they could take care of each other when I wasn't around.

Inside our family home, we still felt Baba's presence. We built an altar for him on top of my mom's piano in the living room. Incense burned in front of his framed photo, which rested next to a bowl of fruit, as is customary for ancestral altars in Chinese culture. Handsome and dignified in the photo, he sent us his love from the great beyond.

My mom also honored Baba by becoming the chef of our family. When he was still alive, she rarely cooked for us. But now that Baba was gone, she started making some of the old dishes he used to make, like chicken and ginger soup. I felt my parents' love in every bowl.

The only thing that felt dire now was my bank account balance, which had dwindled down to only a few hundred dollars. Though my rent was cheap by San Francisco standards, I could not afford another month. I'd been jobless for nearly a year, and my unemployment benefits ran out. I needed money fast. So I did what I always did—go back to the grind.

Before I move on, let me first tell you about my relationship with work and where our love affair began. I was born a hustler. I watched my immigrant parents work hard for our family's survival, so I learned to do the same at an early age.

At fifteen years old, I got my first summer job as a helper at a childcare center. When I received my first paycheck—even though it was just a couple hundred dollars—I couldn't believe it. *All this money? And I could spend it how I wanted? Freeeeedom! Yes, please! More, please!* From that first job, I was hooked.

Work made me feel worthy. Earning paychecks liberated me from the poverty of my youth. Suddenly, I could buy the Gap denim jackets that I wanted, securing me unspoken entry into the millennial cool teens club. At sixteen, I became a barista at Starbucks, where I'd serve coffee above the Moscone Convention Center downtown. Then when I was eighteen, I became a waitress at Uno's Pizzeria, serving up deep dish pizza for hungry tourists and raking in the tip money.

In college, work continued to help me survive. I received government grants that partially helped with my tuition, but I self-funded the rest of my studies at UC Davis. Some days I'd eat leftover sushi after a waitressing shift at a Japanese restaurant. And on other days, as a paid lab intern, I'd extract DNA from saliva samples so we could study the genetics of diseases in dogs.

If this kind of hustle feels familiar to you, I see you and I feel you. Those of us from humble beginnings often work our asses off to overcome our struggles—especially in capitalistic societies like America, where there's a huge divide between rich and poor. And if you're from an immigrant family like mine, then let's add family pressures to constantly work and self-sacrifice to the mix.

I freakin' love to work. It's as natural to me as breathing air. So when I lost my job as an assistant research scientist, my self-worth took a huge hit. The layoff stripped me of my power to make money and provide for myself. It's no wonder why I felt so lost, grasping onto the dream of going to business school to help me find direction. But with no more money, I had to put that dream on hold and head back to work, returning to it like a lover I couldn't shake.

Speaking of lovers, Marco and I were back together around this time. Although he was supportive and caring, I was too ashamed to ask him for financial help.

In fact, I was too ashamed to ask for help from my family, my friends, or anyone else. I kept my money troubles a secret. I wanted to "save face" and avoid shame, just as I was taught by my parents and culture. When it comes to money, sometimes we're too proud, too stubborn in maintaining our independence, and too embarrassed to admit that we need help—even when we're broke.

And I definitely was broke. How could I pay my bills?

A few weeks before I turned twenty-seven, I begged for an early birthday gift from the Universe. As my bank account dipped near zero, I turned my arms up to my bedroom ceiling, pleading to the higher powers that be. "Please, give me something. Anything!"

I kid you not, less than ten minutes later, my phone rang with a number I didn't recognize. Startled, I picked it up. "Hello? This is Jennifer."

A man's voice came through. "Hi, Jennifer. I'm Ed, a recruiter with a staffing agency. I was looking through our database and was wondering, are you in the market for a new job at the moment?"

I wanted to jump up and down. I wanted to scream: *Hell yeah! Ed! My maaaaan! You are my savior!* But I composed myself and played it cool. "Yeah, actually, I am. Thanks for reaching out. What kind of jobs?"

He replied, "I see that you were in research. I could probably place you in another research job. Is that something you'd be interested in?"

I stayed quiet for a moment, not sure if I was bold enough to tell him the truth about my desired career pivot. But then I thought about my father's passing. And how it taught me that I needed to not take life for granted.

"I have to be honest. I'm open to many different jobs, but I'm no longer interested in working in a lab. Something more people-facing would be better." I held my breath, afraid that he'd scoff at the idea.

"Sure, we can work with that," he said.

I couldn't believe it. It was one of the first times in my career that I asked for what I actually wanted.

For the remainder of the call, we talked about how I could tailor my résumé for a more business-oriented role in the life sciences. After all, I had enough non-laboratory experience that I could spin into something positive. At Exelixis, in addition to my normal job as a researcher, I helped organize employee events to foster our company culture. I also interned at the Luxury Marketing Council of San Francisco in the evenings. There, I collaborated with sponsors and venues to produce events that featured council members and products. I took these unpaid roles as a great way to learn about business. The more I was exposed to experiences outside the lab, the more I became convinced that, given my extroverted personality, I should be working with people directly. As to what kind of role, I still had no idea.

That night, after my fortuitous call with the recruiter, I updated my résumé and sent it to him, praying that we could find something that fit.

Luckily, I didn't have to wait long. A few weeks later, the staffing agency offered me the chance to apply for a role at Genentech as a contract project coordinator in the manufacturing department. Located in South San Francisco, Genentech was well-regarded as the birthplace of the entire biotech industry. I jumped at the chance. I had zero experience in pharmaceutical manufacturing and couldn't understand any of the technical jargon that was in the job description. However, my background in biology, excellent organizational skills, and ability to juggle priorities in fast-paced environments made me a reasonable candidate. It'd be a long shot, but it was at least worth a shot. If anyone could handle shit under pressure, it was me, Chief Operations Officer of the Choi household.

Things went real fast from there. Three days after applying, I received an email confirmation of an on-site interview. And four days after that, I got the acceptance call. It was my chance to begin again, the blessing I needed to pick up the pieces of my life and move forward.

On Monday, March 7, 2011, just one day shy of a year since my layoff, I picked up my new badge at Genentech and began a new chapter of my career.

It was even better than I could've imagined. Seriously, I had to pinch myself. I drove every day to a beautiful campus that sprawled across several hills. I worked in a modern office building in a cubicle overlooking the San Francisco Bay. My manager was kind, supportive, and smart. My colleagues were awesome too. They welcomed me with open arms and seemed eager to show me the ropes.

In the beginning, I was mainly updating spreadsheets or taking notes at large project team meetings, where we'd gear up for upcoming production campaigns. From heart disease to various types of cancers, we made important drugs that made me feel like I had a greater purpose working there. Within a few months, I started to facilitate and co-lead meetings, sometimes with over twenty people in the conference room. Most of all, I could finally pay my bills again.

I loved my early days as a contractor and wanted to show my colleagues how much I appreciated the job. To prove my worth as the new kid on the block, I worked my ass off, staying late many nights so I could complete all my assignments. It paid off.

When my department opened up a full-time role on my team three months later, I went for it. Out of numerous applicants, I miraculously made it through. When I read the official offer letter in the parking lot outside our building, I had to triple check the numbers to make sure I wasn't hallucinating. *Holy shit!* The annual salary was 50 percent more than I made before. There was so much to celebrate. I finally felt like I had made it.

But unfortunately, as my salary grew, so did the tension between me and my mom.

My mom and I had always butted heads, but after Baba died, it seemed to hit a high. Without him as the buffer, my mom and I argued more. It wasn't so much that money changed me, but it opened my eyes to the growing divide between my roots and my new reality.

Each time I visited my family's apartment, I couldn't help but feel frustrated. Mold continued to spread on the bathroom ceiling, and used wads of tissue dotted the living room floor like confetti. Towering above the wads was a stack of chairs from the flea market. Without Baba around, my mom's hoarding reached new heights—literally.

I'd grunt in exasperation, standing amidst the growing mounds of junk in the living room. "Mommy, how can you and Stan live like this? And why can't you guys just use the trash?"

I'd motion to the so-called garbage can next to the TV stand. It was the comically small red Duplo Lego box from our childhood, with a plastic bag brimming over and a banana peel teetering on top.

"Dooooon't diiiirect me!" my mom wailed, sometimes lunging at me.

My brother would stand back in the corner. As it turns out, he had stopped going to school due to his own grief about losing Baba and got a job working for a tourist attraction in Fisherman's Wharf instead. Not wanting to piss my mom off more, he'd stay quiet.

In the year after Baba passed, this heated dialogue between my mom and I repeated over and over again. Every time I visited the family home, my entire body tensed up. My mom continued to amass things she'd find at garage sales. To walk forward and wade through the crap, I was like Moses parting the Red Sea.

Worst of all, my mom and I fought about her cancer treatment. Back when she was diagnosed with lymphoma, the doctor told her that it was treatable. That she should comply with the treatment. She did, at least at first. But sixteen months after her initial diagnosis, I rushed her to the emergency room once again when she had black stools. She received another blood transfusion with a round of antibiotics. Though I felt relieved that she was discharged from the hospital that same day, I was suspicious of the return of my mom's internal bleeding.

A week later, at her scheduled appointment with a new oncologist, we received more news.

"Mrs. Choi, I'm afraid that your tumors have grown," a female doctor said, pointing to my mom's latest scan. "Usually, the combination of Protonix and antibiotics is quite effective, but in your case it seems that the ulcers came back, and now there are tumors."

My mom squinted at the computer screen.

"So what does that mean?" I asked.

"At this stage, I would recommend localized radiation therapy to target the cancer cells," said the doctor.

Two nanoseconds later, my mom uttered, "No. No radiation. No chemo."

The doctor pursed her lips and sighed. "It's not chemotherapy, Mrs. Choi. Only localized radiation on one part of the body to shrink the tumors."

"But I feel okay. I can still walk. My blood looks good again," my mom protested.

"Sure, it's your body, and you don't have to decide now, but I would recommend radiation. Why don't you get dressed and I'll be back in a few minutes?" the doctor said.

An awkward silence filled the room in her place. But I couldn't just sit there and do nothing after seeing the spots in my mom's stomach on the screen.

"Mommy, cancer is not like a burn. You know when you burn your hand on boiling water, and you feel it immediately? Cancer's not like that. It grows slowly, and you might not feel much until it spreads to other parts of your body and it's too late." I tried to explain, as if reasoning with a five-year-old.

My mom protested, "I don't want radiation! I don't trust what they say. When Baba got sick, they made him take medicine. Then it made his heart and lungs worse. Look what happened! No."

When the doctor came back, we told her politely that we'd think about it. But on the drive home, any further attempts to explain to my mom why she should consider radiation were futile. Even though I had studied cancer and pleaded as her daughter, she wouldn't listen to me.

So a month later, while my mom was complaining about not being able to pay the bills, I tried a different approach.

"Mommy, what if I give you money? I give you a thousand dollars and you get radiation? Please?" I proposed. I honestly thought that I could bribe my own mother.

"No! No radiation!" my mom shouted, her fists curling into a ball.

Tears suddenly rolled down my cheeks. "But what about me and Stan? Don't you care about us? Baba's already gone. What if your cancer gets worse and you leave us too?" I pleaded.

"Aiya. You're too emotional. I'm fine. I'll go to the Chinese doctor and get some herbal medicine," she insisted.

And just like that, all my nasty feelings of unworthiness came flooding back. It didn't matter that I had an incredible job at a top company, nor that I now made more money than I'd ever made.

It was worth nothing, and *I* was worth nothing if I'd fail to save my mom.

To make matters worse, my grandma's health started declining too. Once an active nurse who seemed like she'd never stop moving, Po Po became worn down by age. Her bones ached whenever it got cold, her hip joints swelled until she needed a walker, and a gallbladder infection landed her in the hospital. Thankfully, she recovered from her infection, and I knew that we were lucky to have her with us at nearly ninety years old. But witnessing people you love succumb to mortality hurts.

To run from my feelings of helplessness and unworthiness, I went back to my old trusty way of surviving—pouring myself into work and studying for the GMAT.

At work, I became unstoppable. Any tension in my family became my fuel, propelling me forward professionally with ferocious speed. Adding to that fuel was the praise I received from my bosses. In contrast to the constant criticism I received from my mom, at my job I felt celebrated for my talents.

I even had a new work persona. There was already another Jenn on my team more senior than me, and sometimes we were assigned to the same campaign as co-leads. To minimize confusion between us, I adopted a nickname. I became JC, which are my initials. JC was badass. JC got shit done. JC confidently led manufacturing campaign teams through challenges, fostered strong stakeholder relationships, and launched process improvement projects. She was detail-oriented and unafraid to ask for more opportunities. A chaotic environment didn't faze her, just like it didn't faze her in her family.

Once, a colleague said to me with a joking smile, "JC, you're so anal retentive." I took it as a compliment and thanked her profusely. I loved that my perfectionist ways were recognized.

With praise that made me feel more worthy and a salary that gave me financial security, I gained the capacity to think about business school again. Sure, I was excelling at work. But I still felt like something was missing. Some senior leaders in my department had MBAs, and I thought it was what I also needed to climb the corporate ladder. To increase my chances of getting into business school, I took the GMAT twice more to boost my scores. Was it excessive—and maybe even crazy—to take the GMAT two months in a row, within the first year of my new job? And five times total? Probably.

I was a fast-moving train that had to keep going, blowing past any signals screaming at me to slow down. Even when I should have screamed from distress, I silenced myself. Like that horrible night in Madrid that I'll never forget.

It was March 2012. One month after I was officially single yet again. I was on vacation in Madrid, wanting to make the most out of my limited vacation time in Spain. Taking time off from work always felt like borrowed time to me. So I decided to go out dancing alone.

At a nightclub, I met two guys and one girl who became my new friends. They seemed nice and chatty. We had cocktails while electronic music bumped on the speakers. Then things got blurry from there. The only way I can talk about what happened now is if I'm speaking very matter-of-factly. When the club closed, I got into a cab with them, heading to a bar. But when we realized that the bar was closed, we decided to have an after-party at one guy's apartment. Just as we pulled up in a cab, the girl and one of the guys realized that they were too tired to continue partying. So they left.

Still buzzing from the club and not wanting to sleep yet, I entered my new guy friend's apartment. He seemed friendly and smart. However, I wasn't attracted to him and gave him no signs of romantic interest, nor did he show any to me. It felt mutually platonic and we mainly chatted about work. Like me, he worked at a huge healthcare company. He even showed me a PowerPoint presentation that he prepared for an upcoming meeting. When it got late, he offered me a spot to crash at his place. I felt safe enough. There were zero red flags at this point. Yawning, I went to bed fully clothed in my leggings and a blouse.

I woke up in the middle of the night. My pants were pulled down. I was being sexually assaulted. I stayed silent. I didn't scream. I didn't shout. I froze. Afterward, I went back to sleep, incapable of making sense of what had happened, hoping that it was all just a nightmare.

In the morning, I left without saying anything. I did not take his contact information. I did not write down his address. I did not go to the police. I did not cry.

I buried the incident inside me. I showered it away. I numbed it like I numbed my abortion. And I buried the trauma for years, feeling ashamed of my body, fearing that if I ever told someone else—even my own mother—they'd tell me it was all my fault.

Moment to Self-Reflect

Before we move on, let me address my sexual assault. I want to be candid because it's important for me to speak my truth—I was raped. When it happened to me at twenty-eight, I repressed it so deep in my psyche and body that I wouldn't face it for over a decade. I did not have the capacity to face it back then, nor process any of the emotions for years. It was so horrid, shocking, and traumatic. But it fucked me up big time subconsciously, eating away at me like an undiagnosed cancer.

The assault reinforced my limiting belief formed since my youth: *My body is shameful. It's not safe to be in my body.*

Later in the book, I'll share how this sexual trauma threatened to destroy me. I'll also dive into how I started healing my sexual trauma.

But for now, I want to say this: If you've been a victim too, I send you immense empathy. I'm so sorry. I want to share loud and clear: **We did not deserve it. It was not our fault.**

12

BURNOUT

AFTER RETURNING TO San Francisco, I pretended that nothing ever happened in Madrid. Pretended that everything was fine. The insanity of it was that I genuinely believed I was fine. That's how dissociated I became.

The train kept pushing forward. I worked even harder, eager to prove my worth. Trying to distract myself as I always did. The rest of 2012 came with plenty of wins that made it possible to feel good about myself on the surface. Making it easy to bury the assault.

On top of being a high performer as a project coordinator, I gained additional career development opportunities within the company. I eventually became lead of a team that enhanced internal communications in our department. I helped colleagues develop better communication skills, consulted on project change communication plans, and partnered with senior leadership on messaging for important announcements. I also joined a company-wide team aimed at developing the next generation of leaders, where I got to network with colleagues in departments outside of mine. Best of all, I kept getting showered with praise, making me feel worthy. JC was a fucking company star. JC drank the corporate Kool-Aid, just as she used to drink cranberry vodkas.

I was winning in my love life as well. After ten months apart, Marco and I got back together again at the end of 2012, in a round that genuinely felt different. You know that feeling when you're absolutely convinced that things have changed for the better in a relationship? That it's *finally* the beginning of forever together? Yeah, it was like that. We talked about how much we'd grown individually in our time apart, apologized for any past hurts, and gushed about how we loved each other perhaps *too* much. The relationship lit my soul on fire.

Things seemed stable again in my family as well. My mom's tumor miraculously did not get any bigger. She also had a steady income again. As a non-native speaker, she had repeatedly failed the English portion of the teaching exams and couldn't get her credentials to become a math teacher. Instead, she started working at a childcare center taking care of small children, which brought her immense fulfillment and joy. Stan was also doing well at his job.

I chugged along, riding high on external indicators of success, believing that my hard work was close to making me feel like I was worthy enough. But I was trying to run away from what happened in Madrid.

The next year started on a high note. By then, my coworker Jenn had become my manager. Once again, the Universe blessed me with a supportive and empathetic boss. In a performance review discussion in her office, she shared that I was performing so well that the only negative feedback I got from peers was that I typed too loud. I've been a lifelong "hunter-pecker," fiercely hunting and pecking the computer keyboard with two fingers instead of ten. The reveal that this silly quirk was the only negative feedback I got had us both laughing.

Full of self-belief from my work reputation and with GMAT scores that seemed decent enough, I finally decided to apply to business school. Not wanting to lose my salary, I applied to the UC Berkeley Evening and Weekend MBA Program, convinced that it could help me gain a more senior role. As to what role that could be, I had no idea. I still did not know who the hell I was at this point, other than JC at work and COO of my family.

A month after applying to Berkeley, I confidently nailed an on-campus interview. But six weeks after that, I received a rejection email that made me give up on the dream of business school entirely. By then, I accepted that it just wasn't meant to be. That, once again, I wasn't worthy enough. But I didn't wallow in my self-pity for long. After all, there were project meetings with catered lunches in big conference rooms to run. And millions of dollars' worth of critical medicines to make. No matter what happened, no matter how unworthy I felt in other areas of life, I could always run back to work. And my boyfriend.

By the summer of 2013, it felt like Marco and I were living in a dream. We traveled to Italy together, swimming in turquoise waters. When we got back from vacation, he hinted that we should move in together. *OMG*, I thought. *It's finally happening! It's the beginning of our shared life together without all the separation of the previous years!* I was thrilled to finally move out of the cheap apartment that I'd shared with roommates since I'd graduated from college.

However, when autumn came, the seasons had changed but our rental contracts had not. There was no further talk about moving in together. I began to believe that maybe I had made it up. As was typical for me back then, I was too afraid to ask about it. Instead of facing my disappointment, I literally ran away from it.

Stan and I signed up to run our first marathon together, to raise money for the Leukemia & Lymphoma Society. On the morning of the marathon, I wore a purple jersey that said in silver bubble paint, "For Mom." Even though we had a complicated relationship, she would always be the person I loved the most. I ran next to Stan, searching for our mom along the route. Searching for her validation. Finally, near the Transamerica Pyramid, we spotted her. Weaving, we ran over to the curbside where she stood bundled up in a brown coat. "Good luck. I'm proud of you kids," she said. I clung to these rare affirming words as we waved goodbye to her. Her approval, so elusive and yet so vital, propelled me forward. Twenty-six miles later at Ocean Beach, dripping with sweat, Stan and I crossed the finish line, smashing our personal records.

I'd love to tell you that I was able to bask in this epic accomplishment and the continued accolades at my job. But by the winter of 2013, something felt eerily off. There was an emptiness inside me that disturbed me. *How could I feel so empty if I had accomplished so much?*

Earlier in the year, I had bought myself a gorgeous dark blue Hyundai Elantra—the first new car I ever owned. I was happy about it at first, but by December, I had an overwhelming fear that I'd purposely drive myself into the center divider on the highway. I could not trust myself to not suddenly crash into the concrete median at full speed. Terrified of my intrusive thoughts, I started driving in the slow lane, trying to override them. I didn't want to die, but what the fuck was happening to me?

Something in me was calling for my attention, something I couldn't see. But instead of paying attention and looking, I just kept running away from myself through work.

I turned thirty in February 2014 without much fanfare. I thanked everyone for their kind wishes in a birthday Facebook post and wrote, "Life has been good."

Good? Really? Was it though? This was the picture of perfection that I wanted to portray online, but the truth was the stress at work had become too much, even for me. When the phone rang at my cubicle, I'd jump back from it. I was anxious that it'd be yet another colleague telling me that something went wrong on one of my projects and that I'd have to fix it with urgency as I always did. The positive news about working in healthcare is that you feel a sense of purpose. The bad news is that anything less than perfection feels like you're fucking up someone else's life.

Unspoken stress also reached a high in my relationship. Marco and I never talked again about moving in together. Once again, I did not question it. It started to feel like previous iterations of our relationship when we barely saw each other. When we were drifting away.

One evening in March, he came over to my apartment with a box of pizza, delivering dinner and a final goodbye. I don't remember much of what he said to break up with me. But I do remember him saying something along the lines of us not being free to be ourselves when we were together. He wasn't wrong about that. My fear of getting hurt caused me to act in ways which made me lose myself—and perhaps he experienced something similar. The whole conversation didn't last long.

I allowed myself to cry for a few days, but somehow this breakup felt less intense than our previous ones. Maybe I had gotten too used to them. Maybe I had changed.

When I told my mom that I was worried about finding a future partner, she said to me, "You? Finding a husband? Hah! You need to be smarter and prettier. Not talk so much at work. Just work harder." So I did.

I worked my ass off so goddamn hard that in June I was promoted to project manager and got a massive pay raise. I should've celebrated my promotion more. But I didn't have the energy to. Instead, I felt suffocated by my additional responsibilities. Furthermore, I received questions from several teammates about how I got promoted when they didn't. So instead of feeling thrilled about my promotion, I felt guilty. The pressure became too much. I needed to blow it off.

I started to drink more again, the nights blurring. I took a vacation that summer, trying to party my stress away. In Ibiza, I danced at a massive outdoor pool party to global powerhouse DJ Avicii. And in Berlin, I visited a friend who showed me the insane nightclub scene where you could rave from Friday through Monday nonstop—with the right drugs, of course. While high, I felt alive again. I felt free. But when it came time to fly back to San Francisco, my entire body went numb.

By October, that had become my new normal. The stellar performance reviews, shiny new title, and pay raise came at a hefty cost—my health. On the hamster wheel of chasing success, I burnt out. Once full of high-voltage energy and emotions, I became hollow. One day, I looked at a picture of me smiling from just a year before and could barely recognize the stranger looking back at me.

"Huh. I don't remember what happy feels like," I said out loud in an empty hallway. Thoughts of crashing my car persisted, causing me to dread my daily commute. At work, I felt like a bird with her wings clipped, trapped in a golden cage that looked beautiful on the outside, but in reality was a prison. I did not know how to get out.

There weren't necessarily any loud negative thoughts to rewrite this round. Nor places in nature I felt called to. Unlike with my depression after Baba's death, this time I had no energy to do anything. I was completely drained and burnt out.

I couldn't turn to Marco for comfort. He was gone. I had reached out to him via email after our breakup to say hello and received a friendly reply. This time, I could feel the distance. I finally had to accept that this was the end for us. I was heartbroken but could barely muster the energy to cry about it. I was that burnt out.

But nature had a gift in store for me. Deep from the moist soil of the earth.

Whenever I think back to the first time I tried psychedelic mushrooms during my burnout, I can't help but smile. It was totally unplanned and so random.

It was sometime in the fall of 2014, on a warm, sunny, ordinary San Francisco day. I was at my friend Shannon's apartment in The Castro because we had planned to meet there prior to an art gallery walk. An effervescent social butterfly with golden blond locks and an insatiable zest for life, Shannon was one of my closest friends. We were hanging out in her apartment when a charming gay neighbor rang her doorbell. Peak Castro, I know.

"I got some more of the magic caramels," he said with a big grin and a wink.

Shannon squealed with delight. "Ooohhh! Awesome!"

Curious about what made them 'magic,' I popped up from the couch. "What kind of caramels are they?"

The friendly gaybor responded. "Psychedelic. With magic mushrooms. Have you ever tried shrooms?"

"Ahhhh, okay. I've heard of them but never done them," I replied.

"WHAT?!" Shannon and her neighbor shouted in unison.

Without hesitation, the neighbor grabbed two magic caramels from his bag and thrust them toward us. "Here. Enjoy!" he said with a twinkle in his eye before turning around and disappearing like a fairy.

I held a caramel, which was in a clear plastic bag, and examined it in my hand. It looked like a gourmet confection from a candy shop.

Shannon started to giggle her mischievous giggle, the one where you know she has a wild idea that you can't resist. "Should we take them?"

"Wait, now? Like . . . right now? Here?" I asked. Then without waiting for a reply, I answered myself. "Yeah, let's do it."

I figured I had nothing to lose. I had already hit one of the lowest lows, feeling hollow and numb inside. The shrooms called me. At least they'd bring novelty back into my life. I also trusted Shannon. I felt like, if anything went south, she'd be able to take care of me. A common way to take psychedelic mushrooms and experience the hallucinogenic effects of its active compound, psilocybin, is to eat them fresh or dried. Would I have done shrooms so spontaneously for the first time if they were in their default form? Probably not. But in this tasty form? Let's go, baby!

The chewy gifts were the blessing I needed to break free from my rut. I devoured an entire caramel. In the first hour, as we walked from Shannon's apartment to Dolores Park in the Mission District, the colors of the trees became crisper, as if I were watching a *National Geographic* documentary in high definition. I audibly ooohed and ahhhed at how beautiful everything seemed, thinking that this would be the extent of the trip.

But then, in the second hour, my trip suddenly escalated, catapulting me through space and time. I saw wolves dancing in the clouds, traveled to other dimensions at a coffee shop, and ventured into an underground music venue for what felt like an eternity. Shannon and I couldn't stop laughing, the two of us doubled over with hands on our knees, wiping away tears of joy from our raucous rapture. We never made it to the art gallery walk. We didn't need to. Art was everywhere I looked, living and breathing in everything. Brightly painted Victorian houses became Technicolor architectural wonders from another planet. Curtains blew in the wind, floating as if they were made of jellyfish. And the sky, OMG, the sky! The dusk sky looked like pink cotton candy dipped in liquid gold and then set ablaze.

Five hours in and toward the end of our psychedelic trip, I wrote on a postcard I picked up at a bookstore with happy tears, "Today I felt joy again. Life is love."

More than that, I felt like myself again, but in a way that truly felt different. The kind of difference that you can feel in your soul. That night, when I got home, I slept like a baby. And the glow of the experience felt sustained.

Weeks after, I still felt the joy of being alive. But it wasn't just the shrooms. It was being around magnificent friends like Shannon. Her enthusiasm for life was infectious. She reminded me of all the beauty in the world, especially during our regular walks together around the city. Every moment with her felt divine.

I finally rested, allowing myself to truly unplug after leaving work on the weekdays. Weekends became fun again. I started to let go of the pressure I put on myself to perform. Work became more manageable. I felt hopeful about the future. And little by little, my energy returned.

Most of all, the experience brought me back to myself. Not JC. Not COO of the Choi family. But my true, authentic self. And the real me was about to break free from the golden cage.

Moment to Self-Reflect

I felt depleted writing this chapter, as if my body remembered the exhaustion from my burnout. I didn't know what rest was back then, as many of us don't when we've been programmed to survive and run from our trauma. I just worked harder, running away from my feelings from living through family illness, sexual assault, business school rejection, and a relationship breakup.

The thing is, I was killin' it at work—which made me feel good, at least on the surface—but my work was killin' *me*. It burned me out.

Burnout and Overwork

Burnout is a state of chronic stress—often work-related—that leads to mental, emotional, or physical exhaustion. This can happen when we try to do too much for too long, feel the constant pressure of responsibilities, and don't rest. Left unaddressed, it could have long-term impacts on our health.

What makes burnout sneaky is that it can happen gradually. In my case, I experienced signs for about a year before I realized what it was. Unfortunately, I'd become so used to ignoring my internal signals that it got to the point where I feared crashing my car on purpose. Looking back, I feel this might've been my body's way of telling me that *it* was about to crash.

Over time, I've learned how important it is to recognize the signs of burnout before it's too late. Some common experiences that people associate with burnout include chronic fatigue, emotional detachment, irritability, feelings of hopelessness, decreased motivation, difficulties with sleep, and digestive issues. If you've experienced some of these in combination, it might be worth exploring whether burnout has played a role in your life. Let's take a pause to check in.

Reflection Questions:

- Do you recognize any of the signs of burnout mentioned, from your personal experience? If so, what did that feel like for you?
- What was going on in your life at that time that made it difficult to slow down, decrease your workload, or reduce your stress?

If you believe you might've burned out before, the root of it may be deeper than you think. As I talked about in Chapter 7, many of us who struggle with self-worth are high achievers, constantly proving ourselves by chasing external achievements. This may make us prone to overwork and perfectionism. When we take on unsustainable workloads, set unrealistic standards for ourselves, and struggle to relax, it can lead to burnout. Furthermore, those of us who grew up with childhood neglect in our families may self-neglect our own needs for rest.

Our tendency to overwork can also be attributed to cultural or socioeconomic factors. I grew up in between two cultures—Chinese and American—both of which place a high priority on productivity as a measure of worth.

Additionally, I watched my parents work hard for our survival, never taking a break. My upbringing led to a limiting belief about work: *Work should be hard and require relentless self-sacrifice.* And my limiting belief about rest: *Rest is unproductive and indulgent.*

Perhaps you've also formed some beliefs from your past experiences, which could make you prone to overwork as well.

Reflection Questions:

- What's your relationship with work like? Do you feel that you overwork?

- Write down any limiting beliefs that you have about work. How do you think your upbringing, culture, or past experiences influenced those beliefs?

- Write down any limiting beliefs that you have about rest. Where do you think those beliefs come from?

Rest is key to recovery. Yet it's not just about physical rest. We could be lying down in bed but still have never-ending worries in our head. Mental rest is also important. That's why it's helpful to delegate to others and reduce workload if you can, talk with friends, or seek help from a mental health professional if it becomes severe or habitual.

I wish that I could've recognized the signs of my burnout earlier. Or reached out to a therapist. However, I got so far into my burnout and felt so empty that I needed a reset. That's when the shrooms came to me.

Psychedelic Medicines

I didn't know it back then, but my first shroom trip kicked off a profound relationship with psychedelic plant medicines that would eventually help heal my trauma. To be clear, I didn't take it with therapeutic intention the first time; it was meant to be purely recreational. However, it was like a reset button for me. It felt like a divine gift, where I got in touch with my authentic self and remembered all the self-love beyond familial, cultural, and societal conditioning. From that place of unconditional love, I was able to allow myself to rest, reduce pressure on myself, and begin to change my relationship with work. It wasn't an overnight fix, but it was a catalyst for deeper transformation, as it's been for many others.

Psychedelic mushrooms contain psychoactive compounds, such as psilocybin, which, when taken, can induce changes in mood, perception, and consciousness, leading to spiritual experiences, hallucinations, and big life realizations. They've long been revered as sacred and ancient medicine. Indigenous cultures in Mexico, Central America, South America, and Siberia have used psychedelic mushrooms for ceremonial, spiritual, and religious purposes for thousands of years.

In modern times, there's been ample clinical research that's studied the use of psilocybin-assisted therapy in the treatment of various mental health conditions. If you're curious, I recommend reading Michael Pollan's book *How to Change Your Mind: What the New Science of Psychedelics Teaches Us About Consciousness, Dying, Addiction, Depression, and Transcendence*. It's astounding how powerful psychedelic medicines can be.

13

CORPORATE ESCAPE

SOMETIMES WE MIGHT not know where we're headed yet, but we do start to question where we are. That's how I felt about my career in the months after I recovered from my first burnout.

Burnout can be wildly destructive, razing to the ground the sense of self you had before. But it can also be a blessing in disguise. It burns down all that doesn't matter to you, clearing the path for what does—allowing you to see what no longer serves you.

At work, I was still performing. But I became disillusioned with my corporate job. I felt like I had to keep myself small to make others feel more comfortable, as if my promotion was somehow wrong. At the same time, I watched multiple colleagues struggle with balancing their careers and raising children. It seemed so challenging, especially when there were high demands at work. *Could I ever manage to juggle it all? Especially when I dreamed of having a family of my own one day?* I was in my early thirties and still single, but something about the relentless hustle culture started to scare me.

JC, my work persona, began to feel like a sham. Once a major part of my identity, she started to feel less and less like the real me. My shroom trip had reminded me that life was about much more than just work. I was the Universe's holy expression of love in the flesh.

Luckily, I was able to feel the love for life again, but I also wanted to find the love of my life. So, I opened up my heart again, much to my mom's delight.

One day when I was sick with a cold, my mom came over to my apartment to bring me soup. But I got more than just soup; I got a two-hour discussion of my dating life, with several servings of unsolicited dating advice. The fact that I was curled up in my papasan chair coughing did not deter my mother.

When I expressed my dreams of love, she said, "Aiya, forget about love. That's for the youth. Just find someone who is willing to marry you."

When I shared that I was trying to meet people on dating apps, she said, "You need to go on the largest dating website possible and meet many, many men. Even the unattractive ones. My friend, who is fifty-six years old, found one hundred suitors."

And when I raised my eyebrows in response, she added, "Jenn ah, your skin should be milky white, not tan like it is. Stop running. Stay indoors for a few months, then date when your skin is lighter again." She then launched into a Chinese folktale to back up her point about milky skin and explained again—for the gazillionth time—how darker skin would make me seem like a rural peasant.

As usual, I did not know whether to laugh or cry. Her advice was so ridiculous, but she was totally serious. In traditional Asian culture, many people marry for convenience over love—and believe that lighter skin means you're in a higher class. I find the skin color classification fucked up in many ways, but then again, I grew up in America where golden sun-kissed tans are venerated, as is the concept of romantic love.

Hell-bent on finding love, I became a pro on dating apps. That Halloween, I even dressed up as Tinderella, my modern interpretation of Cinderella who would swipe right on Tinder looking for her prince. But the truth is, swiping right to strangers didn't provide comfort beyond a few nights. Nor did it help that many men wanted to hook up and have fun but were emotionally unavailable for an actual relationship. I was tired of men going from gung ho to ghosting.

Feeling dejected, I wondered if something was wrong with me, or whether something was wrong with my approach. How was I supposed to find my match when my match was already onto the next date at the flick of a finger?

One Friday evening in December, Shannon took me to an underground Christmas party thrown by some of her friends. The party was at Great Star, a historic theater in Chinatown that used to show Chinese films. I took this nod to my heritage as a good sign. Excited, I shimmied into a tight red dress with long sleeves and a hemline that barely grazed my thighs.

At the entrance, Shannon and I thrusted over a twenty-dollar bill for drink tickets to a guy in a Santa hat. Then we wiggled our butts onto the dance floor—or shall I say, "dance stage," as we found ourselves onstage in between red curtains, looking out into empty rows of theater seats. After sweating out a couple of songs, I grabbed a plastic cup of vodka shots from the bootleg bar.

Suddenly, I felt a tap on my shoulder.

"Having fun?" a male voice with a thick, indistinguishable European accent asked.

I turned around and craned my neck upward to meet the face of a handsome giant with sandy blond hair. The cheap disco lights bounced off his beautiful sky-blue eyes. "Yeah, I guess? Where are you from?" I asked.

"Denmark. I'm Jacob, but you can call me Viking," he said with a smirk.

I imagined him sitting on an old, wooden Scandinavian chair with curves as perfect as his chiseled cheekbones. "Never been to Denmark. But I'd like to visit one day! I'm Jenn."

And then, in typical San Francisco fashion, he asked, "So what do you do?"

I despised that question, especially after my burnout. So I told him what I told everyone when I didn't want to talk about work: "I'm a hand model," I said with a serious face.

"Me too!" he exclaimed. And then he reached out his big hands to mine.

I loved that he got my joke and matched it with his own. As we sat down in the red theater seats, we showcased our hand-modeling poses and recalled made-up stories of glamorous fashion shoots in Milan. Before I went back to the stage to find Shannon, we exchanged phone numbers. But when he disappeared from the party twenty minutes later without saying goodbye, I wrote it off as yet another brief, drunken encounter.

Later, when I got home stumbling, I was surprised to receive a text from Jacob. I smiled and flirted back. Then the next day, I giggled as we exchanged photos of our hands. We texted over the next few weeks, but because of holiday travels, we couldn't meet up.

At the end of December, I flew to Mexico to ring in the new year with Shannon and our friend Faith-Ann in Sayulita. On that magical beach vacation, the three of us started writing a children's story together, inspired by the glowing moon which lit up the entire night sky. Faith-Ann scribbled notes into her notebook as we collectively made up the story, blurting out ideas. I felt so alive. We also started setting daily intentions, which helped me feel more focused, grounded, and hopeful. That vacation, I wrote in my journal, "Everything is manifesting at a manic rate." *Would love manifest soon too?*

Back in San Francisco that January—a month after my first encounter with Jacob—the stars and our calendars aligned. As it turned out, not only was he a busy co-founder of a startup, but he also lived in a massive co-living community in the Mission District. It was there at a house party that we first kissed.

After a few dates, I found myself falling for Jacob's brilliant mind. I loved that he was hyper-intellectual, adventurous, forward-thinking, and nonconformist. We attended a geeky arts lecture together, and over dinner one night, he gifted me five dollars' worth of Bitcoin to introduce me to cryptocurrency. The way he talked about the future of the world and his passion for technology was so sexy.

Over the next few months, I saw this Viking again and again, even though he didn't seem as emotionally expressive as the fiery types that I'd dated before. However, I reasoned that someone who didn't have extreme highs and lows in their emotions could also be a great balance for me.

When I told my mom that I met a Dane, she approved. "Nice country. Good education," she said.

Jacob opened new portals for me. Made me see things I never saw before, like the possibility to break free from my corporate job and do something else. But what could that something else be? I still had no clue. Making a leap of faith into the unknown felt daunting, and I was terrified to leave the financial security of my job.

Though doubts filled me, I had to figure it out.

The good news was I had plenty of opportunities to figure myself out at Genentech. As an employee, I gained access to many personal development trainings, which helped me become more self-aware. Through taking the Myers-Briggs personality test, I discovered that I was an ENFJ, an empathetic extrovert who would be great at leading and helping others. By taking the CliftonStrengths assessment, I learned about my top strengths, such as positivity and communication, which could be applied both in and out of the workplace. And in a team workshop where we were asked to write our story in six words, I unearthed a dream I didn't even know I had: *Live the chapters. Share the book.* That's what I wrote on a Post-it note in March 2015. *But wait . . . a book? What could I possibly have to say that would be worthy of sharing?* I did not know back then. However, the vision of a book would show up again and again.

A few weeks later, I told my boss Jenn that I was going to take a day off to "think about life." Not long after, in her office during our weekly one-on-one, she handed me a piece of paper.

"Here. They're questions I think you should consider. Maybe they'll help," she said.

"Wow, thank you," I said as I held the paper in my hands. On it were three questions handwritten in ink: *Who will you become? What will satisfy your soul? What is your battle to take up this year?*

They felt like big questions that I didn't have the answers to yet, but I loved that my boss shared them with me at that particular juncture. She'd always been extremely supportive of my growth and understood that I was in a period of deep contemplation about my life.

Oh, I thought about life all right. I thought about it so much that it'd end up changing the entire trajectory of my life.

That April, on a clear Friday morning, I drove up to Calistoga with Jacob, where I had booked a night at a wellness resort. Located an hour away from

San Francisco, the Indian Springs resort had thermal geysers, a swimming pool, and acres of lush gardens. It was the perfect place to reflect in nature. After lunch, I took some time to contemplate alone. I grabbed my pen and a small notebook and hiked up to a grassy spot on top of a secluded hill. There, on a bench surrounded by lavender flowers, I allowed myself to be completely guided by my intuition. I wanted to listen to my true self, which had risen from the ashes of my burnout.

What came to me on that hill can only be described as divine intervention. Out of nowhere, I got the idea to ask my Future Self—ten years in the future—for guidance, seeking her advice. I asked her the three questions from my boss's prompts: *Who will you become? What will satisfy your soul? What is your battle to take up this year?* I also sprinkled in my own questions about what her daily life was like, where she worked, and what advice she'd give to my Current Self. I closed my eyes, waiting, unsure of what response I'd get—if any.

Fortunately, I didn't have to wait long. Within minutes, the words flowed effortlessly out of my pen as I channeled my Future Self. And not only did she respond, but my Future Self wrote me a letter eleven pages long! Here are the highlights, abbreviated from the original version:

Dear Self in 2015,

It's now 2025 and I am so damn happy. Sometimes I want to pinch myself because I don't believe this dream that I live in waking life. I am now a nurturing mother, loving wife, and someone who inspires others—as a profession! I've turned my early writings into a published book, and it has ignited a chain reaction of inspiration . . . using my voice and narrative to make loved ones happy, and strangers too across the globe. It satisfies my soul to know that through my connections, I've helped others connect to others and to themselves. This makes my soul smile. I've traveled to over thirty countries, and my writings are in multiple languages.

I remember turning the corner in 2015. I pushed myself out of my comfort zone and made a big move and career shift. I was able to help others in healthcare, but I was also able to capitalize on my skills in communication. It was scary at first, but I knew the world was better served by my courage, not my comfort.

You should not give up on the love you want because look at me now. I have the love I want. I am madly yet peacefully in love with someone who loves me, grows me, challenges me, stands by me, and chooses me. Now, we have this special tribe of a family.

I want to tell you, Jenn of thirty-one, to keep at your dreams no matter how crazy. Remember that your mom named you "weed that grows on the side of the road" because you are tough, resilient, and determined. Use that and your overwhelming positivity to achieve your dreams. It only takes one—you!

I look back at the past forty or so years and think, "Damn, I am so fucking blessed." But really, I've created all of this for myself. I seized the opportunities. I saw light in the darkness. I listened to my heart. I saw the steep uphills, ran up them, and now at the hilltop, I admire the view of the vast open reality before my eyes.

When I reached the end of the letter, I dropped my pen and cried tears of awe. It was like looking into a crystal ball and seeing a version of myself that I actually loved. One that was older, wiser, and full of self-belief. While ten years felt like a lifetime away, I was encouraged by my Future Self to start making changes immediately. That afternoon, I marched down the hill in Calistoga, empowered to step into a new version of myself.

Later, when I reunited with Jacob at the pool, I gushed about the dreams in my letter. Rather than call me crazy, he celebrated my ambitions. And over dinner, we brainstormed ways that I could create something impactful, like hosting a podcast. But when he asked me about the practicalities of my desired career transition, I felt clueless. Like someone who could talk the talk but couldn't walk the walk—at least not yet.

However, I did feel within me a deep knowing. A deep knowing amidst all the uncertainty that everything would turn out just fine. That *I* got me. My Future Self told me so.

———

When I returned to San Francisco, I felt like a caterpillar spinning a cocoon, wanting to become a butterfly but needing to go inward first.

I reread the letter from my Future Self again and again. The gap between where I was and where I was destined to go was shocking. *Inspiring others as a profession? Publishing a book?* I didn't know how the hell I'd get there, but I finally accepted that I had to quit my current job. What should've been a difficult decision suddenly felt easy. Old me would've felt pressured to stay at her job and please others, bending and twisting to prove her worth. But ever since I started connecting to my authentic self after my burnout and shroom trip, I felt empowered to choose what *I* wanted. Besides, staying was no guarantee of security, as I'd seen already from my last layoff.

Did the idea of leaving still feel scary? Yes! But did I feel hopeful nonetheless? Absofuckinglutely.

I spent the next month giving myself space to think about how to make my career shift. I started going to a café downtown after work, where I'd research options on my laptop.

One evening, I watched a YouTube video of two Stanford professors who taught a course called "Designing Your Life." In the talk, Dave Evans and Bill Burnett explained how to use a design-thinking approach to figure out your life and career. It blew my mind. In their words: "Don't try to decide your way forward; just do something." They discussed how to take action and prototype big changes, reframe dysfunctional beliefs, and trust yourself as the expert of your life. More than anything, they gave me the permission I needed. Permission to jump in, say fuck it, and just do it.

Encouraged, I started mapping out ideas for my next career move. I created a visual mind map to brainstorm all the possibilities. From traveling the world for a year to finding a startup job to building my own communications consultancy—no idea was deemed too wild. I even considered looking for an internal transfer at Genentech's parent company, Roche, so that I could work abroad in Switzerland. The possibilities were endless!

After a week of contemplation and research, out of fifteen options, one lit me up the most: build my own consultancy. I'd been successfully leading a department-wide communications team already and loved helping people with their messaging. My main role as a project manager also heavily relied on my innate communication skills. *Shouldn't I be able to turn that into a business?* But this option also felt the scariest.

I'd always believed that I had to work for someone else to prove my worth. Now, for the first time in my life, I entertained the idea of entrepreneurship. However, the memories of my mom freezing at Fisherman's Wharf drawing portraits made me shiver. Sure, she made money as an entrepreneur, but it seemed like such a struggle. *How would I find customers? Would I make enough money? Am I even good enough?*

Not wanting to look like a fool going blindly into uncharted territory, I enrolled in classes to beef up my skills. That May, I became a student at the General Assembly tech-learning campus downtown, taking classes like marketing, copywriting, and website building. The classes gave me more confidence to start my own consultancy. Additionally, they reminded me that living in San Francisco gave me incredible access to resources that many in the world didn't have. Generations of wide-eyed hopefuls had come to the city, eager to find their version of gold.

It was time for me to shed my cocoon and uncover my own treasures too.

Everything that happened next seemed to unfold at warp speed. Sometimes things in your life can appear to drag for a while, until shit becomes abundantly clear and you hit the gas pedal.

When I told my mom that I was thinking of quitting my job, she was surprisingly supportive. On one hand, she was concerned that I'd make no money. But on the other hand, as someone who'd changed her career many times to follow her passion, she seemed proud of me. That was the last signal I needed.

On a warm afternoon in June 2015, I walked into my boss Jenn's office for our weekly one-on-one, half determined, half racked with guilt. She was an amazing manager, and I didn't want her to take the news I was about to drop personally.

"So . . . I've been thinking a lot. You know I love working with you and the team . . . but here's my official letter of resignation." My heart breaking a little, I handed her a piece of paper as I sat down across from her.

"Damnit. I knew I shouldn't have given you those three questions!" she said, part-dismayed, part-smiling.

We both laughed. We'd become close over our four years of working together, and I sensed that although she was sad to see me go as my manager, she was proud of me as a friend.

"It's a one-month notice, so there's more time for a smooth transition on each of my teams. I promise to leave things good before I go," I said.

She gazed at me pensively. "JC. Are you sure about this? Would you consider staying until the fall?"

I smiled slyly, fantasizing about an epic summer vacation in Europe, sipping champagne with no work meetings in sight. But I kept my response professional. "No, I've given it some thought. This is my final decision."

We spent the remainder of our meeting discussing practical items, such as my handover plan, but we also couldn't help but blink back the moisture in our eyes. Goodbyes are hard, even when they're necessary.

One month later, in mid-July, I sat down in my cubicle for the very last time. That morning, I opened my laptop and sent a farewell email, notifying my colleagues of my "reflective pause." Feeling profound gratitude in every word I typed, I thanked everyone for being part of a huge chapter of my life, for inspiring me, and for growing me.

Heartfelt email responses from my coworkers trickled in over the course of the day. My team even threw me a goodbye party. I hugged everyone I could, our embraces filled with bittersweet emotions and promises to stay in touch. Around five that evening, I turned in my company laptop and my work badge, an extension of my identity for the past four years.

And that was it. I had loved being JC, but JC was no longer me.

***

The next week, I flew to Europe by myself with a one-way ticket and no itinerary. I landed first in Zurich to visit a friend, but after that, I let my intuition guide me on where to go. My six-week soul-searching sabbatical had begun.

Back when I was twenty-two, I had studied abroad in Paris and fell in love with the more relaxed lifestyle. After graduation, I'd dreamed of moving to Europe, telling my friends that I was "American by birth, Chinese by blood, and European by heart." But the filial duty of staying close to my aging parents had kept me home. Now with Baba gone and my mom in stable health, I could enjoy Europe, at least for my reflective pause. Through traveling, I hoped to find joy, meaning, and the next steps for building my consultancy.

Oddly though, leaving my job didn't feel as daunting as I'd imagined. It helped that after quitting, I was able to cash out on company stocks that I'd forgotten I had. So while I didn't make a financial plan before leaving, at least I had enough money for the next few months to pay my bills.

The first week of my sabbatical, I was sitting at a café overlooking Lake Como in Italy when I couldn't believe what I saw on my barista's shirt. Printed on her T-shirt were the words: *If you dream it, you can do it.* I nearly spit out my cappuccino. They were the exact same words printed on the cover of my new blue leather journal, which my friend Nikki had given to me right before the trip. *What were the freakin' odds?!* It felt like a high five from the Universe, telling me I was on the right path.

Jacob also encouraged me to fly free. I guess I should also mention that at this point, we weren't officially a couple yet, even though we'd been dating for six months. I didn't ask about it before, scared that if I did, it would scare him away. But now, when my whole life was up in the air, I needed some kind of certainty to grab onto.

The second week of my sabbatical, when I was in Istanbul by myself, I didn't want to avoid the topic of us anymore. After cranking up the air conditioning in my Airbnb to escape the sweltering July heat, I called Jacob to discuss our upcoming reunion. He'd be in Copenhagen to visit family in August, so I'd meet him there.

"So . . . how are you going to introduce me?" I asked. Nervous, I pulled at the tassels of the Turkish cushion on my lap.

He replied, "My girlfriend? That would be the easiest to explain."

"I think so too," I said nonchalantly, trying to play it cool.

However, after we hung up, I could barely contain my excitement about the relationship news. I practically danced through the streets all the way to the Blue Mosque. Standing beneath its stunning tiled ceilings, I prayed he was the partner prophesied in the letter from my Future Self.

A few days later, I jetted off to Berlin to visit Niels, one of my best friends who I'd met when I was twenty-four in a hostel bar in Vienna. Though he was Dutch, he lived in Berlin. He had first introduced me to the city in 2014, and I immediately felt at home in this city of graffitied buildings, insane nightlife, and layered German history. There was an intense energy in Berlin—a duality between the horrifying darkness of its past and the lightness of its new, multicultural incarnation. You could eat a döner kebab by the river, just steps away from buildings where innocent people were once dragged from their homes and tragically sent to their deaths. Parts of the city's past were heavy and brutal. The future, hopefully, vibrant and bright.

One early August afternoon by a pool on my sabbatical, I read Tim Ferriss's book *The Four-Hour Workweek: Escape 9–5, Live Anywhere, and Join the New Rich*. In his book, Tim talked about how to live a life with more freedom and not be weighed down by the outdated dogma of working nine-to-five. Feeling inspired, I scribbled in my journal: "Maybe I can work remotely and live here one day?" I also jotted down ideas of what I could do for a business, like bringing together communication, emotional intelligence, and people. Later, when I shared my business ideas with Niels at his apartment, a grasshopper hopped in, a sign of good luck.

I'd love to tell you that my whole sabbatical was as joyful as I've described so far. But I must admit that I had several emotional breakdowns as well. In the third week, I sobbed on a bench alone in the seaside city of Split in Croatia. As I watched families gather in a plaza, I grieved the loss of my dad.

I also bawled in Sarajevo at a film festival, where I learned of the devastating Bosnian war in the early 1990s, in which around 100,000 people died. As I walked by bombed-out buildings riddled with hundreds of bullet holes, I could feel the heavy energy. And in packed theaters, I watched documentaries commemorating the twenty-year anniversary of the end of the war, sitting with survivors who grieved. I grieved with them too. Holding a wad of tissue paper soaked from my tears, I jotted down in my journal: "If Sarajevo can rebuild, there is hope for me too." Sometimes there is beauty in the breakdown, reminding us that even when we feel lost or lonely, we can rebuild.

I carried this hope to rebuild my life into the fourth week of my journey. I danced with friends at a music festival in Poland and walked solo through the charming islands that make up Stockholm, Sweden. However, whether I was with friends or by myself, by the fifth week I felt there was something big missing. That something was my boyfriend.

When Jacob and I finally reunited in Copenhagen at the end of August, I jumped straight into his arms at the train station. In my five weeks in Europe, I felt like I had lived five lifetimes already. Pushing, questioning, and resetting myself at each new place. Against my boyfriend's chest, I was elated to physically grab a slice of home again. Even thousands of miles away. I met his mom over coffee and felt immediately welcomed in his hometown.

The next morning, he took me to visit his dad, who had Alzheimer's and lived in a care facility. Dressed in a white T-shirt, blue jeans, eyeglasses, and sandals, his dad looked like he was ready to go on vacation. As the sunshine burst through a big window in his room, I studied the smiling faces of father and son. *His dad definitely didn't look sick*, I thought. But when he repeated the same story about digging a hole in the ground and emerging in Russia three times, I could see that the neurodegenerative disease had taken hold.

I flashed back to my visits with Baba in the care facility. My heart filled with crushing guilt again as I remembered how detached I was before he died. I envied how present Jacob was in comparison. How he and his father could play together, laughing like children, even when his dad was nearing his end.

For the next few days, we continued with a whirlwind friends-and-family tour. Jacob has seven lovely half-siblings and numerous adorable nieces and nephews. At birthday parties and brunches, I felt embraced by his family with *hygge*, the Danish term for comfy coziness. I felt so content in Copenhagen that I decided to stay a few more days to explore the city by myself.

One morning, I went to Assistens Cemetery to visit the famous Danes who lay there, such as the fairy tale writer Hans Christian Anderson and Søren Kierkegaard, the existentialist philosopher. Amongst the rows of trees and tombstones, I sat down on a bench, reflecting upon how we must live life fully before we die. Then I pulled out my journal and wrote down one of my favorite Kierkegaard quotes: "Life can only be understood backwards; but it must be lived forwards."

If I could dream it, I could do it. Keep living forward. After six weeks of looking inside myself in nine countries, I was finally ready to fly home.

I landed back in San Francisco in early September, excited to design a new chapter of my career. During my sabbatical, I had dreamed up so many ideas for building my first business. I also felt like I went to a bootcamp, where I mentally and emotionally toughened myself up to prepare for entrepreneurship. Now, it was time to hunker down and take action.

I unpacked my bags, climbed into bed, and slept soundly with a new appreciation for everything I already had. While I loved being abroad, I knew that I was meant to build my business in my hometown. My family was here. My boyfriend was here. And my professional network was here.

My bedroom became my first office. Sitting at my desk, I worked every day to refine my business ideas. I probably drank way too much coffee, stared too long at my laptop, and became delusional about what I could accomplish. But hey, every successful business comes from some kind of crazy, right?

Soon it became clear to me that I wanted to help companies communicate with more emotional intelligence. I could work with clients to develop their communication strategies so that they could connect better with their customers and their employees. This would ultimately increase their business results. After all, it's what I'd already been doing internally at Genentech.

I even came up with a name for my company: Bon Intent. It was a worldly-sounding name that meant good intent. Within a week, I built my own simple website with the consultancy motto scrawled across the home page: *Good communication matters*. It all happened so quickly, everything coming together faster than I could've imagined. I felt unstoppable.

In mid-September, a mere two weeks after my return from Europe and just two months after I quit my job, I was ready to register my business. That morning, I marched into the same marbled halls of San Francisco City Hall where my mom first got her business license decades back—and where I'd danced as a raver in my teens. When I walked into the Treasurer's office to file my application, I couldn't believe it. The clerk who received my application was a childhood friend! A few minutes later, she handed me a document. "Congrats," she said with a huge smile.

It was official. I, the small girl from Chinatown, was now an entrepreneur, fluttering free like a butterfly. What a fucking metamorphosis.

Moment to Self-Reflect

I cried happy tears writing this chapter, feeling so blessed. You've been with me on my journey. You've witnessed how heavy it was for me, fighting through what felt like my personal war from my layoff to family illness to the loss of Baba to my burnout. Then came this pivotal turning point.

I can barely believe how quickly everything happened, from me quitting my job to me starting a company. And how it just flowed naturally once I started to follow my intuition and my heart. But it did. As it can for you too. I'm also grateful to have met my boyfriend during this period. Just as I'm grateful to the Universe—or God, or whatever we may call the higher powers that be—for showing me signs that I was on the right path of breaking free.

Wherever you are on your journey, I hope you're noticing the signs that come to you too, be it people that inspire you, synchronicities, or moments of sudden clarity. You're divinely guided.

Listening to Your Future Self

For most of my life, I had searched for the answers outside of me, looking at others to tell me what to do and who to be. Perhaps you've done that too. But after my burnout and getting in touch with my own desires through channeling my Future Self, I felt empowered to listen to myself more. Apparently, I was a whole lot wiser than I originally gave myself credit for—as are you. There's magic when we learn to listen to ourselves and start to let go of the need for external validation.

However, sensing what you truly want deep inside can feel overwhelming. Especially if it's difficult to imagine getting out of your current situation, where you may feel stuck. That's where your Future Self comes in. They can help you see more clearly what you want and reveal a world of possibilities.

Reflection Exercise: Letter from the Future

- Find a quiet place where you can reflect in peace and connect with your own intuition.

- Write yourself a letter from your Future Self, who is ten years older than you.

- Some questions for your Future Self to answer:

  - Where are you? What's around you?
  - Who's around you?
  - What does love look like for you these days? What about family?
  - How do you feel at this moment in your life?

- Who are you in your personal life? What about in your professional life?
- What satisfies your soul?
- Any advice for your Current Self?

- Share anything else that comes to you. Let it flow.

Designing Your Life

It can be incredibly empowering to get in touch with a future version of yourself. But turning dreams into reality also requires taking action. Learning about design thinking and the *Designing Your Life* tools radically changed my life because I was able to "mind map" my ideas and prototype. It allowed me to play with my options without getting stuck in analysis paralysis or perfectionism. That's how I got the idea to create my own communications consultancy and take practical action toward building it.

When I was making my career shift in 2015, the bestselling book *Designing Your Life: How to Build a Well-Lived, Joyful Life* by Bill Burnett and Dave Evans wasn't available yet. But good news for you: Now it is! I'm a certified Designing Your Life coach and highly recommend reading the book. It's full of hands-on exercises to help you design a meaningful life and career.

14

I LOVE YOU

I BELIEVED THAT once I courageously broke free and became a butterfly, everything would suddenly be breezy. But of course, as with most things in life, there's often a gap between our expectations and reality.

What people don't tell you about major transformations—even the positive ones—is how jarring they can be. There can sometimes be an emotional split between one area of our life versus another, especially as we start to realize what no longer aligns with the new version of ourselves. This was certainly the case with me. Shortly after I founded my company, I felt like I was living two parallel lives: one where my work life was thriving and another where my personal life was falling apart.

Following my heart career-wise was liberating. Work opportunities poured in with ease. After I left my job, I fantasized about consulting for Genentech. As a former employee, I knew their communication needs intimately, understood the corporate culture, and still resonated with the company's mission to change patient lives. I felt it'd be a dream to land them as a client.

One day in October, a month after making a public announcement on social media to promote my new business, I received an email from a former colleague. She had heard of a project that needed a communications consultant and asked if I'd be interested in an intro. *Was she forreal?!* Within a week, I was on a call with the lead project manager, gushing about how it was a mutual fit. A month after that, I started a consulting gig on a huge IT project as the communication lead.

It was a true blessing. The hourly pay rate I negotiated was phenomenal. So were the flexible work hours. While I'd work on-site at Genentech most days, I also had the freedom to be remote. Soon, I was making more money than I'd made as a full-time employee—with less stress and on my terms. My new global project team members were awesome too.

My work life was a dream. I felt empowered and worthy as an entrepreneur. I wish I could've felt as confident in my romantic relationship.

That December, Jacob asked to temporarily move in with me, so that he could save on rent while he looked for another place to live. By then, I already had three other roommates and knew it'd be tight in my Richmond District apartment. But I happily obliged, making room for him in my home, just as I made room in my heart for a deeper commitment.

I was so hungry for his love. Though we'd been dating for almost a year, I still hadn't heard "I love you" from him. Just like I never heard it from my parents. *Was something wrong with me? Was I that unlovable?* Scared to tell him "I love you" for fear of never hearing it back, I hate to admit that I didn't say it either. Instead, I loved him through my actions, like buying a Danish language book to learn his native tongue. And welcoming him into my home. Was it passive aggressive of me to wait for him to say it? Probably. But I didn't know any better back then.

When Jacob and I flew to Mexico City for Christmas and New Year's, I felt hopeful. I had so much fun visiting the historical sights and finding the best street tacos together. However, Christmas came and went with no "I love you" from either of us.

Then came New Year's Eve. Champagne flowed as Jacob and I danced amongst hundreds of strangers at the W Hotel in Polanco, surrounded by silver balloons. Even in a crowd, it seemed like we were in a world of our own. When he pulled me close, I felt a rush of euphoria, intoxicated by his cologne and my hope. *OMG, this is finally the moment*, I thought.

He looked me in the eyes. "I've been thinking about us. We're growing at a nice pace. Each day I care about you more. But it's different than in my past relationships."

"Okay . . ." I muttered.

He continued. "I know you've probably been wanting to hear that I love you. And I just want to tell you . . . I love you as I love my family, but I'm not in love with you."

My heart shattered into shards. I gazed at the bits of confetti on the floor, trying to hold back the tears. "Okay . . . but do you think you *can* fall in love with me?" I asked.

"Probably. I would like to and I do care about you a lot," he replied.

I didn't know what else to say.

When the disco ball dropped at midnight, the rest of my self-esteem plummeted with it. The transition into the new year was a blacked-out blur.

After we got back to San Francisco, I was desperate for any kind of reassurance that my boyfriend still wanted to be with me. I was terrified that he'd suddenly leave me—that nothing I did would ever be good enough.

My lifelong fear of abandonment, which had always been present subconsciously in the background of my relationships, sprang to the forefront of my life. The paralyzing fear of Jacob abandoning me consumed me on the nights that he came home even thirty minutes later than usual from work. My chest would tighten. My pulse would race. I had to remind myself to breathe. When he finally rolled his bicycle into the garage of my apartment building, the door would make a loud click. Only then would my anxiety subside.

The belief that I formed in my childhood haunted me: *I am not worthy enough to make people stay*. I was embarrassed that I seemed so insecure but didn't know how to get out of the loop. Whenever I freaked out about us, Jacob would reassure me, telling me that everything was fine. I convinced myself that it was only a matter of time before he'd fall in love with me. If only I could prove that I was worthy of his love.

I thought that I was going crazy in my relationship, especially when coupled with my increasingly chaotic family situation. The punches came in succession.

First, our beloved family cat, Faybee, died. Although she was already nineteen years old, watching Faybee take her last breaths at the vet clinic was like watching Baba die for the second time. She was his constant companion, and in spirit, they felt intertwined.

Then Po Po got sicker and could barely walk at ninety-three years old. Day in and day out, my mom took care of my grandma. Though I was in awe of my mom's strength, I felt bad for her. She always seemed to be putting aside her own needs to caretake others in this era of her life. If not Baba, then Po Po and the kids she now took care of as a part-time daycare nanny.

And remember the foreclosed home in Richmond that my mom forced me to buy so I could "be a good daughter?" Well, our tenant stopped paying rent. My family gave them a generous grace period, but the payments never came. It was a mess. We hired a lawyer to consult on the eviction case, but I had to represent myself as the legal owner in court. I grew numerous white hairs from the stress. Thankfully, I could take time off work to deal with the house drama.

After we finally won the court case in February 2016 and obtained eviction orders, a county sheriff escorted me and Stan to reclaim the house. My mom couldn't make it, and, as usual, I was the COO of our family, expected to manage the mess.

The sheriff didn't even have to open the front door, which was left wide open. As he stepped in, his jaw dropped. "Didn't take the news well, did they?" he asked.

When I walked in, my jaw dropped too.

The house was left in chaos. Someone had tagged all the walls with graffiti. The rooms were full of dog shit and mountains of trash that made it difficult to walk through. The backyard looked like a cemetery for rejected flea market items, full of junk. I nearly slipped on a pile of peeled potato scraps, thrown on the floor by squatters who had taken over.

After the sheriff cleared the house to make sure no one was there, Stan and I assessed the situation in a state of numbed shock. I started taking pictures of the kitchen as he documented the condition of the bedrooms.

Suddenly, Stan ran toward me with eyes as big as saucers. "We gotta go, we gotta go! Somebody's here! He was hiding behind a door!" he shouted.

We sprinted like Olympians out of the house and threw ourselves into my car.

Stan pointed at the fence around the backyard. "He's right there!"

A man with a *V for Vendetta* mask lunged over the fence.

"He had a knife!" Stan shouted as we drove away, my driver side door still swung open.

Once we reached safety, I called the cops to come to the house. "Only squatters," they said. "Probably harmless. Make sure you secure that house."

That night, I cried myself to sleep, shaking with fear. I hated that fucking house. I hated that my mom expected me to deal with the drama of a house I never wanted in the first place.

It was maddening. I felt trapped. However, I couldn't say no to my mom, afraid that if I did, I'd be called an ungrateful daughter. And how could I say no when she had sacrificed so much for my family?

When spring came that March, my fear of abandonment became unbearable.

One evening, in a fit of panic, I sent an email to a psychotherapist I found online. Her website mentioned cross-cultural issues, and she was Asian American too, so I felt like she might be able to help me. Tired of hiding my emotions behind polite smiles and stuffed inside boxes of shame, I was ready to talk. Anything to relieve this gnawing pain.

Two weeks later, I dashed into a skyscraper downtown. Sweat seeped through my blouse as I squeezed into the elevator going up twelve floors. Panting, I burst through the door and said hello to a therapist for the very first time. For the purposes of this book, I'll call her Susanne.

"Please, take a seat," Susanne said, gesturing to the armchair by the window overlooking the rush hour traffic below. With warm brown eyes, she emitted an aura of genuine care. Care that made me feel safe enough to open up to her, eager to seek calm in the storm of my psyche.

"I never feel good enough in relationships. Like my boyfriends are just going to suddenly leave me," I said, my voice shaking.

Susanne nodded empathetically. "I can imagine how difficult that feels. Let's explore where that might come from."

Time flew by during that first session and the next. I recounted how I was raised by busy Chinese immigrant parents. How I was often the last one to be picked up at preschool. How on multiple occasions the teachers had to call my great-uncle, our emergency contact, because my parents couldn't come get me.

When I shared how I was regularly left alone at home at the age of four, Susanne gasped.

"I'm sorry that you were left alone like that. While I understand how they probably didn't have a choice, that's illegal. It's child endangerment," she said.

"Huh? But . . . but . . ." I protested, my voice trailing off.

Endangerment? Illegal? Those were some serious words. How then could it feel so normal to me?

It's funny what we consider normal all our lives, until someone tells us that it's not.

Telling my therapist the truth of my trauma after repressing it for decades felt like opening Pandora's box. I described the painful aspects of my relationship with my parents. To my mom, I was not smart enough. Not Chinese enough. Not pretty enough. Not a good enough daughter. Baba stayed silent when she berated and hit me, so I took his silence as agreement.

All of this came out, squeezed through tears, in my weekly therapy sessions. I met Little Jenn again—the small girl abandoned at home, sitting on the floor while Mommy studied at university and Baba bussed tables at the restaurant. I waited like a Pavlovian dog, conditioned to salivate at the sound of keys turning at the door.

On one hand, my childhood trauma created a powerful sense of independence, of being able to take care of myself from a young age. On the other, a deep sense of longing, an intense anxiety of being abandoned by a loved one, of seeking approval and wanting to know that I'm worthy enough to make people stay. I genuinely believed that if I just worked hard enough on myself in therapy, that things would magically change for the better in my relationship—that I would hear those three elusive words *I love you*. But no.

One day, Jacob announced that he'd found a studio apartment to rent by himself. I was crushed. I had convinced myself that the next apartment would include me. After all, we seemed to have gotten so close in the four months that we'd been living together, and our families had already met. His move shouldn't have surprised me—he'd already been viewing apartments without me. But I was naïve. And afraid. I didn't have the guts to ask why he hadn't asked me to move in with him. I was scared that I'd seem too needy.

My friend Rene got married in Palm Springs that May. Her wedding weekend was like a festival, the perfect place to bask in the glow of love. Friday was amazing. Jacob and I arrived at the resort and mingled with seeming ease. But by the next day, things took a turn.

Fueled by chardonnay, a girl standing next to us cheekily inquired, "So . . . are you guys getting married anytime soon?"

Before I could even look over at Jacob, he jumped in. "No. We don't have any plans to get married."

Ouch. To save myself from the embarrassment, I smiled and chimed in, ". . . yet." Outside, I laughed. Inside, I felt as tiny as the blades of grass beneath my toes.

Over the next few months, I carried the weight of feeling rejected into therapy. I told Susanne how I felt like a small, unworthy girl left sitting on the carpet alone. Thankfully, in my therapist's office I never felt alone. I felt heard, even when my anxiety about my relationship heightened to crippling levels.

"Where in your body do you feel that anxiety? Can you try to scan for it?" Susanne asked.

I closed my eyes. "I feel it in my feet. It tingles, like little electric shocks."

"What other times do you feel this?" she probed.

Like an emotional map, the body remembers where pain has traveled.

With anxiety electrocuting my feet, I told her about the Richmond house. I told her how much I hated it. How it made me feel small when my mom forced me to sign for it. How I couldn't say no to my mom. With my therapist's help, I realized that a major trigger for my anxiety was feeling like someone crossed my boundaries but not being able to express my own feelings or needs.

"You are allowed to feel for yourself. And you are allowed to tell people what you need," Susanne said.

I was stunned. *Me? Allowed to feel for myself? And have needs?* What an alien concept. I'd spent thirty-two years of my life shoving down my emotions and hiding my pain, even from myself. I didn't allow myself to feel what I'd deemed too negative or shameful regarding my own experiences. Could I feel anger and sadness regarding other people and their situations? Absolutely! I was the ultimate empath, the bleeding heart who cried with others when they cried, feeling all their emotions as if they were mine. But to feel anger or sadness about my *own* situation? Oh no no no. I didn't feel safe expressing these emotions in my family. Not as a child and not as an adult. Healthy emotional processing was absent in my family.

My therapist gave me the permission I needed to finally feel self-compassion, treating myself with the same empathy and kindness as I would offer to Little Jenn or a friend. And with this self-compassion, I was able to see how I prioritized everyone else's needs above my own, trying to please others in exchange for their approval.

Week after week in therapy, I grew bolder with acknowledging my own needs. I needed my mom to stop guilt-tripping me and respect my boundaries. And from my boyfriend, I needed to know whether he saw a future with me.

However, expressing my true feelings in the safety of therapy was one thing. Taking practical action in the real world was another. I was still too scared to bring things up in my relationship. My fear of abandonment was that big and that deep.

As I struggled in my relationship, feelings of unworthiness crept back with a vengeance in my career. The more I performed well on my consulting projects, with a growing client portfolio, the more I started to feel like an imposter. *Would I be found out as a fraud? Who am I to deserve success?* I also wanted to inspire others through public speaking but was afraid to be seen and heard by a larger audience. *Was the letter from my Future Self just bullshit? What the fuck am I even doing with my life?* Frustrated by my self-doubt, I decided to reach out to a coach.

It was awesome that I had therapy to talk through my childhood trauma and relationships, but I also wanted to work with a professional coach to help me overcome imposter syndrome and start public speaking. At first, I saw working on these different areas of my life as separate, but soon I'd come to understand that everything overlaps—in love, in life, and at work.

One day, I reached out to Lindsay, a coach that I'd met at a networking event. Drawn to her friendly vibes and empowering spirit, I sent her an inquiry. After an initial call where we chatted about my career goals, mental blocks, and how she could support me, I knew it: She was the perfect fit.

When Lindsay and I met in a coffee shop in San Francisco for our first coaching session, it felt like chatting with a longtime friend. Her bright smile welcomed me immediately. So when she began asking about what she called "Mean Monkeys," beliefs or things that held me back from my dreams, I felt safe opening up.

Though the conversations around us were loud in the café, I revealed that something was even louder—the inner critic inside my head. *You're not good enough. You don't deserve success. People will leave you. No one will listen to you. You imposter!* Gosh, my inner critic sure was mean.

Lindsay met my sharing with empathy. "It's okay to feel what you feel. But don't feed the Mean Monkeys. They keep you stuck."

Through talking about my self-doubt with her, something clicked. She helped me realize that *I* was keeping myself small. That I didn't just fear abandonment—I also feared success. It seemed so ass-backward. Who the hell fears success? But it turns out that many people do.

Lindsay introduced me to the "Upper Limit Problem," coined by Gay Hendricks in his bestselling book *The Big Leap: Conquer Your Hidden Fear and Take Life to the Next Level*. Reading the book after our first session helped me see that I had set a subconscious upper limit for myself. Whenever I exceeded that perceived limit of how much success and happiness I believed I was worthy of, I'd kick myself back down to a more comfortable place. I also realized that I felt like an imposter because I feared outshining others and being disloyal to my roots. It felt safer to stay small. Just as I was taught by my family and culture to stay small, obedient, and quiet—to not cause a fuss.

To become the Future Self I envisioned, I had to believe that I was worthy of success and raise my bar on how good I was willing to have it. But how?

The answer for me was taking practical actions that aligned with my authentic self. Not the kind of actions driven by external validation and people-pleasing, but the kind of actions that made the *real* me happy. This is where coaching became the ideal complement to therapy for me. Therapy helped me understand the roots of my challenges. Coaching empowered me to move forward with action.

Through my weekly coaching calls with Lindsay and the homework she suggested, I was able to implement actions that embodied self-worth. In the beginning, my coaching journey was mainly focused on the career stuff. With her encouragement, I launched a podcast called *Cup of Comms*, where I interviewed people about communication. Soon, I started to feel more comfortable being seen and heard. I also began public speaking, delivering a talk about embracing uncertainty at a women's empowerment event.

However, what I didn't expect was that our coaching journey would also focus on my personal life. Soon everything started to merge. I shared my relationship and family struggles with Lindsay, who held me accountable for making changes. I wrote a breakup letter to my Mean Monkeys. I spoke to my mom about the Richmond house.

I was on fire. My actions shifted my mindset and vice versa. I was on an epic self-help binge that made me feel like a badass. Yet despite all my progress across coaching and therapy, I still wasn't ready to ask my boyfriend about our future together.

Until loss hit my family yet again and thrust me onto a stage.

One morning in July, I got a call from my mom that Po Po wasn't doing well. By this time, Po Po had already moved to a care home in Daly City, where she received round-the-clock care. I raced down the highway in my car.

When I got to Po Po's, I immediately rushed to her bedside. Here was the woman who had helped raise me and Stan with such tenderness and love.

"Po Po, I'm here," I said.

Her eyelids flitted open. "Jenn ah," she mumbled. And within seconds, her eyes closed again. I watched her chest rise and fall.

Uncle Bo sat in a chair at the head of Po Po's bed. He had come all the way from China once he heard about Po Po's rapid deterioration in the days leading up to this one. My grandma lay so peacefully. As if she no longer felt pain in her hips. As if nine decades of living and raising five children had satisfied her soul. As if she was ready to finally rest.

I smoothed her small bundle of white hair and leaned in next to her. "Goodbye, Po Po, I love you. Thank you for everything," I whispered.

I took one more look at her and knew it was likely the last time. Less than thirty minutes later, in my car, I listened to a voicemail from my mom. Po Po had let go. And I let the tears stream down my face.

Losing my grandma shook me, but it also shook out some of my self-doubt. Just a few days before Po Po died, I had received a big speaking opportunity. I'd been volunteering as marketing lead for TEDxPeacePlaza in San Francisco, and Glenn, the main organizer, had asked if I wanted to be the emcee for our upcoming event. When Glenn had first asked me, I told him I was unsure. *What if I choke onstage? What if I let everyone down?*

But after I lost Po Po, I decided that I didn't want to play small anymore. I wanted to use my voice. After all, hadn't she? I remembered how Po Po used to perform at the On Lok Senior Center, singing in red lipstick and wearing a traditional qipao onstage. To say yes to emcee-ing at a TEDx event would be the best way to honor her legacy.

Two weeks later, in Japantown, I stood onstage in front of a hundred people wearing an emoji shirt and blue pants. After Glenn's intro, my voice made its debut into the mic.

"Hi, everyone! I'm Jenn Choi, and I'm very honored and humbled to get to share the stage with our incredible speakers who will share their diverse perspectives on fun."

The next three hours whizzed by. In between speaker intros, inspirational talks, and networking with audience members, I found my voice. I found within me a powerful roar.

Unfortunately, the high of the successful event didn't last for long. When I got home, I felt a hollow sadness. *Would I ever be able to voice my needs in a romantic relationship?*

I'd soon find out.

One August evening in Montenegro, I watched longingly as couples dined by the seaside. Perched above them on a cliff at dusk, I sat with my feelings alone. I had asked Jacob to join me for this vacation, but he couldn't take time off work. Ever the busy entrepreneur, building his company was his main priority. I kept checking my phone for texts from him. But all I received was a reminder from T-Mobile to pay my bill. The loneliness stung—not just from the solo trip, but from the ache of unrequited love.

The next day, I sat on a bench by the shore, reflecting upon my relationship. The longer I reflected, the more things became crystal clear. I wrote into my journal with emboldened fervor: "I see clearly that there's no point in keeping anything in my life that no longer serves me. I want to feel hope, optimism, and confidence in my relationship. I should have what I deserve."

No longer in a state of denial, I saw the chasm between us. I saw a future with Jacob. I wasn't sure if he saw one with me. However, to his credit, there were a lot of positives. He was kind, smart, adventurous, and open-minded. He'd also influenced my career, empowering me to build a business. In many ways, I loved and admired him.

But as I reflected upon what I really needed, a painful truth appeared. I wrote into my journal: "Why am I in a relationship with someone who isn't in love with me? What would I say to a friend in the same situation?"

I channeled the love for my best friend, Lily, and tuned into the response I knew I needed, writing it down: "I would say, friend, you need to address this head-on or move on. You should not feel so heartbroken and rejected. No more."

I closed my journal immediately. What else did I need to hear?

———

A week after flying home, I finally gathered the strength to say what I'd buried beneath fear deep inside. We were cuddling in Jacob's bed when I finally allowed myself to let it out. Although I felt nervous, I knew I could no longer hide my pain.

"I feel so sad. Like a small, rejected kid. I still feel like you don't love me. Do you even want to be with me?" I managed to blurt out before the tears welled up.

Jacob's eyes started to water too. "I care about you and love you as a person, but I don't see a future with you. I asked myself, why aren't you asking Jenn to move in? It's because I don't see it happening. I wish I did. I wish I could tell you, but I can't."

My heart tumbled into the alley below where a homeless druggie pissed on it. Then I felt my frustration rise. "Why were we even in this relationship for so long?!" I exclaimed.

Feeling defeated, I shoved the clothes I'd left at his place into a garbage bag. I felt like the stupidest fool in the world. I thought I could make him fall in love with me. I was wrong.

———

The next few weeks were awful. We didn't talk again, leaving me without closure. Thankfully, I had both a therapist and a coach to help me process the heartbreak. They were true saviors, guiding me through my grief.

I felt a huge hole in my life after the breakup. I hid in public bathrooms to cry. I couldn't even manage a yoga class without a packet of tissues.

But I couldn't focus all my time drowning in tears. I had shit to do. After all the drama with the last tenant, my family decided to prepare the Richmond house for sale. We got rid of the squatters, put new locks on the doors, boarded up the windows, and paid a neighbor with a loud chihuahua to guard the house. After hiring contractors to fix up the foundation and haul five truckloads of junk out, we were ready to let this cursed house go.

Talking to my mom about the house remained difficult. Every time I tried to state my boundaries, she gave me the same old guilt trip. "Jenn ah. Be a better daughter. Do you know how much I've done for you?" she'd say.

To make things worse, she constantly asked me why I was single. It was relentless. It felt like no matter what I did, no matter how much I achieved in other areas, I couldn't escape her incessant questions about my dating life.

"When will you find a husband? Maybe you shouldn't look for love. Just look for a man that is honest. That's what I did with Baba. Stop wasting your time with entrepreneurs. They won't have time for you. Date an engineer or a doctor. I want grandkids," my mom would say.

"Mommy, stop . . ." I'd plead. I could feel my blood boiling.

Whenever I told my therapist about my mom pestering me about my dating status, my blood would boil all over again.

"What reasons could she have for saying these things?" Susanne asked.

"I don't know, to make my life miserable? To make me feel bad? She's always so critical. It never seems enough," I blurted out.

"Any other possible reasons?" she asked.

"Ugh. Probably because she wants me to get married and have kids like her. In Chinese culture, it's the ultimate goal. Get married and have kids. But we're in America. I want to work on my career. I can't live with all these ridiculous pressures," I said.

A light flashed in Susanne's eyes. She began, "Sometimes with our loved ones, we can become enmeshed. It's not clear whose feelings are whose. And it's hard to separate, so I understand how you feel pressured. Perhaps you can try separating from what's going on with your mom. Give it a little bit of space."

I mulled it over and slept on it, still not knowing whether it was possible to separate my mom's needs and feelings from mine. Slowly though, over the next few weeks, I started setting more boundaries. I started saying "no" more to my mom. I was even able to laugh it off when she pelted me with dating questions again.

Like muscles, my boundaries became stronger every time I exercised them. Soon my exercises would pay off.

One foggy Saturday, my mom, Stan, and I were at the cemetery visiting Baba. The scent of burning incense filled the air.

Suddenly, without warning, and as if possessed by some ghost, my mom said, "I love you kids."

Mouth wide open, I stared at her without saying anything. I didn't want to jinx or scare whatever it was away.

She continued. "Having you kids has been the best thing in my life. Living life and not having children is like wandering the world yet not seeing anything."

With both shock and a feeling of long-sought redemption, I replied, "Thank you, Mommy. I love you too."

And there in that cemetery, truths sprang up from the dirt beneath our feet. For her, the Richmond house was meant to be a financial buffer for all of us. The pressure to have kids was her wish for me to experience the same joy.

I turned to Stan. "Did you hear that?! Did you hear what she said?! Hah! I have to tell my therapist."

A few days later, as I sat in my therapist's office with the busy traffic rushing by below, it felt less chaotic. I felt a sense of calm I hadn't felt in a long time.

A miracle had happened. I may not have heard "I love you" from my boyfriend, but I finally heard it from the first love of my life—my mom.

Moment to Self-Reflect

Life is wild. We could spend our whole lives chasing love from others, all while lowering our self-esteem by abandoning our own needs. The longer we don't stand up for ourselves, the longer we diminish our own worth and feed fear and anxiety.

Reflecting back, I can clearly see how my childhood trauma led to my fear of abandonment and fear of success. I believed: *I am not worthy enough to make people stay*. And *The world is unsafe. I have to stay small to stay safe*. Filled with fear, I spent decades abandoning myself and keeping myself small, thinking that would get me the love I craved. I can't believe that I was thirty-two years old when I finally understood that I was allowed to have needs, express needs, and set boundaries.

However, I'm glad that I was able to get professional support through therapy and coaching. They were worthy investments in my mental health, well-being, and happiness. Through getting support, I finally learned the truth, as I hope you're coming to see as well: Only when we honor our needs and befriend our boundaries can we break free.

Honoring Your Needs

It can feel scary to awaken to your own needs. This is in part because awakening to your needs means giving yourself permission to even *have* them, which exposes you to the vulnerability of people you love denying those needs. We can fear the loss of our relationships, or even the loss of the *self* we have constructed out of that fear. We can become attached to the version of ourselves that we've known for so long—the version that helped us survive.

Like me, you might also find it difficult to acknowledge your needs in a relationship. This makes sense, as having or expressing needs might've backfired on you in the past. However, you can choose for things to be different now. *You* are different now.

Sure, my boyfriend and I broke up when I finally spoke up for my needs (instead of continuing to assume that he knew what I wanted), but I'm proud that I chose to honor myself. When we choose to be our authentic selves, we can create healthier relationships that honor our self-worth.

Sensing into your needs is an important step to breaking old patterns.

Reflection Exercise: Sensing Into Your Needs

Part 1

- Close your eyes and do a head-to-toe scan of your body as you think of a recent memory of being upset or triggered.

- How does it feel in your body and where?

- That feeling can indicate the presence of unmet or unexpressed needs. Imagine for a moment that no one would judge you for having those needs. Imagine that if you expressed your needs, someone would be there to meet them. If you could express a few unmet needs out loud, what would they be?

Part 2

- It can help to write a letter to a friend, and then write a letter back to yourself, as if you were your own friend. We're often kinder to our friends than we are to ourselves.

- If you were writing a letter to one of your best friends describing your current situation, desires, and needs, what would you say?

- What questions would you ask your friend as you're seeking their insight and support?

Part 3

- What would that friend write back to you, in a loving tone?

- How does that change your perspective? What actions might you want to take as a result?

Befriending Your Boundaries

On top of getting in touch with our own needs, setting boundaries can positively transform our lives. You can think of boundaries as invisible lines that we draw to define what behaviors are okay versus not okay. You can set emotional, physical, psychological, or even energetic boundaries to protect your feelings, space, values, and time.

Boundaries can sometimes feel like barriers against others, but they're like our close friends. They look out for our well-being. They bring us more happiness. They come from a place of love, rather than fear.

Boundaries have been a big topic in my life, and I'm still working on mine. However, I can share that with practice, it's become easier for me to identify and communicate my boundaries. Becoming aware of my relationship with them was a huge first step, as it can be for you too.

Reflection Questions:

- What's your relationship with boundaries like?
- If you struggle with setting boundaries, where do you think that comes from?
- How can you befriend your boundaries in an act of self-love?

15

EAST MEETS WEST

HEARING "I LOVE YOU" from my mom felt like a dream come true. I just wish it didn't have to come with her cancer.

The invisible wall between my mom and me, built up by years of unacknowledged family trauma, had started to fall as I began to heal through therapy and coaching. I was able to receive her affection with a more open heart. Our conversations became less tense. However, her lymphoma lurked in the background, threatening to raise hell at any moment, even when there seemed to be temporary peace in our family. Unfortunately, with her refusal to opt for any Western medicine, her tumors only grew. As did my anxiety about losing her.

Thankfully, other aspects of my life seemed to be going well. Through working with Susanne and Lindsay, I found a stronger sense of self. One that could begin to express my needs, boundaries, and voice. Because I felt like I was in a better place, I decided to stop both therapy and coaching. My therapist and my coach had empowered me with tools that transformed my life and relationships. Now, it was time to put those tools into practice.

With clearer boundaries between my mom and me, the drama with the house in Richmond finally came to an end. Within two months of listing the house for sale, my family sold it. We paid off the remaining mortgage loan and resolved some of our outstanding debt from other bills. I was also able to keep some of the profit from the sale, redemption for all the years I'd spent paying the mortgage for the house I was forced to sign for. It felt like sweet justice.

At work, I stepped into my power. At my consulting gig at Genentech, I claimed my seat near the head of the conference room table, no longer feeling like an imposter. I was also a guest on multiple podcasts such as *The Tao of Self-Confidence*, where I talked about overcoming self-doubt. By this point, I had retired my podcast, *Cup of Comms*, realizing within only three episodes that I preferred to be a guest on other podcasts instead of producing my own. Old me would've stuck with it for longer, pressuring myself to continue even though I didn't want to anymore, holding myself to an impossible standard. But the new me was different. I knew when to cut my losses. Besides, I needed my energy for my new obsession: making videos.

By the fall of 2016, I became one of the top creators on a social media app called *AskWhale*, where I shared communication advice and life lessons. I was hooked. Making videos made me feel wanted—in contrast to my seemingly unsuccessful dating life. Sure, I'd finally heard "I love you" from my mom, but I still felt unworthy unless I performed. I wasn't consciously aware of this at the time, so I kept blindly chasing achievement. Every like, comment, or share stroked my ego, giving me the dopamine hits and external validation I craved.

Embracing a new version of myself that was publicly seen and heard was confusing though. For so long, I'd been conditioned to stay small to stay safe, to be modest and obedient—just like generations of women before me in Asian countries such as China. I felt I was betraying my roots. Would Confucious scorn me for my disgrace? Yet staying quiet no longer served me. I was ready to speak like the kind of loud American that I'd see on TV—if only I could resolve the identity clash within me between Eastern culture and Western culture.

The dichotomy between East and West permeated my life. Not only did I have to constantly code-switch between two languages, but I had to endure unrealistic expectations placed on me. I was expected to remain modest amidst my family's Chinese collectivist upbringing while living in America where individuals are encouraged to self-express and shine. I was expected to never question my parents while questioning authority in Western cultures is seen as a healthy exercise of critical thinking. And most annoyingly, my relatives expected me to already have kids, when everyone around me in Silicon Valley seemed to be focused on their careers. From a cultural and societal standpoint, nothing I did ever seemed good enough. I was a walking contradiction.

———

As a few months dragged on without talking to Jacob post-breakup, I was surprised that I still thought about him. Here was yet another contradiction in my life: *Shouldn't I just move on?* But I found myself missing our deep intellectual connection. After we broke up, I went to a blockchain technology conference by myself and started investing in cryptocurrency, just as he'd inspired me to. Sure, I had more self-love than before, but there was also a part of me who still loved him and wondered if he ever thought about me too.

Then one day in December, three months after our breakup, I received a flirty text from Jacob asking to meet up. Though I was surprised that he reached out, I was also intrigued.

Overcome with curiosity, I invited him over to my apartment the next afternoon. But instead of talking about our breakup or our emotions, we spent hours in bed, entangled in each other. There was a part of me that felt wanted again. That felt redeemed. *Was he trying to get back with me?* I wondered.

I didn't know. But I did know that we couldn't resist seeing each other again. That winter, we'd hang out at my apartment, but I set a boundary not to go back to his, not wanting to relive the pain of our breakup. We'd draw out this not-girlfriend-not-boyfriend-thing for months.

If you're noticing a pattern here, yes, it's true. Getting caught in situationships with exes was my toxic trait. Once again, the push-pull dynamic felt familiar to me. Just as it did in my family.

Speaking of family, when I turned thirty-three years old the following February, the pressure from my mom for me to have kids reached an all-time high. She asked when I would have kids at every conversation. To get her off my back, and to give myself space to breathe, I decided to freeze my eggs. Many of my single friends in Silicon Valley were already doing it, so I decided to do the same. I was making good money from consulting and knew that I wanted kids one day. *Why not buy myself more time?* I considered it an insurance policy for my fertility. After two months of fertility clinic visits and hormone treatments, it was done. My potential future was cryogenically frozen. And my anxiety about needing to settle down was significantly decreased.

When I told my mom about my frozen eggs, she was displeased. "Aiya. Those hormones aren't good for your body. Not natural," she said. Once again, I felt nothing I did was ever right in her eyes. But at least the decision felt right for me.

Meanwhile, Jacob and I continued to hang out without discussing what it meant. I asked myself many questions. *Did he finally realize what he'd lost? Was he dating others?* But rather than discussing it directly with him, which seemed too scary, I casually dated other people and automatically assumed he did too. Not the healthiest approach, I know. There were many weeks when we didn't see each other. But inevitably, we'd pick up where we left off. Even in romance, I was internally conflicted.

The truth was, in some ways I was proud to be a walking contradiction, much like my mother. She didn't fit into any neat box either. And despite her unpredictable behavior, she was still the woman I admired the most.

When I was a little girl, I used to wander in parks together with my mother. She'd encourage me to admire little details that people would often miss, such as the soft flower petals dancing in the wind.

Then in adulthood, visiting the annual "Bouquets to Art" exhibition at the de Young Museum became one of our favorite mother-daughter traditions. Each spring, florists would create unique floral arrangements to mimic the art pieces that inspired them. Cascading white lilies mirrored a waterfall painting. Yellow daffodils shone against a pastoral sunset on canvas.

My mother taught me how to find the extraordinary in the ordinary. I wanted to honor that gratitude practice through art. While I was crappy at painting, I knew I could write. So when my former coach, Lindsay, announced that she was co-leading The100DayProject—where participants would document and share their creative process online for one hundred days—I jumped at the chance to join.

On Day 1, I announced in a post on Instagram: "Today marks the beginning of my 100-day project, in which for one hundred days straight I will find the extraordinary in the ordinary. Oftentimes, we go hunting for things to make us happy. We buy things. We seek happiness in others. But you know what? The extraordinary can be found in the ordinary. Just look. It is within you and around you."

I was ready to use my newfound voice to share my musings through an artistic microblog. At the beginning of the project in April, it started off lighthearted. Just a long hashtag and some colorful filtered pics. On Day 15, I happily shared that I'd booked a two-month summer trip to Berlin, where I wanted to work remotely and channel my inner artist.

Then, as if struck by lightning, things took a dark turn in May. On Day 38, I shared a photo of Victorian homes on a steep slope and wrote: "Perspective. Today my world was shook up . . . going downhill even, as I heard from my brother that my mom's cancer was worsening. We had planned to go together to China next week, to take my mom to the homeland she hadn't seen for thirty years. But life has a way of giving you that new look on things, just when you think you've adjusted. It keeps you on your toes. But it's beautiful even in its melancholy brokenness. I find that extraordinary."

Though I tried to put a positive spin on it, I was devastated. We were supposed to go on a two-week trip to China to visit family in Hong Kong, Hunan, and Guangdong. It'd be our first family vacation in decades. But I should've known not to get my hopes up. I couldn't trust that anything good would ever last. I had already bought all our plane tickets, wanting to repay my mom for all the years she'd sacrificed for our family. I had believed that lack of money was the reason why she hadn't gone back to her native land for so long. But when her black, bloody stools showed up again, my hopes to take us to China seemed to go down the toilet.

A couple days after shit looked bad—literally—I took my mom out for Mother's Day. Though she insisted that the doctors told her she was getting better, I witnessed otherwise. When we sat down at a café by Chrissy Fields, I watched her struggle to eat a cup of chili. And in a selfie of us by the Golden Gate Bridge, she looked too thin for her puffy coat. Her complexion told the truth too. Once fleshy and pink, her cheeks sagged and appeared almost gray.

When she insisted on keeping her ticket to China, my jaw dropped.

"Jenn ah. I'm coming. After my singing class final," she said.

My mom loved her singing class at City College, where she had learned how to sing opera in her late sixties. Missing her final performance was out of the question for her, so we'd previously agreed that Stan and I would fly to Hong Kong first to celebrate his birthday, and our mom would join us a few days later.

"Okay, Mommy," I replied.

The adult in me wanted to protest in concern for her health, but the child in me cheered in jubilation. So, we stuck with our original plan.

A few days later, Stan and I boarded a plane headed to Hong Kong. However, I couldn't help but feel a deep unease within me, not wanting to split from my mother. I felt the tension within me rising, just as I'd felt the tension within me between East and West.

But there was no turning around now.

Moment to Self-Reflect

Reflecting back on this period feels bittersweet. Although I was able to reclaim my power in my professional life, it was hard to truly celebrate for long because there was so much uncertainty in my family. On top of the constant, unpredictable ups and downs with my mom's cancer, I also felt inner conflict about my situationship—just as I continued to feel inner conflict about my cultural identity.

Cultural Identity and Clashes

Sometimes, as we go through big life changes, we're pushed to examine our cultural identity. Cultural identity is the sense of belonging that comes from our connection to a particular group or culture. It includes the beliefs, traditions, values, social norms, and language that can form our views about who we are and how we should behave. When you think about cultural identity, concepts such as nationality, ethnicity, or family might come to mind, but it can also include religious or political affiliation.

In times of personal transformation, cultural identity can create internal conflict as we let go of parts of ourselves that we no longer identify with and make room for what does align with us. In my case, I experienced tension growing up between Eastern and Western cultures. I felt like a walking contradiction, never quite Chinese enough nor American enough. However, even if you don't live between two or more cultures, you might still feel tension in your identity between who you are in your family versus who you are outside your family.

Reflecting upon our cultural identities can bring us greater self-understanding. But it can also bring us grief. There's even a term for this type of grief: "cultural bereavement," which therapist Sahaj Kaur Kohli explains in her groundbreaking book *But What Will People Say?: Navigating Mental Health, Identity, Love, and Family Between Cultures*. When I reflect upon growing up between cultures, I grieve for what was lost in translation between me and my parents—not only literally in terms of language, but also metaphorically in terms of our cultural divide, differences in beliefs, and challenges understanding each other emotionally. It's no wonder why my identity felt so split and confusing at times. However, I'm glad that I get to take the parts I like of each culture, mixing them together to create an authentic version of myself.

Reflection Questions:

- In what ways do your family and cultural background influence your beliefs and behaviors?

- Are there areas in your life where there's a clash between who you're expected to be (in your family or culture) versus who you want to be? How does it impact you?

- How do you want to honor your family or cultural background while also staying true to your individual identity?

16

SINKING IN THE SWELL

ON A HUMID day in mid-May, Stan and I arrived in the bustling streets of Hong Kong. Modern skyscrapers towered over us as we passed by shops packed with people speaking Cantonese. I was glad to be back in one of my favorite cities, which felt like a much larger version of San Francisco Chinatown, but with 7 million people. After we got our bearings, we headed to our Airbnb in the center of the city. We'd be in Hong Kong for six days total, visiting Baba's side of the family, then heading to Changsha afterward to visit my mom's hometown.

The morning of Stan's thirty-first birthday, we feasted at a dim sum restaurant, scarfing down shrimp dumplings, pan-fried turnip cake, and steamed rice rolls with beef. We both smiled at the thought of eating as Baba did in Hong Kong in his youth.

After dim sum, we continued celebrating Stan's birthday by hiking Dragon's Back, one of the city's most scenic hikes with sweeping coastal views. The sun beat down on us as we dripped sweat from head to toe. When we reached the summit, we could finally see the trail's end in sight. Soon enough, we'd be hanging out at Big Wave Bay, where we planned to have lunch.

As we started the steep descent on the path toward the beach, I smiled. I loved this bonding time with my brother. He was the perfect travel partner. Easygoing, never complained, and full of jokes. It was our first proper vacation together in decades.

When we finally arrived at an outdoor café close to the beach, we each ordered a plate of fried noodles.

Suddenly, as we were eating, Stan's phone rang. "It's mom," he said as he accepted the call.

She probably wants to wish him a happy birthday, I thought.

"When will you get out?" Stan said on the phone. And then, "Okay. Okay," as he hung up, looking upset.

I set down my chopsticks. "What's up? She packed yet?"

"Mom's not coming. She's back in the hospital," Stan revealed.

My stomach dropped. "What?! Again?!"

"She felt dizzy and pooped black again," he said.

"I hate this! I hate it!" I clenched my fists. "Let's go home."

Without ever touching the sand on the beach just footsteps away, we got on a bus headed back toward our Airbnb. When we finally stepped into the apartment, the sun had already set. I showered and put on pajamas, too upset to make it back out.

For the next few hours, we hopped on and off the phone with our mom. I felt terrible for being so far from her, especially when she was so sick.

"Stan and I can get on a flight back to San Francisco on Friday," I said to her.

"No, you can't," my mom replied. "*Dai Gu Maa* is getting old and sick, and you have to go see her on behalf of our family. Anyway, the doctors gave me blood, and I'll be okay again."

I sighed. Going against my mom's wishes was futile.

Dai Gu Maa was our Big Auntie, Baba's oldest sister, who lived in Taishan. Dai Gu Maa had been getting sicker, and my mom feared that we wouldn't have much time left with her. It was one of the reasons for our trip back to China.

The rest of our Hong Kong stay was a blur. Stan and I had dinner with uncles, aunties, and cousins from my dad's side of the family, but I struggled to engage in conversation. These were Baba's three beloved half-brothers and a half-sister from Yeh Yeh's second marriage. I should've been more present. Especially when they went out of their way to welcome us at a beautiful restaurant with banquet tables. But nothing felt right without my mom and dad there. On top of that, there was the language barrier. I spoke enough basic Cantonese to get by, but everything felt surface level. My mom's cancer eclipsed my ability to connect.

With an emptiness inside our hearts, Stan and I left Hong Kong and headed to our next leg of the journey: Changsha in Hunan Province, in the south-central part of China.

To get to Changsha, we first rode a metro train from Hong Kong to Shenzhen, where we officially crossed the border into Mainland China. I could feel the shift immediately. In Hong Kong—a vibrant, international city shaped by both Chinese and British influences—I blended in easily as a Westerner. But just a forty-minute ride away, on the other side of the border, I felt more like a foreigner. Even in my ancestral land.

I quickly closed the social media apps on my phone as we crossed over the Great Firewall of China, which restricted internet access to foreign websites such as Google, Facebook, and Instagram. At the crowded station, where we needed to catch the train from Shenzhen to Changsha, only one thing looked familiar—the golden arch of McDonald's.

This leg of our trip felt different. We had to be more mindful of what we said, and relying on Cantonese was no longer an option. Although we were in the Guangdong Province, where my family is from in southern China, Mandarin was the main language here. Ah, the great Eastern motherland. Our cultural roots.

Every single person at the train ticket counters spoke Mandarin, which Stan and I couldn't speak. Luckily, we found a young dude in line who could help us translate from Cantonese. A while later, we sat on the bullet train, speeding north to Changsha.

Three hours later, we arrived in our mom's hometown. It felt strange to arrive in Changsha without her. She was supposed to be our guide, our translator, and the reason for us being here. Our Uncle De, who we called *De Kau Fu*—the eldest of my mom's younger brothers—picked us up from the train station. We all acknowledged the sorrow of being without my mom. But at least we found comfort in dining together. When Stan and I settled into a hotel room that night, I lay awake tossing and turning. Four million people lived in the sprawling capital, but I felt abandoned and alone.

Thankfully, Stan and I had a trip planned to Zhangjiajie National Park just a few days after arriving in Hunan—something to take our minds off the fact that our mom was getting sicker. With its tall, stunning, otherworldly limestone formations, Zhangjiajie inspired the scenery in the movie *Avatar*. My brother and I took a bus from Changsha, arriving at a village close to the park. Uncle De had arranged for an English-speaking tour guide to accompany us so we wouldn't be totally lost.

The next day, the three of us headed into the park, an alien world on earth. Stone karsts shot up from the ground thousands of feet toward the sky like giant vertical fingers. When we finally got to one of the highest points in the park, a golden arch appeared once again. "Damn, now this is a Mickey D's with a view!" Stan exclaimed.

Inside the McDonald's, we ordered almost everything we could off the menu. I stared out the window at the magnificent scene before me, seemingly from an ancient Chinese watercolor painting. Crazy to think that our mom had once touched these stones before all the modern infrastructure was up—and well before any international fast-food chains infiltrated the country.

After a long day hiking, we finally descended via the Bailong Elevator. Translated as "hundred dragons sky lift," the glass elevator took us down over a thousand feet. When we got to the base, Stan and I both checked our phones to see several missed calls from our mom.

My heart racing, I listened to her voicemail. "Jenn ah. I'm at the airport in San Francisco coming to Changsha," she'd said. No further explanation, no details.

Stunned, I shared the news with Stan.

"She's crazy," he said.

"Classic Mom move, though," I replied.

Two days later, we headed back to Changsha. As Stan and I arrived at the street where Uncle De lived, the silhouette of a woman appeared. Her back was facing us, but we could instantly see her shape. Hair up in a bun. A black crocheted cardigan draped over a beige long sleeve shirt. For a moment,

I thought I saw a ghost. Then the figure turned around. Her ankles were swollen. Her complexion was pale. But it was definitely my mom.

"Mommy!" I said, running up to her. "Did the doctors say you could fly?"

"I got the tickets myself in Chinatown," she said. She pulled out an envelope from the travel agency on Stockton Street and a printed itinerary. "See?"

"So . . . that means they let you fly?" I asked again.

She quickly looked away, avoiding my question. Then she turned to Uncle De and spoke in Hunanese, yet another Chinese language which sounded different from Cantonese and Mandarin. From what I could make out, it was regarding dinner plans.

When we got back to Uncle De's house, I decided to share some good news with my mom. "Mommy, I want to give you my car. Since I'll be in Berlin this summer, you can have it." I imagined her sitting in my shiny Elantra after decades of her driving old beater cars. The car had served me well, but I wanted to give it to her as a gift.

"No. You better rent it out or sell it to someone," she replied.

"Ugh! What do you mean *no*?! And who will I rent my car to?!" I yelled. I felt small, useless, and rejected.

Stan looked at us in silence, once again caught in our crosshairs.

"You look like a lunatic," she said to me.

I shut up, ashamed by my outburst, which reminded me of growing up with hers.

The next morning, my mom got a lymphatic massage from a masseuse. She firmly believed that it would help her manage her cancer.

"Less swelling already," she said, pointing to her ankles. "My kidneys hurt less too," she added.

"Great!" I said. I ignored the comment about her kidney pain, choosing to focus on the news of reduced swelling instead. Ah, the things we do to remain in denial. And I was deep in denial about the severity of her cancer, as was my mom.

That day, Stan and I traveled back in time to our mom's childhood. First, to her favorite public park. She eagerly led us through the paths and along the lake, telling us stories about her childhood as we strolled through the

300-acre park. "Wah, all these buildings weren't around when I was young," she said.

That evening, we gathered in her childhood friend's loft. My mom and her three friends recounted the times they shared well over three decades ago. That was how long they'd been apart. How long my mother missed them.

Though Stan and I couldn't understand their Hunanese jokes, we appreciated the aromatic flavors of the food. Pickled cucumbers, dry heat chicken and, of course, plenty of the region's famously spicy chili peppers. I snapped photos of all the dishes, hoping to find them again back in the United States.

After two more days in Changsha visiting relatives, my mom, Stan, and I headed to our next stop on our whirlwind tour: my family's ancestral villages in Chaolian and Taishan, in Guangdong Province.

———

The last of the sun's rays glistened over the Pearl River as we arrived back in Guangdong via high-speed train. Uncle Bo picked us up from the train station in Guangzhou, the province capital, and we piled into his car as we drove toward my mom's paternal ancestral village. The village in Chaolian, part of the larger Jiangmen city area, was where many generations of my Chen ancestors lived. Unfortunately, due to our rushed schedule, we only had one full day there. There was no time for sightseeing, just family business.

Two weeks was the maximum I wanted to take off from my consulting project for our trip. At the time, I couldn't understand how important this trip was. Sure, I knew it was important for my mom to reunite with her motherland and for us to visit relatives, but it felt like just another family obligation. Just like visiting Baba at the care facility. When we went to bed in a hotel that evening, I collapsed, feeling relieved to have made it through another day.

The next morning, the four of us strolled through the village's narrow alleyways with stone buildings. We passed by a wall made of oyster shells and then reached a tiny school building.

"This is where my dad taught for years," my mom said.

I had not known that Gung Gung was a teacher, only that he became an engineer later on in Changsha. I realized that I still didn't know much about my family's history. I made a mental note to learn more one day. But for now, the focus was on my mom's precarious health. Her feet had started to swell again, so she had on tennis shoes instead of her usual leather flats.

After eating lunch, we dutifully headed to the ancestral grave to visit Po Po and Gung Gung. Uncle Bo led the way with my mom trailing behind. Stan and I each carried a red plastic bag filled with ancestral worship offerings. In Chinese culture, filial piety isn't just in the human world, but it extends beyond death into the afterlife. Our bags held incense, tangerines, and joss paper, which is fake paper money to burn and send to the deceased. Chinese people believe that even in the spirit world you need money. Maybe that's why we're so damn frugal.

After hiking through bushy pathways, we made it to the hillside cemetery. The last time I'd seen Po Po's face was in an open casket in San Francisco, and here was a photo of her imprinted on a tombstone in China. Beside her photo was an image of a handsome man, my Gung Gung, who died before Stan was born. At last they lay together, reunited again.

I watched my mom go through the motions of paying her respects. My uncle, brother, and I followed her lead. We burned the incense and joss paper in a giant flame atop the stone grave. We stacked tangerines on a dish in front of my grandparents' shared tombstone. We then bowed in turn. Our duty here to send them love in the afterlife had been fulfilled, at least for now.

That afternoon, whisked away in Uncle Bo's car again, we drove to Baba's ancestral village in Taishan. Taishan, about an hour away from Chaolian, is also located in the larger Jiangmen area. As we zipped by dirt roads, green fields, stone houses, and villagers biking in flip-flops, I wondered where we'd stay. The last time I'd visited Taishan, in 2005 with a friend, we stayed in a tiny apartment with a toilet in the ground. I remembered how I had to squat, trying not to fall in.

Suddenly, we pulled up to a modern industrial zone with cement buildings. It was the production campus where our cousin, whom we called *Biu*

Go, worked. He was Baba's nephew, the son of Dai Gu Maa. Biu Go pulled up in a new car, threw his cigarette to the ground, and warmly welcomed us.

"Your rooms are ready," he said as he grabbed my mom's suitcase with a smile. The building where we'd stay was close by, and its floors shined with economic success.

"Wah, China really has changed," my mom said, grinning.

I must admit—I was impressed by the country's rapid developments too.

After touring the facilities, we feasted at a restaurant close by. I felt overwhelmed by the sound of chopsticks clamoring against dishes as the crowd dined.

When Biu Go got up to pay the bill, I leaned in next to my mom. "Mommy, why is our itinerary so packed? It's too intense. Can't we just get a break?" I asked.

"Hah. You're the one who has to go back to work, so don't blame me," she snapped.

She was right. Here we were on this journey to the ancestral motherland, yet I felt the need to rush back. I'd told my project team I was off the grid, but every now and then, I checked my emails. In some ways, work was a mental respite from my mom's cancer.

The next morning, Uncle Bo drove us into the village where Baba grew up. When we arrived at Dai Gu Maa's house, she looked like she was going to cry when she saw us. She didn't look sick at all, with round and rosy cheeks.

"It's been so long! Look at you!" she said to me and Stan. Then she turned to my mom and quietly said, "You made it. But you lost a lot of weight."

She didn't directly address my mom's cancer, but we knew what she meant. She was worried about my mom, as were all of us.

As more relatives assembled at the house, the energy started to pick up. After some tea, together as a clan of eight people, we marched through the village, once again carrying plastic bags with ancestral offerings. There were so many relatives, I couldn't keep track of who was who. Nor did I take the time to understand, perpetually confused by the Chinese kinship terms.

When we reached Maa Maa's house, the humble ancestral home where Baba grew up—and many generations of my family before—I felt a wave of sadness. Maa Maa, my paternal grandma, was alive when I was here a decade prior. But she had crossed over to the spirit world since. After her passing, no one lived in the home anymore.

We entered through the wooden doors to the gray stone house, hundreds of years old. A wooden ladder led up to an ancestral altar in the main room. Red incense holders and painted vases with silk flowers decorated the altar. Some relatives had set up a wooden table with cups, chopsticks, steamed chicken, crackling pork, and stacks of joss paper.

My mom, the guest of honor, bowed first, facing the altar to pay her respects. Then the rest of us bowed. I paced through the house after, exploring every nook and cranny. Old photographs clung to the walls. There were black-and-white photos of the generations before us. And a picture of my mom and dad on their wedding day. It was like walking through a family museum. I wish I'd had the curiosity to ask for family stories, but I just didn't care enough back then.

After a quick breath on the rooftop, we marched forward in a procession through the village with umbrellas shielding us from the searing summer sun. The mood was cheerful as we passed by the green fields, relatives chatting with one another.

But when we finally reached the village cemetery, it felt somber again. One of the men in our clan whacked through the tall, overgrown grass with a sickle as we followed behind. After what felt like forever walking in the heat, we made it to Maa Maa's grave. We laid our offerings. We burned incense. We bowed. Once again, I wish I could say that I was more present. But I couldn't focus. Two things kept attacking me: the mosquitoes eating me alive, and anxiety about my mom's health.

Thankfully, after we left the cemetery, there was some comedic relief. One of the older ladies in our clan grabbed my arm. "Why is your mom so skinny?! Aiya. She must be sad that you're not married. You must get married immediately, and she will be fat again. Do you have a boyfriend?"

When I shook my head no, she continued. "August is a very good month to get married. I feel it! You still have a few months left to find a husband. Okay?"

I laughed as I grabbed her arm too. "Okay."

After we reached Dai Gu Maa's house again by foot, our family clan piled into several cars to head to a restaurant for lunch. Biu Go had gathered additional relatives and family friends, and we took over two round banquet tables in a private room in the back of the restaurant.

Our visit to Taishan ended on a high note when my mom suddenly stood up and announced that she'd sing opera for us. She looked so regal, even though she was wearing black leggings, a brown shirt, and a blue denim button-down wrapped around her shoulders. My mother's beautiful voice filled the room as Italian words from the song "Sancta Maria" transported us to lands far away. I beamed with pride as I recorded a video of her performance on my phone. After she sang her last note, the room exploded in applause. "I have no idea what she just said," a relative exclaimed.

It was all so funny and wonderful—because our mom didn't care that she was singing Italian to a bunch of Chinese relatives who had no clue what she was singing. She didn't care that there were half-eaten dishes scattered across the dining tables. What she cared about was living her life and sharing herself unapologetically.

My mom was a goddamn queen. For a moment, I forgot that she had cancer.

Until things unraveled in Shenzhen.

By the time we arrived by car in Shenzhen, I could tell that my mom was feeling worse. Stan and I checked into a hotel across the street from Uncle Bo's apartment, where my mom was staying. Then we met my mom, Uncle Bo, and his wife—my Auntie, who we called *Kau Mou*—for lunch in the neighborhood.

"Less salt and no MSG please," my mom said to the waiter at the restaurant. "The salt is bad for the swelling," she said, motioning to her ankles, which had become much plumper.

The waiter nodded as he poured tea into our cups. Stan and I both drank our tea silently, both wanting to ignore the state of my mom's cancer.

When my mom decided to stay in and relax at Uncle Bo's that afternoon, we were all relieved. Some time off her feet would be good for her. Besides,

Stan and I wanted to go explore the city. Both in shorts and T-shirts, we set out to enjoy the summer day.

Shenzhen is a major global technology hub, known as the Silicon Valley of China. Shenzhen manufactures a large percentage of the world's consumer electronics, such as smartphones and laptops. It's one of the most populated cities in China, with over 17 million inhabitants. Walking in the streets, you'd see billboards from tech giants like Tencent and Huawei.

As Stan and I stepped out of the metro station to head to the world's largest electronic market, my phone rang. It was Uncle Bo telling us that my mom was feeling better and that he, she, and our aunt would come to meet us.

Thirty minutes later, the five of us headed into the electronics mall together. When we stopped by one of the booths, I picked up two cute phone covers, both with cats on them.

My mom looked at my choices with disdain. "Jenn ah, why don't you grow up and get something more elegant?"

"Why can't you let me make my own decisions, Mommy? Why are you always so damn critical?!" I shouted.

That soured our adventure at the mall, and after visiting just two more booths, we left. I hated that we butted heads so much. As the sun set, the mosquitoes attacked my legs more aggressively. My itchiness rose with the guilt I felt that we were fighting, even though my mom was so sick.

By the time we sat down for dinner at a restaurant around the corner from Uncle Bo's apartment, I scratched until I bled. When we ordered, my uncle took charge of the instructions. "Can we do less salt and no MSG?" he asked the waitress, looking at his older sister.

The waitress nodded.

I hated that our last meal together in Shenzhen, before Stan and I had to leave for Hong Kong to catch our flight, was so depressing. I hated watching my mom suffer. I couldn't suppress my feelings anymore. "This meal is too sad," I said, poking my chopsticks into a bland pile of rice and tofu. "What's the point of even eating this?"

No one reacted. We sipped our tea in silence. Talking about the situation directly would make the cancer all too real.

When we got back to Uncle Bo's home, I broke the awkward silence by entering the guest room where my mom was staying. "Mommy, here's all our money. Take it," I said. I reached into my purse and pulled out all the yuan collected from me and Stan. I released the big clump onto the bed.

I figured the money would help her since she'd decided to stay in China longer. She had booked a train to return to Changsha, where she'd stay with Uncle De for a few weeks. Since our mom didn't trust the doctors in America, she wanted to get medical treatment in China.

She looked at the yuan on the bed and then at me. "Thank you. But take some back to exchange in Hong Kong," she said, thrusting some bills into my hand.

I was confused. I didn't know who was taking care of whom anymore. I felt a strong urge to protect her, to keep her safe. To give her everything I had. "Mommy, please be careful. Call us as soon as you're in Changsha. And update us every day, okay?"

"Okay," she said.

We rarely ever hugged, but I grabbed her. "I love you, Mommy," I said.

"I love you too," she replied.

Stan came in and said his goodbyes before we left for our hotel across the street.

That night, I fantasized about pouring boiling water on my legs to get rid of the insane itch from the mosquito bites. And to distract myself from the grief I felt for separating from my mom.

The next morning, Stan and I took a train from Shenzhen to Hong Kong and boarded a flight to San Francisco. It felt wrong to leave my mom behind, but it also felt right to go back home.

The first days back in San Francisco, gratitude filled every cell in my body. I had my usual comforts back and was thrilled to see my friends. Thankfully, my mom also seemed to be doing alright in Changsha, so I had the mental space to work and socialize.

But as with everything, there's ebb and flow. Just four days after I got back to San Francisco, I received a call from Uncle De that pulled me under a tidal wave. My mom was in a hospital in Changsha. Her whole body had started to swell, most alarmingly her abdomen. "It's as big as a balloon," Uncle De explained to me over the phone.

A few days after that, he said with urgency in his voice, "The cancer scans look very bad. One of you kids should come back."

Whenever he put my mom on the phone, though, she pretended things were fine.

"The food here is okay. Don't worry about me. Many nice doctors here. How's work?" she'd ask.

"It's good. Very busy," I'd reply.

"Busy is good. That means they need you," she'd say.

The knot in my stomach grew each day she was in the hospital. I regretted going back to work. I regretted leaving China without her. I regretted going to Hong Kong with Stan in the first place and not being with her when she was in the hospital in San Francisco. *Could I have stopped her from flying? Did the flying exacerbate her cancer?* I went online and looked. "Flying can increase pressure on the body," one website said. *Fuck!* I felt like a failed daughter.

Anticipatory grief is tortuous. It's brutal to watch a loved one's health decline. One day the news is good, then the next day bad, then good again, then bad. It's like a never-ending roller coaster that's possessed by demons. One you can't get off until someone dies.

Racked with guilt and overwhelm, I didn't have the psychological capacity to face going back to China. Despite her willpower and faith in the Chinese doctors, my mom continued to deteriorate. Finally, one day she set her pride aside and agreed to come back to San Francisco. At least she had health insurance in America, unlike in China where she was paying out of pocket. My brother, bless him, said yes to the mission to get our mom home.

After coordinating with our uncle, we found a last-minute flight for Stan to Changsha and back. Fearing that my mother wouldn't make it back alive, I printed out a will for her to sign that I found on the internet. She still owned the house in Pinole that she rented out. It was morbid to think about her eventually dying, but over the phone, my mom and I had agreed that it was smart to prepare in advance—just in case.

Meanwhile, my other dreams came crashing down. Days before heading to Berlin for my two-month trip to live and work abroad, I sent my Airbnb host a note to cancel my stay. Softly, I cried—for the dream summer in my dream apartment that wasn't going to happen. For the colossal nightmare that washed it all away.

What helped me survive through all the turmoil was writing, which let me process my emotions. On Day 68 of the 100-day project, I posted a photo of roses and wrote: "Even in the face of death, there is life, still, all around. There is so much life even though all living things expire. What matters is what we do in the time that we have living."

On the day of Stan's flight to Changsha, I picked him up from our family home. As my brother got in the passenger seat of my car, I shoved the printed will in his hand. When we pulled up to the curb at San Francisco International Airport, I turned to Stan. "Be safe and good luck, bro. Make sure the doctors say it's okay for her to fly."

"I got it. Call you when I'm there," he said.

It'd be a short trip of just a few days. Carrying only his backpack, Stan disappeared through the revolving door.

I drove back on the freeway. On Highway 101 again, just like the day of the layoff and the first time I took my mom to the emergency room seven years before. As I looked out the passenger window to the bay on my right, I felt like I was sinking in the swell. Drowning.

Moment to Self-Reflect

Every time I come back to this period, enormous waves of pain wash over me again. I'd become used to dealing with family illness, but nothing could have prepared me for my mom's rapid decline. It's no wonder why I dissociated again. Why I was unable to be present in what should've been a profound ancestral pilgrimage in China. I was just trying to survive through overwhelming anticipatory grief, an experience that's inevitable for all of us.

Anticipatory Grief

I used to think that grief was something that appears after a death or loss. However, I've since learned that grief can also be experienced *before* a loss. When our loved ones are very sick or we're about to go through significant life changes, such as a layoff or a move, anticipatory grief can show up. It can bring fear, sorrow, guilt, anger, anxiety, social withdrawal, or exhaustion in response to an impending loss. You may even experience all of these feelings, signs of anticipatory grief, at once. In my case with my mom, I felt denial, anger, anxiety, and guilt. However, anticipatory grief can also bring meaning to what actually matters in life. It can offer us a chance to say what's been unsaid to our loved ones before it's too late.

If you've dealt with, or are dealing with, the declining health of a loved one, then I'm sorry. It's the fucking worst. It sucks the life out of you as it does them. And even if you haven't experienced this kind of heartbreak yet, you may still be dealing with other big upcoming changes in your life. It's healthy to allow yourself to grieve in advance, so each emotion can be presently felt.

Reflection Questions:

- Are there any significant changes or expected losses coming up in your life? If so, how do you feel about them?
- Is there anything left unsaid that you want to say to anyone before it's too late? What do you want to tell them?
- What would it look like to be compassionate to yourself during this time of uncertainty?

17

ALL IS LOST

I DID NOT know if I'd ever see my mom alive again.

Each day she spent in China, as I awaited her return to America, felt like an eternity. Thankfully, the doctors allowed her to leave the hospital to fly home. And she was in Stan's care as they boarded a flight back to San Francisco.

The day of their planned arrival, I paced back and forth in my bedroom frantically, awaiting any word from Stan. When I finally received a text from him that their flight had landed, I shoved on my sneakers and bolted out the door. On the drive down Highway 101 again, song lyrics blasted through my speakers, but I couldn't make them out. All I knew was that my mom had made it back from China. Nothing beyond that.

As I pulled up to the same curb at SFO from just four days before, I reminded myself to breathe. Our mom was under our watch now, making the situation feel less out of control. However, minutes later, when I saw her come out of the airport door, I nearly choked. Stan pushed a wheelchair with one hand while rolling my mom's suitcase with the other. My mom, hunched over in the wheelchair, looked like a skeleton. Her hair was disheveled, falling out of what once was a bun. Her black leggings and beige cotton shirt swam around her in a sea of fabric.

I popped out of the driver side and thrust the backseat door open. "Oh my God! What the hell, Stan?!" I screamed.

"We need to go straight to the hospital. She's been like this for the last few hours," Stan said.

My mom moaned as we carried her into the backseat.

"Can you sit up so we can buckle you?" I asked, trying to prop my mom upright.

"Jenn ah, hurry up. I cannot," she whispered, lying horizontally across the backseat.

For a moment, we considered dialing 911 for an ambulance. But my mom didn't want to cause a fuss. So, as I had done so many times before, I drove her to the hospital. On the freeway, I tried to calm my nerves and stay focused on driving.

Twenty-five minutes later, we pulled straight into the emergency drop-off at St. Mary's Hospital. Once a nurse rolled out a wheelchair, my mom immediately threw up all over the curb.

The nurse rushed my mom into the triage area, where a doctor took her vitals. "You got her here in time," the doctor told us. "Her vitals were fading fast."

I imagined what would've happened if the last leg of the flight were any longer. If Stan hadn't been there taking care of our mom on the flight back. Chills went down my spine.

The doctor looked up from the computer. "I see from her files that she has lymphoma and was in this hospital as recently as last month. Any idea what they did to her in China?" he asked.

"From what she shared with me, she was given some antibiotics by IV and then fluid drainage from her stomach. She also had a bunch of scans," I replied. "Right, Mommy?" I asked, turning to her.

She nodded and pointed to her purse. A thick wet bandage oozing with yellow liquid seemed to hold in my mom's stomach. She looked pregnant, a belly full of cancer. I fished into my mom's purse, pulled out a booklet with cancer scans, and passed it to the doctor.

He raised his eyebrows. "Ah, I see. The cancer has metastasized. It's now here, here, and here," he said, pointing to several spots on the scans.

When I saw where his finger pointed, I was shocked. Her whole body had been taken over by her lymphoma. *Shit! How long had it been like this? Did my mom know, or was she that naive? How did they even let her out of the hospital in this condition?* I had so many questions, but no one to ask.

Not long after, my mom moved to the ICU. Hooked up to machines and fluids, her skin, thankfully, started to plump up. Her vitals were stable again too.

Stan and I sat next to her bed.

"I thought I might die on the plane," my mom said.

My brother and I looked at her with surprise. We thought she was invincible. She hated showing any weaknesses. So, her admitting this was a big change. She must've finally accepted that she was that sick. But I didn't want to accept it. Even as she stayed in the ICU that night, I believed my mom would somehow fight her way through as she always did.

The next morning, Stan and I sifted through her luggage at our family home. The nurse had told us to pack a bag of clean clothes that she could wear home from the hospital, so we complied with optimism. After putting a pair of leather flats, a fresh pair of leggings, and a T-shirt into a bag, we headed back to the hospital.

As we stepped into the ICU, I gasped in delight. My mom sat upright in bed, looking like herself again, with rosy cheeks filled back out by fluids.

"They said I can move to another room today!" she said with a smile.

Before we could talk further, a new doctor walked in, who looked like a young Santa Claus. He introduced himself as the oncologist assigned to my mom's case and sat on a stool next to her bed.

"Mrs. Choi, your cancer has progressed aggressively. We would like to start you on chemo as soon as we can. Is that something you're willing to discuss?" he asked.

I wanted to hide, shielding myself from her usual stubborn revolt against Western medicine.

"Okay. I'll do it. I just want to play badminton again," she said. The doctor stayed silent, giving her a chance to explain. "I was so active and healthy! Just two months ago, I was playing badminton with my friends," she said.

The doctor stared into her eyes with empathy. "I can imagine that you did," he said.

Yet as he looked down at the floor after, I could tell that her obliviousness didn't compute in his head either. I could almost hear his thoughts. *Is this woman that naive or simply in denial?*

Then he spoke again. "Alright. We'll make an appointment to start chemo on Monday at seven in the morning." He shook her hand and left the room.

I could barely contain my excitement. At long last, finally she said yes to chemotherapy! The helplessness that I'd felt for so many years started to dissipate. Hours later, my mom was transferred upstairs to a normal hospital room.

That day, I felt like a good daughter as I sat on my mom's bed feeding her. I carefully cut up beef patties into little bits with a spoon and rolled them into potatoes to make a mash. As she looked up at me, I thought of how she must've fed me when I was a baby. I poured my love into each spoonful as I recalled how she also fed Baba and Po Po when they were sick.

It felt so peaceful that afternoon. We dreamed about what we'd do together when she got out of the hospital and finished chemotherapy. I talked about how I still wanted to spend time in Berlin, and she promised to visit me. She mentioned how much she wanted to visit Liechtenstein, the tiny country where she believed a collection of her favorite artist Peter Paul Rubens's paintings were still housed. I promised I'd go with her. I also pitched the idea of hosting a gallery exhibition to showcase her art. She smiled at the thought of dusting off her paintings in our hallway and bringing them out to be seen.

As the sun started to set, she shared a confession. "Jenn ah, I regret not being a better mom."

I was surprised. All along, I believed she thought she was a great mom, while I was just a shitty daughter who needed to be better. "Huh? What do you mean?" I asked.

"I should've cared more when you guys were in school. Other parents tutored their kids, took them to sports, and paid more attention. I didn't do that for you and Stan," she said.

I held her hand. "But you did your best. Stan and I turned out fine. We take care of each other. That's what matters most, right?"

"I still feel bad," she said as she started to doze off.

I kissed her forehead. "I love you, Mommy. Be back tomorrow."

Her confession was the closest thing I ever got to an apology. I did feel a sense of acknowledgement and vindication that day. However, I couldn't think too much about it because I was so worried about her health.

That night, I put on a pair of heels and headed to a bar downtown. As I raised a glass to celebrate a friend's birthday, I thought about my mom's upcoming sixty-ninth birthday. It was nice to allow myself to laugh and have fun. Sometimes, when there's a challenge, we let it wash over the rest of our lives, but it doesn't have to be that way. We can live each moment as a capsule moment, each one a container for whatever feelings come up. We can just as much allow ourselves to feel joy as we feel sadness. I learned that after losing Baba. We can just as much celebrate life in the face of death.

Besides, I hoped that there would be a lot more living to do together. When I went to sleep that night, I felt a sense of peace and surrender.

The next day, my phone jolted me awake at eight in the morning. I placed it next to my ear.

"Jenn ah, I'm too hot. I can't stop sweating. Find me a hairdresser. I need to cut this hair off today," my mom said, her voice piercing through the phone.

Was she serious? How would I find a hairdresser who would travel to the hospital last minute? And on a Sunday? But instead of laughing off her ridiculous demand, I chose to be an obedient daughter.

"Okay, Mommy. I'll try," I replied.

She hung up without saying bye.

Growing up, I admired my mom's luscious black hair, a sign of her vitality. As far as I could remember, she had thick, long hair that she'd sweep up in a bun or weave into a braid. Like her strong willpower, her hair was part of her core identity. So, I had to find her a hairdresser.

Determined, I hopped online to hunt for stylists but had no luck. Failure was not an option, though, at least not for my mom. My temples throbbed from my hangover. I fell back asleep. After snoozing for thirty more minutes, I woke to a text from Lily asking me if I wanted to go for a walk on the beach.

I gave her a call. "Lil? My mom needs a haircut at the hospital today. Know anyone that can help?" I asked.

"Um . . . I dunno, girl. It's hella early. Salons aren't even open yet. Guess I could try the lady I usually go to, but you might be assed out."

"Damnit. I'll join you for a walk then?" I replied.

I figured the sea breeze would be good for me, help me walk off the vodka from the night before. The fresh air rejuvenated me, and while playing fetch with Lily's dog, Smaz, at Baker Beach, I almost forgot all my worries. As I picked up the tennis ball and tossed it over the sand, Lily reached into her jacket pocket.

"Hi, Fiona! Okay, let me put her on," Lily said, handing me her phone.

A tender voice greeted me. "Hi . . . Jenn? Lily left me a message about your mom. I can come to the hospital during a break at the salon. One o'clock okay?"

After saying thank you, I hung up, squealing with joy. I looked at Lily as if she had just handed me ten bars of solid gold. Best friends always come in clutch.

"Ahhh! You're freaking amazing! Let's go get some pizza? On me?" I asked.

I was starving and figured it'd be another long day at the hospital. And besides, with my mom's compliance to start chemotherapy the next day, I felt optimistic.

Mid-bite, I saw a missed call from my mom.

"Jenn ah, hurry up and come. What's taking you so long?" my mom asked over voicemail.

The guilt punted my appetite away, though I forced myself to eat.

At one in the afternoon, I met Fiona in the hospital lobby. She was Chinese too. With a flannel shirt, blue jeans, and stylish short hair, Fiona seemed like someone my mom could trust.

As we entered the hospital room, the nurse unhooked the IVs from my mom's arm and turned off the white fan by her bedside. Leaning on the nurse, my mom hobbled over to a chair in the middle of the room.

"Your mom's been really hot today. But we managed to scour the entire hospital to find a fan for our special guest," the nurse said with a wink. Then she pulled the privacy curtain across the room and left.

Fiona set her tote gently on the bed and pulled out her magical tools. First, she draped a peach-colored salon gown over my mom's shoulders and then unfurled my mom's hair. Long, wavy, and soft, it caressed the back of the gown. Then Fiona gracefully flitted around my mom with a comb and scissors. They spoke like long-lost friends in Cantonese.

Thirty minutes later, a heap of hair lay on the ground. With her new short hair, my mom looked more like Baba than her former self. Her cheekbones jutted out and wrinkles splintered across her sallow skin. I felt an overwhelming sadness engulf me, a deep longing for my mom from before. But fuck it, I guess the chemo would soon take her hair anyway.

"Wah, much better!" my mom exclaimed. It was the first time she'd smiled all day.

As I escorted Fiona back down the elevators, I shoved six twenty-dollar bills in her hands—forty bucks more than her quoted rate. She tried to push a few bills back, but I cupped her hands with mine. "You saved our day."

When I got back upstairs, my mom was already back in bed hooked up to IVs. The floor had been swept clean of the long hair that I'd known all my life.

"Jenn ah, my mouth is dry," my mom said softly.

I grabbed a pink sponge from a plastic cup filled with water and gently swabbed the insides of her mouth.

"Jenn ah, turn the fan back on," she said.

I turned the fan on.

"Higher!" she shouted.

"You're not a princess, Mommy! Why are you so demanding today?" I asked, gritting my teeth. Nothing I did ever felt good enough for her.

She stared into the center of the room. "I saw a dark man in all black in the room this morning. I asked him what he was doing, but he didn't say anything."

I shrugged it off. Probably just a male nurse or a figment of her imagination.

When Stan walked in at four in the afternoon for his caretaking shift, I left to take a nap. It was a clear June day, so I walked home. I started recording a voice memo with thoughts on caretaking sick parents. One of my friends also had a parent with cancer, and I figured I'd write an article with helpful tips. Besides, if my mom was starting chemo soon, I wanted to document the long journey ahead.

By the time I climbed into bed for my nap, I was totally wiped out. When I woke up two hours later, I saw a few missed calls and texts from Stan.

"She's transferring back to the ICU. She's got a fever and stomach swollen," he wrote.

Panic rose from my heart to my throat.

And then I read the text timed forty-five minutes after that. "Hurry, come back now! They say she might not make it."

Shit, shit, shit. The panic moved from my throat to my brain, setting it on fire with self-berating thoughts. *What idiot has their phone on silent during a time like this? Why do I do such stupid things?* I hated myself for ever leaving the hospital. For choosing to have pizza earlier instead of sitting by my mom's bedside.

I catapulted out of bed. Then jumped in my car as I did seven years before, racing to the hospital when I didn't know if Baba was still alive. When I got to St. Mary's, I ran toward the elevators and bolted through the ICU doors. When I reached my mom's room, I burst into tears from relief. She was still alive.

Hooked up to machines and monitors, she whispered, "It's still too hot."

I took her hands and held them as time stood still. But her hands weren't hot. They were as cold as the heartless bitch we call cancer.

As a nurse came to check her vitals, I pulled Stan into the hallway.

"What the fuck?!" I asked. "She was supposed to be okay!" I doubled over and slid down the wall to the floor, clutching my head in my hands.

Stan shrugged. "Yeah, I dunno. She seemed fine until she wasn't. Things got bad, and the nurse told me to call family when we got to the ICU. Uncle Four and family are coming soon."

Uncle Four's family was extremely close to ours. We'd spent many Thanksgivings and Chinese New Years together at their house. Auntie Four and my mom also shared a close bond, almost like sisters, especially after Baba's passing.

When we got back to my mom's room, a nurse with short blond hair explained what was happening. "She's got sepsis from the infection in her stomach. Her body is in shock. We put her back on antibiotics, but it's not looking good. Has your family discussed her last wishes?"

I shook my head no. Even though we knew her cancer was getting worse, asking for her last wishes would've been acceptance of the unthinkable.

The nurse turned to my mom. "Mrs. Choi, you need help to breathe now. We need to connect you to a machine. Is that something you're okay with?"

My mom nodded yes. But as soon as they put the CPAP machine over her mouth, she clawed the air and shook her head violently. The nurse took it off. And then came the sickening déjà vu again, the question we'd heard at Chinese Hospital when Baba faded away.

"If she codes, do you think she would want to be resuscitated?" the nurse asked.

I wanted to be selfish. I wanted to scream, *YES, of course! Please do anything you can to save my mom!* I wanted to beg my mom to accept the CPAP. To do anything to stay alive.

But Stan answered for us with the only answer we knew to be true to my mom's wishes. "No. She wouldn't want that."

"Okay, I'll give you guys a moment," said the nurse, lowering her eyes.

My brother and I stood there stunned, like chess pieces in a locked game. Any move could be deadly, but not moving didn't help either.

I sighed. "I think it's time for the will."

I fumbled in my purse for the unsigned will that I'd printed. Back in Changsha, Stan said he couldn't find the right time to get her to sign it. Who could blame him? We were a family in denial. Our matriarch could never die.

"Mommy, can you sign this will?" I asked, holding a pen next to her hand.

She nodded and picked up the pen. Then immediately dropped it as it rolled in the creases of her bedsheets. The woman who'd conquered so much in life now didn't even have the strength to pick up a pen. I didn't try again.

Stan cleared his throat. "They're here."

We stepped into the waiting area outside the ICU and met our uncle, aunties, and cousins from Baba's side of the family in San Francisco who could make it. They set Styrofoam containers filled with noodles, rice, and stir-fried dishes onto the table in the middle of the chairs. In small groups, they marched in to see my mom, the matriarch of our entire extended family.

When one of my relatives burst into tears, I felt myself crack. *Shit, this really isn't good*, I thought. *If our relatives can't even keep it together, how can I? How can I possibly keep it together when my worst fear is coming true?*

With my mom on a morphine drip, we waited. *Was the dark man in mom's room that morning Death? Could she have known?* Reality and fantasy started to blur. I could not believe anything anymore. My entire world was falling apart all over again.

Our older cousin, Judy, came through the ICU door as I chewed on beef noodles in the waiting room. "Your mom is asking for you," she said to me and Stan.

My brother and I rushed to her bedside. Everyone else left the room.

"Yes, Mommy?" we asked in unison.

"You kids go home and get some sleep," she whispered, her voice full of a mother's love.

My heart shattered. Even in her final moments, she wanted to make sure that Stan and I got some rest. I stood there, feet planted into the ground. I stared at her hair, cut short in an act of defiance. Chemotherapy wouldn't get to take her hair away. But to even get to chemotherapy, she'd have to live another day.

Just one more day. One more day, Mommy, I pleaded inside my head, too stunned to speak out loud. Hot tears seared my cheeks.

Five minutes later, the nurse walked in with pupils glistening. "I think it's time."

My legs turned to jelly. I looked down at my mom, who seemed to be drifting into a dream.

"I love you, Mommy," I said as I touched her face.

Stan bent down to kiss her cheek.

At 10:01 p.m., just a few weeks shy of her sixty-ninth birthday, our mom went to sleep forever.

My worst nightmare came true. I became an orphan, abandoned at thirty-three years old.

18

A CELEBRATION OF LIFE

WHO AM I without my mother?

I did not know. My mother was my idol. My biggest love. Making sense of my life after her death felt like a daunting voyage—one after the collapse of my world.

Right after she died, I sent my sorrow out. *We lost my mom tonight,* I texted my closest friends. They immediately responded with messages to comfort my wounded soul.

After crying myself to sleep in my apartment, I woke up the next day feeling called to share the news online. Along with a photo of my mom standing on a bridge in Changsha, I posted on social media: "Last night, my mom crossed the bridge to the other side. With my brother and I next to her, she peacefully let go of this life to join my dad. One can never be ready for the loss of a parent, at any age or time, but we've had the privilege of exchanging heartfelt last words and 'I love you's.' "

The love I received from my community blew me away. Comments, texts, and calls came pouring in. Friends I hadn't talked to in years offered their support from across the globe. Colleagues from my consulting project sent me flowers and a signed group card. I realized that I didn't have to go through my grief alone.

My best friends swooped in like rescue helicopters. Rene took me out to sushi the day after my mom died. It was hard for me to speak, but I could eat. Then Lily invited me to *The Defiant Ones* premiere in Los Angeles to cheer me up. Her boyfriend, Lasse, was one of the editors on the HBO series and grabbed an extra ticket for me. Walking on a Hollywood red carpet just a few days after my mom's death felt like the perfect break from all the heaviness. I may have felt like shit, but at least I looked like a million bucks.

Most importantly, I had my brother, who shared the gravity of our loss. I appreciated his zen calmness amidst our family's seeming collapse. We divided the family duties. Stan called the people closest to our mom on her cell phone to let them know of her passing. He dealt with their tears and shock. I organized the funeral and burial arrangements, familiar to me after Baba's death. It's crazy how many administrative items one can knock out while in survival mode.

My mom's funeral was a week after her passing, in June.

I spent all night putting together a collage for her funeral, sifting through hundreds of photos to find the most meaningful ones. A black-and-white rectangle with Po Po and Gung Gung cradling mom as a baby. A wedding picture with Baba. Stan and I holding her hands as kids at the Grand Canyon. We chose a gold-painted frame for the collage, from my mom's collection of unused frames in our family home. Treasured memories surrounded the centerpiece: a photo of my mom in her forties and the words, "In Loving Memory, Juli Chen Choi, 1948-2017."

The next morning, I put on a black suit. With the gold frame of my mom's life in my arms, I headed to the funeral in a Lyft. I didn't want to deal with parking and figured a rideshare car would make things a bit easier. However, I didn't account for how awkward it would be to answer my driver's questions. Chitchat can feel so strange after a loss.

"How are you?" he asked as I got in the car.

"Oh, just living the ups and downs of life," I said. I felt that was a nice way to answer without lying. *What was I supposed to say? My mom died and I feel like crap?* So, I held my tongue.

For a few minutes, we sat in silence. But when a hip hop song came on the radio that we both liked, we started talking again. He was from the

Dominican Republic and was surprised to hear that I was a San Francisco native.

"Are your parents still in San Francisco?" he asked.

I sat quietly for a moment and decided there was no way I could get around dodging his question. "Both of my parents died. I just lost my mom, and I'm heading to her funeral now," I said as a matter of fact.

His voice cracked as he responded. "I'm sorry. I . . . lost my mom too. Last year."

Suddenly, just a few blocks later, this big-ass man started bawling his eyes out.

I leaned forward. "Hey, man. It sucks, but it's going to be okay. You know what I've been thinking? Our grief is a sign of love."

He turned around to face me at the next stoplight. "Wow, we feel the same things. It doesn't matter about being Black or white or whatever. We're the same. Human."

Eyes moist, I nodded enthusiastically.

When he dropped me off at Green Street Mortuary, I showed him the gilded collage of my mom. Then I stepped through the doors to face the funeral. If anything, it felt familiar. Just a year before, I was here for Po Po's funeral, and seven years prior to that, Baba's.

Thankfully, Stan and I had help from our aunts, uncles, and cousins, who played important roles so we could honor Chinese funeral traditions. One of them collected the red envelopes with cash from guests to contribute to funeral costs. Another greeted the guests, many of whom only spoke Cantonese, Mandarin, or Taishanese. And someone affixed red bows made from yarn onto family members, so we could receive spiritual protection.

When the time came to walk into the chapel, we filed in one by one. Stepping in, I felt both devastation and pride. The chapel that Stan and I had chosen was beautiful. Light burst through a colorful stained glass window. In the center of the room, a chandelier hung above the majestic red carpet and wooden pews. Though our family wasn't religious, my mom was a true Renaissance woman who appreciated the classical arts. This room seemed to do her justice.

At the front, our mom lay in an open casket. It was both strange and wonderful to see her again. I had forgotten that her hair was cut short, her last act of willpower against cancer. Her lips were rosy with lipstick, and her cheeks blushed with pigment. My mom wore a flower dress that we'd found in her unpacked suitcase from China and the new heels we bought for her. A friend of our mom whispered, "She looks so peaceful, like she's asleep." It was true.

When I got up to deliver my mom's eulogy, I felt her spirit fill the room. After a deep breath, with notes in hand, I spoke in a mix of English and Cantonese. With tears brimming in my eyes, I talked about her life in China and how much she loved America. I told stories of her immigration, how much she'd sacrificed for our family, and how she'd lived her life fully as an artist, teacher, and world traveler. As I concluded my speech, I said, "She will live on in us, and we will live on for her. I feel everything right now. I am not numb. The best way for me to honor her life is to feel everything alive. The world is not gray right now. I see it all in full extraordinary color, just as she did. Mommy, thank you. I love you. I miss you. I promise to keep you alive in me always."

I looked around the room at all the people she loved. As tears trickled down my face, I felt a great sense of pride in being my mother's daughter.

I nodded at Stan as he stood up and started his speech next. Unlike mine, which had a more poignant tone, my brother's touched everyone in a different way—through humor.

He recounted funny stories about our mom. Like how she got Faybee drunk with bourbon so that we could give our poor cat a flea bath. We all laughed and rejoiced in the good times with Juli. For a moment, it almost felt like the joyous part of a wedding, where the best man makes a hilarious speech expressing his love for the groom.

My brother reminded us why we were here in the first place: Not only to mourn a death, but to celebrate an extraordinary life. This was perfectly captured by one of his closing remarks. "Some of you may think that sixty-eight is too young to go, but my mom lived more in those years than most will in three or four lifetimes!"

When he said that, we all knew without a doubt that it was the truth.

Once he finished, we turned the video monitor on in the front left of the room. We wanted to surprise everyone with something in true Juli style.

"Everyone, we'd like to invite you to our mom's last opera performance," I said.

There in the chapel, she appeared on screen, alive again, standing in between the dining tables in a restaurant in Taishan. Her angelic voice filled the chapel as we watched air fill her chest again with each deep breath. She sang with every fiber of her being.

When the video ended, everyone erupted in thunderous applause. It was an encore worthy of celebrating her life.

After my mom's funeral, she joined Baba at the cemetery in Colma. It brought me peace to know that they could rest together. However, something haunted me like a ghost—the thought of her unseen art as she went to her grave.

When I was a kid, my mom submitted her paintings to galleries in the hopes of showcasing or selling them. Sadly, she heard no after no. This tormented me after her passing. She'd sacrificed so much for our family, only to have her artistic dreams unfulfilled. I felt like we were sitting on a great artist's treasure chest, holding onto a secret that needed to be released.

After lamenting about it with Stan, we decided to host a posthumous art gallery exhibition for my mom's art in July, a month after her death. Luckily, we were able to find the perfect gallery to rent for a weekend in North Beach. It had wooden floors, white walls, and a long track of lights dangling from a vaulted ceiling. When I talked to the owner, he said he could remove all the current art, leaving a blank canvas for us. It was destined to be.

Over the next few weeks, Stan and I sifted through hundreds of our mom's artworks in our family home. Thirty-two pieces made it into the final cut. We'd have two dates during the exhibition: a private Friday event for friends and family and a Sunday afternoon open to the public. I created a digital flier for "Extraordinary Human" and sent out invites, hoping that people could join us to see the beauty of being human through my mother's eyes.

Once again, the power of communal support amazed me. The morning of the exhibition, one of Stan's friends came to pick us up in an SUV. We piled his trunk with snacks, plates, cups, and bottles of wine. Then we stacked our mom's art carefully like Tetris pieces in the backseat.

When we unloaded at the gallery, my friend Annie's cheery face appeared, knocking at the glass door. "Goood moorning!" she said as she stretched her arms out for a hug.

With blond pixie hair, a heart of gold, and a love for art, Annie had volunteered to help me set up. Over the next three hours, we sorted through my mom's art, figuring out where to place each piece. Like a conductor at a symphony, Annie orchestrated the final ensemble. The still lifes came to the front, near the entrance. The painted nudes and charcoal sketches went to the left wall. The celebrity portraits from my mom's days sketching at Fisherman's Wharf went to the right. And my mom's personal favorite, the painting of a woman who looked like a queen, sat in the most prominent spot on the back wall. When we were done, we took a break, preparing for the crowd to come.

At six in the evening, right on time for our grand opening, a loud voice cracked through the door. "Ah Jenn ah! Stan ah! Wah!" said our Auntie Four.

Our aunt, uncle, and cousins clamored in. Just a month ago, they'd assembled with tears outside the ICU, and now here they stood, smiling with bags of clementines.

The rest of the night buzzed with energy. To our delight, over a hundred people came from all chapters of Stan's and my life. From longtime childhood friends to former coworkers to people we had only met once or twice, they kept pouring in. Friends brought their romantic partners. Coworkers brought their children. And everyone brought their empathy.

When I spotted my dear friend Nicole, I gave her a giant hug. She had lost both of her parents several years prior. When I had beaten myself up for failing to convince my mom to do chemotherapy sooner, Nicole had comforted me over a call. She'd explained how brutal chemotherapy was for her parents. And how maybe it was better that my mom had a high quality of life in the end.

Now in the gallery, Nicole admired my mom's charcoal sketches with misty eyes. "It's beautiful that you and your brother are honoring her life this way."

I raised my plastic wine cup to hers. "Our parents would want us to celebrate them. To them and to us!"

Later, another friend pulled me aside. "I just wanna tell you how much it means to me when you share about your mom. Because of it, I've been reminded to spend more time with my own mom in the time we still have together," he said.

I was floored. In speaking about dying, we can inspire more conscious living.

This realization emerged again when we opened the exhibition to the public the next day, and a woman with gray hair waltzed in. After fifteen minutes, she asked for a piece of tissue. "You're making me cry in a good way," she said, sniffling.

There were so many of these beautiful moments that blended together like oil paints on canvas. By the time we emptied the gallery of our mom's art and put them back up in our family home, Stan and I had come to a little more peace with her death.

I wish that the peace I felt after our mom's art exhibition lasted. But the journey of grief is nonlinear, the pain coming back to hit you hard when you least expect it.

Every time I stepped out of my apartment, I'd envision my mom walking toward me on the street. Sometimes my arms would reach out to grab her. But she wasn't there. She'd never be there to greet me again. No more meals together. No more calls.

Desperate to hear her voice, I'd play her last voicemail to me again and again. Tears soaked my pillow every night. The voice inside me taunted me. *I am not worthy enough to make people stay. I am a fucking failed daughter.*

Drowning in my grief and self-loathing, I needed to get the hell away. There were too many reminders of her in San Francisco. It became unbearable. I needed space to figure out who I was without my mother. For so many years, I'd dreamed of living in Berlin, but I didn't want to leave my parents behind. Now that I was the one left behind, I didn't see a reason to stay.

On the romantic front, Jacob ended up coming over and comforting me a few times after my mom died. However, I still felt confused about what we were to each other and wondered if it was finally time to put our situationship to rest.

A week after the exhibition, I flew out to Europe by myself to do some soul searching and finally prototype my dream of working abroad. I let my clients know that I'd be working from Europe for a month, and no one had concerns. By then, I'd already started consulting on another IT project with Genentech, mainly remotely, and with more colleagues based in Switzerland.

On a bright summer day in July, I landed in Berlin. Years ago, when I first visited the city, I fell in love with the brightly colored buildings on Oderberger Strasse, convinced it was the most beautiful street in Berlin. I had been thrilled to find a small apartment on Airbnb on Oderberger Strasse for my original trip in June, but sadly, that trip wasn't meant to be. Yet, lo and behold, when I rebooked my Berlin trip after my mom passed, by some miracle I was able to find an even bigger apartment on Oderberger Strasse! The street is only two blocks long. What were the odds?! I felt my mom watching over me.

With a huge smile, I stepped into the gorgeous apartment with high ceilings. Like a hug, this home away from home welcomed me. Enveloped me. Made me feel somehow whole again, even with a hole left from my grief.

A week into my stay, I went with my friend Niels to a rooftop party, hosted by a German guy named Stephan. Over beers, we danced late into the night, and everyone became fast friends.

"I think I want to move here next summer! Start over, you know?" I shouted to my new friend Stephan over the heavy techno beats blasting from his speakers.

"Why wait 'til summer?" Stephan asked. "Bedeir moved here in the winter," he said, motioning to a friend on the couch.

"Isn't it too depressing to move here when it's cold and gray?" I asked.

Bedeir smiled. "No! It means that you'll get to settle in and build your foundation before the summer."

Hmm, his logic seemed sound. Perhaps it was time to rebuild. Find a new life and maybe even love in Berlin? Lily had just moved to Helsinki, where her Finnish boyfriend Lasse was originally from. Having my best friend a two-hour flight away was a major selling point. And working abroad had been seamless so far. My client deliverables were digital, and project meetings accommodated both United States and European time zones. But I still wasn't sure. I loved my community in San Francisco. Could I ever find that in Berlin?

Later, as I was leaving Stephan's party, I took a picture of the mural on the wall. In large letters was a quote by artist Robert Montgomery: "The city is wilder than you think and kinder than you think. It is a valley and you are a horse in it. It is a house and you are a child in it. Safe and warm here in the fire of each other."

I definitely felt that warmth in Berlin. But I also wanted to check out some other cities in Europe before making a decision to move. The stunning nature in Norway called me next.

After I flew to Bergen, I took a train to reach the fjords. Nærøyfjord is one of the most stunning fjords in the world, known for its dramatic green cliffs reaching toward the sky on both sides. Goosebumps crept up my arm on the deck of the Nærøyfjord cruise. As we passed by a small village with red houses at the base of a waterfall, I burst into tears, realizing that I would never get to share travel stories with my parents again. Waves of grief cut deep. Just when you think you've found stable footing, you're pulled under and drowning again.

However, nature has healing powers. As I blinked through my tears at the vast scenery before me, I imagined that I was sailing into a painting. The details became crisper, the sun bounced off the glistening water, and green leaves leapt off the high gray rocks. It reminded me of a painting that my mom would love if she saw it in a museum. Suddenly, I realized in a moment of perfect clarity that she'd see the world through me now. Baba too.

With that newfound perspective, I felt a sense of duty to carry on for my parents. This epic, month-long vacation was also an homage to them. Even though I only spent a few days in each European city, except for Berlin, I was fully present. I admired the flowers in my friend's family garden in Pärnu, Estonia, and I hugged Lily tightly as I reunited with her in the cobblestone streets of Helsinki.

I also found hope in romance again in Stockholm, where Tinder served up some Swedish hotties. There was one guy—let's call him Erik—that I became infatuated with. He was an artist with a stellar eye for capturing beauty. I didn't know where our fling would lead—if anywhere—but I felt adored in the few whirlwind days we spent together. He cheered me on as I headed next to Liechtenstein, where I fulfilled a promise to my mom.

Nestled between Austria and Switzerland, Liechtenstein is a tiny German-speaking country. Before my mom died, I had promised her that we'd go see the Peter Paul Rubens collection there. But as I wandered through the Kunstmuseum in Vaduz, the capital, I hunted for the collection with no luck. When a staff member said there were no Rubens in the museum, I searched in the Treasure Chamber across the street. I saw jeweled crowns but still no naked biblical scenes characteristic of Rubens. Perplexed, I ran to the Landesmuseum, where I found gothic scrolls. What the hell? Where was the collection?

Exasperated, I pulled up my phone to investigate and finally question my mom's facts. I'd trusted her in blind obedience without question, even after her death. But now I had no choice but to question. The internet's answers revealed a cosmic joke to me. As it turned out, the artworks had moved to Vienna, my mom's favorite European city! Happy tears sprang from my eyes as I thought about how my mom's adventurous spirit still lived on.

Afterward, I went back to Berlin to close out my trip in the place where it had begun. Everything started to feel familiar. I partied with Stephan and his crew again. I hung out with Niels and his friends. My social network seemed to grow with each passing day. It was clear to me that I could indeed build a community in Berlin. That I wouldn't feel alone if I moved.

On my last night in Berlin in August, I looked up at the starry sky and flashed back to a happy memory with my mom. When I was sixteen, she picked Stan and me up from school and drove many miles away from the city's light pollution so we could catch a meteor shower. She even rented a new car for the occasion, since her old car was unreliable and could break down at any moment. But as we drove further out from San Francisco into the night, the sky remained hazy with clouds overhead. Frustrated, she drove us back home. We went to bed defeated.

But suddenly in the middle of the night, my mom shook me awake. "Jenn ah, let's watch on the roof."

We carried two blankets and plastic stools up the backstairs of our apartment building. Then we plopped down on the gravel on our roof. Other than the occasional foghorns in the bay, the air was silent. We waited in the damp cold, unsure if it'd be worth it. However, bit by bit, the clouds started to clear from the dark sky.

At around three in the morning, she grabbed my arm and pointed up. "Wah! Look! Look!" she said.

Above us, the sky exploded with meteors streaking across. We had gone so far searching for them, only to see them back at our own home.

It was then, standing in Berlin under the twinkling stars after my mom's passing, that I knew. I didn't have to look anymore. My mom was with me no matter where I went. In the fjords. In the museum with no Rubens. Here standing in the streets. She was inside me. Home, wherever I went.

When I landed back in San Francisco, I felt like a different person. I had left for my trip feeling so lost. Yet I came back with more direction for my future—a future based in Berlin. The question was whether I was actually capable of moving. Logistically, I could probably figure it out. But psychologically, I doubted my survival skills without my mom.

Sure, I'd already adulted at an early age due to my childhood trauma, but could I really stand on my own? All my life, I'd looked to my mom to do the impossible. When Baba got sick and then died, she was our rock. Even when she was sick herself, she was our rock. *Did I have it in me? Could I ever live up to her strength?*

To test my survival skills, I went for an extreme challenge—Burning Man. Growing up in San Francisco, I'd heard of Burning Man, an annual, weeklong, world-famous event that takes place in a desert. Although many people call it a festival, I think of it more like a city. Imagine a temporary city of around 70,000 people that's built in a Nevada desert every year. You bring in what you need to survive for a week in the extreme heat, and at the end, you take it all away. It's a celebration of human possibility, and a true test of the human spirit.

Luckily, I found a last-minute spot through a friend in a camp called Flat Tire Cafe, which would gift free coffee and bike repairs to attendees. In case you're confused, let me explain how Burning Man works. One of the ten guiding principles is Gifting. There's no money exchanged on-site. Everything is gifted from the community. You could camp solo or with friends, or you could join a larger camp. To join, I had to buy my own ticket and pay camp fees for food and infrastructure. Each camper was also required to work shifts, so I volunteered in the camp kitchen and café. There's a lot of news reports of Burning Man being just a giant party, but I can tell you firsthand that it can require a ton of actual work—physically, psychologically, and emotionally.

In the weeks prior to Burning Man, I obsessively studied how to prepare. I made a huge checklist of over a hundred items to pack: A solid tent, check. Dust masks, check. Gallons of water, check. Outfits prepacked per day in Ziploc bags to prevent them from getting dusty, check.

By the opening Sunday of the event in late August, I felt like I was ready for the apocalypse. At dawn, I packed my car with everything, strapped a used bicycle I'd bought off Craigslist onto my trunk, and drove alone toward Black Rock Desert in Nevada.

After six hours of driving, I arrived in a flat barren land with mountains in the distance. Bikes hung off the backs of RVs and cars in front of me, each vehicle creating a mini dust storm as they drove. It seemed like something out of a sci-fi movie.

Inside the temporary city, I passed by makeshift streets filled with tents, scaffolded structures draped with fabric, and bright LED lights. When I finally reached my camp, everyone welcomed me with giant hugs as if they'd known me for years, even though most were strangers to me except my friend Siska. We were about twenty campers in total, from various ethnicities, countries, and professional backgrounds. I felt like I'd landed in the United Nations delegation of an alien world. After pitching my tent, I sat in it, trying to get my bearings for the days ahead.

When I opened the event guidebook, I was blown away. There were pages of events scheduled at every hour. You could learn ballet, taste wines at a bar, attend workshops, dance all night, marvel at the moon's craters through a telescope, or even run an ultramarathon. And everything was gifted by attendees! What a glorious social experiment!

The creative can-do spirit that permeated everything at Burning Man was something my mom would've loved. I channeled her as I wore my handmade costumes from home. One day, I dressed up as water, with flowing silk ribbons attached to a blue bathing suit.

She would've also loved the incredible art. One sunset, I attended a symphony at a tree made of 175,000 LED lights. Wherever I went, whether it was within the city or the vast open desert area known as Deep Playa, I would stumble upon more art. A metal wasp sculpture breathed fire. A rainbow cathedral beckoned visitors to climb it. And at the center, the Man, a towering multistory wooden sculpture symbolizing creativity, transformation, and impermanence that would burn at the end of the week.

Everything was amplified in the extreme conditions of the desert, including my fears. It may sound silly to you, but one of my biggest fears was riding a bike. Growing up in the hills of San Francisco, I'd never learned to ride one. But I was determined to learn at Burning Man. Because of the huge distances between places, it's more convenient to bike.

When I first rolled out my used bike and tried to ride it, my entire face turned red. I stopped every few feet, paralyzed by my shame. But one by one, camp members came out to show me how to pedal.

They say it takes a village to raise a child. I learned that it takes a camp to raise a baby biker. On group outings, I was always the very last one, peddling awkwardly behind.

"Please go on without me!" I'd shout.

"We don't leave our family behind!" camp members would shout back. I came alone and orphaned. But I was adopted into a newfound family.

On the fourth day, I mustered up the courage to bike out by myself for the first time. I refilled my CamelBak with water, packed a letter I'd written to my mom and dad, and headed out to the temple. Like a colossal wooden pagoda, it rose from the dust. The temple is a place of deep spiritual meaning, where we grieve what we've lost.

As I entered the temple, I read hundreds of letters to lost loved ones that were posted all over. I reached into my backpack and pulled out mine. It was a printed photo of my parents on their wedding day. In the middle of the temple, I fell to my knees and cried. All around me, people were mourning and celebrating simultaneously. *I know the heartache of your loss and the joy of your love,* our watery eyes would say. One stranger came by and offered me a tissue. Another offered a hug. We all sat in silent remembrance.

On Saturday, I gathered with my camp to watch the big finale, the Man Burn. As flames engulfed the massive wooden structure, it struck me then how everything is ephemeral. Cities are built and then destroyed. Civilizations rise and fall. People are born and people die. Nothing lasts forever. I stared into the blaze and imagined the silhouettes of my mom and dad walking toward each other and then embracing as they vanished in smoke. Their souls were now set free from their bodies. No more lung disease. No more cancer.

The flames reminded me of a phoenix rising from the ashes. When it all burns down, what do we have left? We have memories etched into our brains. We have a reminder to live and love in the present moment. We have each other. In the end, and what matters most, is that we are left with the gift of presence in the fleeting ephemeral.

One of the ten Burning Man principles I admire the most is Leave No Trace. Whatever you bring in, you must bring out. On the last day during camp breakdown, we combed our entire plot several times to make sure not even one tiny piece of lint was left. As we picked up the last traces of our existence from the ground and the sun rose over a city slowly vanishing, I felt more alive than ever. Not only had I survived, but I had thrived.

In death we see life. In destruction there is a new dawn.

Moment to Self-Reflect

Losing my mom was the worst experience of my life. I revisit our last days together again and again, wishing that I could've saved her. While the journey of grief was—and still is—nonlinear and painful for me, it's also been hauntingly beautiful. Beneath all the grief is the love. And on the other side of death there is life.

For those of you who have lost someone you love, I send you my deepest condolences. You may know what a brutal ride grief is. It can feel so lonely and isolating. However, I want you to know that you're not alone. As I came to learn through my own grieving process, we are never alone in our grief. It is a shared universal experience.

Making Sense of Life and Death

Many people in the Western world avoid talking about death, like it's some big taboo. But as I learned through losing both parents, talking about death can actually inspire more conscious living. Making sense of life in the context of death can be life-affirming. Whether you've lost someone or not, thinking about death can really make clear what matters in your life. I invite you to reflect upon your life through the lens of mortality. Although it might feel morbid, it can also be incredibly enlightening.

Reflection Questions:

- If you were to leave this earth, what would you want to be remembered for?

  - It can help to think of a loved one giving a eulogy to celebrate your life. What do you hope they'd say about you, in terms of your personality, identity, and the legacy you'd leave?

- Think about your life as it is right now. Is it in alignment with how you eventually wish to be remembered?

- What are the top five things that matter most to you? How can you spend your time and energy in this precious life on those things that matter, before it's too late?

19

THE BONDS OF LOVE

AFTER I GOT back from Burning Man in September, I met Jacob for dinner. It'd been over six weeks since I'd seen him, and there was so much I needed to tell him about how I was moving on—both physically to Berlin and emotionally from our situationship.

I'd already bought a one-way ticket to Berlin for November, with no clue where I'd stay yet. But I was convinced that I could figure it out. On top of my Berlin dream, there was something else that tugged at my heart in Europe: Erik, the Swedish guy, and I had continued to stay in touch. I had a flight to Stockholm to visit him at the end of the month. I didn't know where my infatuation would lead, but at least Berlin and Stockholm weren't that far apart.

So when I met Jacob at an Italian restaurant in Hayes Valley, a neighborhood in San Francisco, I was ready to deliver the news. It wasn't long after ordering pasta that I blurted it out. "I'm moving to Berlin in November," I said as a matter of fact.

He looked surprised. "Wow. That's . . . interesting. Because we're opening an office in Berlin."

Thoughts raced in my head. *What the hell? How come he never mentioned this before?!* After a long pause, I finally exclaimed out loud, "Wait . . . what?!"

He proceeded to explain how his company was expanding internationally, though he'd remain working in San Francisco.

I pretended to be happy for him, but I felt conflicted. I saw Berlin as a new beginning for me, and now my decision felt clouded by this news. We continued to eat and talk about other things like our latest travels. I felt nervous about mentioning Erik, not knowing when was the right time. I didn't say it when the tiramisu came. I didn't say it when we got the bill.

Finally, when we were outside the restaurant, I let it out. "I met someone in Stockholm. We're not in a relationship or anything yet, but I want to see where it goes."

Without saying anything, Jacob walked away from me. I didn't expect such a strong reaction, and I ran after him. I don't remember much of what we said to each other on the busy street corner, but it wasn't much. I wanted to explain and make myself feel less guilty about hurting him, but he pulled away from me. So, I let him go—or so I thought.

I flew to Stockholm at the end of September to visit Erik. Unfortunately, he wasn't who I thought he was, and perhaps he realized the same of me. My visit ended in a drunken argument where I stormed out of his apartment. When I flew out of Stockholm, I felt relieved. Old me would've felt like I'd failed yet another attempt at romance. But the new me felt proud of myself for even trying.

Most surprisingly, I realized how much I missed Jacob. The way he reacted outside the Italian restaurant made me wonder if he might've cared about me much more than I thought. There was a part of me that wrote him off as unavailable, given our past. But maybe *I* was emotionally unavailable, closing my heart to any possibility of true reconciliation? I needed to find out.

So, in early October, I reached out to Jacob. Once again, we picked up where we left off. We saw each other every few days, but we didn't talk about our feelings verbally. Instead, we expressed them through kinky sessions, where I felt my body was celebrated. When we had first met, I'd sent a provocative text about rope and told him I liked being tied up in bed—but we never acted on it while we were dating.

Now, though, the heat intensified between us.

I'd been into bondage since my twenties and was excited to play with him. I'd engaged in kink before, with various partners from my past. During sessions with others, I'd become a different person—someone who could let go of my need to control. When I was blindfolded and tied up, I surrendered. When I was flogged, I felt pleasure explode with the pain. And it wasn't just physical. I got a psychological and emotional high as well. That's one of the many reasons why I love BDSM. It's not just hot—it's liberating.

If this is one of the first times that you're hearing about BDSM, an umbrella term for sexual activities involving bondage, dominance, submission, sadism, and masochism, then you may find some of what I've shared shocking. I understand. It's still considered taboo in mainstream culture, and it's often misunderstood. Why would someone want to play with power in the bedroom? Isn't it weird to derive pleasure from pain or restraint?

However, what people don't often talk about is how healing BDSM can actually be. When it's consensual, it can create a safe space for partners to explore their relationships with vulnerability, intimacy, trust, power, and boundaries. During play sessions, my partners would always check in with me and my boundaries, adjusting to my needs. Consent was key. Every time I said no, I got to reclaim some of the power I'd lost when I was hit as a child. And every time I said yes, I got to experiment with my sexual desires, tuning into what I wanted and who I was beyond my past conditioning. With kink, I felt worshiped, adored, and cared for. It was the total opposite of neglect.

I won't get into the specific details of my play sessions with Jacob. However, I will share that each time we connected, I felt a piece of me let go. I also started to let go of something else—the guard around my heart. It felt like the deeper we dove, the more we became emotionally bonded to each other.

What we shared transcended the bedroom. We'd gaze into each other's eyes over dinner, lost in deep conversation. And though he was still busy with work, he made time for me in a way that felt more committed than ever.

I didn't know what it'd all mean, nor what would come, but I did know my heart swelled when I saw him—even as I was about to move to Berlin.

As for my family, there was still a huge hole in my heart from missing my mom. It'd been three months since her passing, and the pain still felt fresh. The grief was omnipresent.

Probate was one of those things that tormented me. Because my mom owned a house in Pinole that we still rented out and didn't sign a will before she died, I had to file for probate in court. Probate is the legal process of administering a deceased person's assets to make sure they're properly distributed to heirs and beneficiaries. Stan and I were too cheap to hire a lawyer, so once again, the duties fell on me. I hated having to comb my mom's death certificate for details as I filled out countless forms.

In the void without my mom, I was always searching for the next high. So when my brother proposed we fly to Nepal in October and trek the Annapurna Circuit, a popular route in the Himalayan mountain region, I said yes. At first, I was terrified and said no because I'd never trekked before, but my fear of losing Stan if I allowed him to go alone was too strong. The route wasn't easy, and trekkers had perished before. Before my mom died, I had promised that I'd take care of Stan. I couldn't let her down.

Leading up to our trip, Stan tried to alleviate my anxiety. He sent me YouTube videos of the trek, took me on practice hikes, and explained how we'd sleep overnight in teahouses, where we could pay for food and lodging. We had seventeen days total in Nepal, with about twelve days allocated to the Annapurna Circuit, depending on how fast we hiked. Many trekkers allocate more time, but I was in a rush to get back to client work and begin preparing for Berlin.

In terms of emotional preparation, my brother and I were both inspired by Cheryl Strayed, my favorite author. In her bestselling memoir *Wild: From Lost to Found on the Pacific Crest Trail*, she beautifully captures her epic trek after losing her mother. If trekking helped her process her grief, perhaps it could help us as well?

When Stan and I landed in Kathmandu in mid-October, each carrying just one hiking backpack, I felt overwhelmed. Swarms of scooters zipped by us, and we had to cross busy dirt roads with no traffic lights. If I was already scared to cross the street, how the hell was I supposed to trek the freakin' Himalayas?

The bumpy nine-hour bus journey to the start of the Annapurna Circuit wasn't any more comforting. Passengers toppled over each other as we wound on narrow mountain roads. However, I did feel blessed to be in such pristine nature. On the first day of the trek, I was blown away by how everything else seemed worlds away. My client deadlines and the rat race of metropolitan life melted away like the snowy white mountain caps that turned into turquoise rivers. Yaks trotted down the trail. Stan and I trotted upward, gaining elevation as we aimed to reach the highest peak of the trek, Thorong La.

Many days involved the same routine: breakfast at a teahouse at sunrise, lunch at a scenic stop along the way, and hiking for over ten miles until we managed to reach whatever village we could by sunset. We passed by rice paddies, bamboo forests, waterfalls, and children in small villages.

As we trekked, I realized that my brother wasn't so little anymore. The wide-eyed toddler had become a man. When I didn't know how to place my footing safely across difficult terrain, he'd show me. When we woke up at the crack of dawn, he'd planned how far we'd go and how. I had become so used to leading and caretaking others in my life that it felt good to be led instead.

But even with routine and Stan's leadership, many days were brutal. We'd fight against gravity on what felt like nearly vertical slopes, staking our hiking poles into the ground to prop us up. I had several emotional breakdowns, crying and screaming at my brother to slow down. Every day, a medical helicopter would fly over our heads as trekkers suffered from injuries or altitude sickness. I wondered, *would that be us too?*

As the days wore on, my anxiety grew. We'd have to cross dangerous scree slopes to get to Tilicho Lake, one of the highest altitude lakes in the world. Landslides were a real threat, and I was terrified of sliding down to my death.

The night before we headed to Tilicho Lake, I saw my mom in a dream. She looked healthy and cancer-free. "Jenn ah. You'll be okay. I'm happy you're doing it with Stan," she assured.

My mother was right. The next day, we made it safely to the lake. The blue lake looked like a giant mirror that reflected the snow-covered mountains encircling it. It was magical.

What impressed me, as much as the scenery on the trek, was the people we met along the way. Often on these arduous journeys, you meet fellow souls walking on the path to healing. At a restaurant in a village, we ate lunch with a trekker named John. Over fried noodles, he shared how he trekked in memory of his wife, whom he'd lost to cancer. The pits of grief are a bond. We parted after our meal, but I'll always remember John. Somehow, I knew his love for his wife would carry them over any mountain.

On the ninth day of our trek, Stan and I woke up to face Thorong La at an altitude of over 17,000 feet above sea level. As we walked out on the trail, I shivered in the cold, even while wearing two pairs of pants, a fleece pullover, and a down jacket. But at least we weren't alone. As we pointed our headlamps onto the dark trail, other trekkers' lights twinkled too. Like fireflies, we followed one another on the steep switchbacks.

I was breathless within thirty minutes. My thighs burned like hell. At some point, though, we got used to it and hit a nice rhythm. We marched on like this for hours.

Finally, sometime midday, colorful Tibetan prayer flags flew in the wind before us, welcoming us to the peak.

Stan grinned the biggest grin. "Jenn, we made it."

We ran to the hundreds of flags and crouched down by a sign that said, "Thorang La Pass - Congratulations For The Success!!!"

"Mom would be so proud of us," I said softly.

Her spirit accompanied us as we descended the mountain. And sat with us on the flight out of Nepal a few days later.

I came to Nepal to be my brother's guardian. But I discovered that he was also mine. As the plane pulled off the ground, I could hear my mom's voice: *You take care of each other now.*

When I landed back in San Francisco at the end of October, things continued to escalate romantically between me and Jacob. I also found out some devastating news.

The first time he came to my apartment after I got back, he mentioned the death of his dad. He'd been notified of his dad's sudden decline from Alzheimer's while I was in Nepal, and he'd flown to Copenhagen to say his last goodbyes. That night, I squeezed him tightly, silently promising his father that I'd take good care of his youngest son.

Once again, the pits of grief became a bond. I let the guard around my heart drop further. And feeling less guarded, I finally felt ready to go back to his apartment. I did not regret my decision. At his place, we'd spend many hours lost in lust.

The more Jacob and I saw each other, the more we got closer, culminating in even more shocking news. I can remember the night clearly. It was early November. We were having dinner in a dimly lit restaurant. As we cut into our steaks, he looked me in the eyes.

"When I was in Copenhagen for my dad's funeral, I told my brothers and sisters that I could have a kid with you," he said.

I was dumbfounded. After what felt like forever, I finally responded. "Umm . . . a kid? Really?"

Jacob took my hand, responding casually like it was no big deal. "Yeah, that's what I told them. You'd make a great mom. You're smart, kind, and structured. And I like that you're always open to exploring new things."

I was floored. He didn't tell me that he loved me directly that night, but this was pretty damn close. I was scared to admit it, and withheld telling him, but I was falling in love with him all over again. The rest of the evening felt like a dream.

A few days later, we finally said "I love you" to each other. I had wanted to hear "I love you" from him for so long, only to realize that although the words were unspoken throughout the three years that we'd known each other, the love had always been there.

The fortress I'd built to protect myself started to crumble—and fast. But could I really open my heart again when I'd be moving thousands of miles away to Berlin? And how the hell would we make it work—or not?

I did not know. But I was eager to find out.

Moment to Self-Reflect

Leaning into our sexual desires can be so liberating and healing. Looking back, I can see this was a period of personal awakening for me as I explored my sexual desires with less shame. As a result, it brought me more love as my bond with my partner deepened.

I'll be honest though. Speaking about sex publicly feels embarrassing, especially since I was raised by my parents and culture to be modest. Additionally, I know that many people still consider BDSM to be taboo. Part of me also fears unwanted sexual attention, believing that if I talk about sex, others will objectify me. But this discussion is important.

There are so many things that I want to share about BDSM. However, when it comes down to it, I realized that the point of this chapter isn't to sell you on kink nor create an in-depth guide to it. Instead, I'd like to begin diving into a larger theme that we'll continue to explore in this book—sexuality.

Exploring Sexuality

Why explore sexuality? Because it's a way to uncover who we are authentically. Sexuality is the way people express and experience their sexual desires, feelings, orientation, and identity. When we're in touch with our sexuality, it can bring us closer to our true selves and into deeper connection with others. However, when we're disconnected from it, it can bring us feelings of shame, guilt, low self-esteem, and loneliness.

It might feel uncomfortable to reflect upon your sexuality, as it did for me before. In my family, we didn't talk about sexuality, especially since it was considered taboo to discuss sex in Chinese culture. On top of that, I had a distorted relationship with my sexuality, exchanging my body in my teens and twenties for external validation. I also had significant repressed sexual trauma from my assault, confirming the limiting belief I'd formed at an early age: *My body is shameful. It's not safe to be in my body.*

Exploring my sexuality in my thirties, especially with BDSM, allowed me to tune into what made me feel good. I didn't know it back then, but this would begin my long journey to recovery from sexual trauma and help me find safety in my body again—with pleasure and on *my* terms.

I invite you to reflect upon your own relationship with sexuality.

Reflection Questions:

- On a scale of 1-10 (where 1 is very disconnected, and 10 is very connected), how connected do you feel to your sexuality? Why?

- What beliefs about sexuality did you inherit from your family, culture, society, or past experiences?

- When thinking about sexual experiences that feel fulfilling to you, what comes to mind?

PART 3

BREAKING THE CYCLE

20

A FRESH START

AT THIRTY-THREE YEARS old I began again, excited to start a new chapter in Berlin. Like a tree preparing to shed its autumn leaves in anticipation of the winter, I was ready to shed layers of my old identity to make room for the new. I wanted to discover who I was—and on my terms—outside of my hometown and birth country.

Battered and beaten by the losses in my family, I was eager to move on. There was a part of me that wanted to leave everything behind. But there was also a part of me that couldn't let go of my past. Instead of letting go of my rent-controlled apartment that I shared with roommates in San Francisco, I kept it. I wanted to keep it as a backup, just in case. Just in case things didn't work out in Berlin and I had to come running back.

I told myself moving to Berlin in November was going to be my fresh start, but I couldn't seem to fully commit to my move. I couldn't trust that bad things couldn't happen, especially when I still hadn't found a place to live in Berlin. As was normal for most of my life, I was always preparing for shit to hit the fan.

There was also Jacob, a big-ass question mark in my life. *What are we now that we openly love each other? How do we proceed?* I asked myself these questions, but I didn't bring them up. Our last night together before the move felt uncertain, like we were standing at the edge of a cliff. However, we did manage to make plans to see each other in December, when I'd be back in San Francisco for an expected court date for my mom's probate case.

I also kept my consulting work, which allowed me to move with financial security and career continuity. I told my clients at Genentech that I was moving, and they agreed to let me work fully remotely from Berlin. In terms of flexibility in my career, I felt pretty fucking blessed.

I also felt blessed to have a bittersweet send-off with close friends at Amelie, my favorite bar in the city. Toasting with glasses of French wine, we gushed over our profound love for each other, promising to stay in touch. No distance could divide us.

It was under these conditions, with one foot still in San Francisco, that I flew to Germany alone. Floating above the clouds on the plane, I felt closer to heaven than to hell.

On a crisp day in mid-November, my teeth chattering in a too-thin jacket unprepared for the cold, I arrived in Berlin with two small suitcases. I didn't bring much aside from my clothes, but I carried hope, the flint to spark a new era of a new me in the wake of my mom's death.

Since I still didn't have an apartment of my own yet, Niels let me crash at his place in the trendy, vibrant, and expat-friendly neighborhood of Prenzlauer Berg. He was away on vacation, and I could stay at his apartment with his orange tabby cat, Sammy, until I figured out the next steps. After stepping into his apartment, I gave Sammy the squishiest hug.

In my imagination, Berlin would immediately feel like home. After all, I had already visited six times before. I was eager to find my routine. But reality proved to be the opposite. Although I had a growing community of English-speaking friends in the city, I couldn't speak German, which made it difficult to accomplish tasks like signing up for a bank account. Berlin is a relatively diverse city. Non-German immigrants from about 170 countries make up nearly one-quarter of the total population of over 3.5 million residents. However, many older Germans in Berlin don't speak English. And for anything bureaucratic or administrative, German is required. I hadn't realized how big the communication gap was when I was previously on vacation. But now that I was living in Berlin, I felt voiceless and disempowered.

Beyond the huge language barrier, I encountered other struggles. I had no home of my own, which made me feel anxious and insecure. I didn't even have a plan for how I'd stay legally in Germany beyond my ninety-day Schengen visa. I also didn't have the right clothing for the plunging temperatures. I had never visited during the cold months before and was shocked by how frigid it actually got. In short, I felt like a total foreigner, swimming in a sea of unknowns. *Damn, was this what my parents went through when they moved to America? Was my move to Berlin a big mistake?*

Driven by panic, I strategized my next steps in a manic whirlwind. By the fourth day after my arrival, I'd miraculously found a furnished flat with a three-month lease starting at the end of November. The short lease would at least get me an *Anmeldung*, a crucial document registering my address in Germany. Then I grabbed the earliest available appointment at the immigration office, where I'd pray for a chance to get a residence permit. Though my appointment wasn't until January, at least I had a date I could prepare for. As for the freezing weather, I bought a long winter puff coat that could help me survive even an Arctic expedition.

With the next steps in motion, I had the headspace to tackle my next obstacle: learning German. I signed up for a weekday intensive-learning class at a German language school. In the morning, I'd learn German, and in the afternoons and evenings, I'd work. For the next few weeks, I came to know other immigrants and their dreams of starting over too. My class had about eight students, organized in a U-shaped configuration of desks with the instructor at the front of the room. I made friends with a South Korean female cellist who played in an orchestra, a guy from Pakistan who needed to learn German before enrolling in university full-time, and another American woman who was working remotely. Our shared immigrant experience took down walls.

One morning, I decided to finally reveal my story of why I'd moved. For homework, our teacher had asked us to write about our families. I stood at the front of the classroom, held up a photo, and spoke in my broken beginner's German. "We are the Choi family. My dad's name is Kong Shing and my mom's name is Juli. My brother's name is Standish. Unfortunately, my parents are dead. This June, my mother died from blood cancer. She was only sixty-eight years old. I've moved to Berlin to begin a new chapter of life."

My teacher and classmates listened in silence and then breathed out compassionate sighs. I returned to my seat, questioning whether I had overshared. A few minutes later, my Pakistani classmate revealed that he'd lost his mom too, just six months prior. We connected in our grief, two foreigners bonded by the familiarity of loss. Grief knows no borders.

By the end of November, I'd already started to feel more settled in. That Thanksgiving, my friend Anna and I shared a meal at an American diner. I thought Thanksgiving without my family would be brutal, but it's amazing how the familiar flavors of roasted turkey and pumpkin pie were able to soothe my heart.

What made me feel even more at ease was moving into a place of my own, even if it was just for a few months. The one-bedroom *Altbau* apartment, meaning "old building," on Gartenstrasse was in the central neighborhood of Mitte. It was the first place I'd ever lived in by myself. No family members would invade my privacy. No roommates would fight me to use the shower. As I gawked at the high ceilings, modern gray and white Scandinavian-style furniture, and hardwood floors, I exhaled a deep sigh. Finally, I had the physical space to be me.

I also had the space to run free in the wide-open streets of the city. One of the things I love most about Berlin is its relative spaciousness compared to many other metropolitan cities. Berlin is seven times bigger than San Francisco in terms of land area, but with 60 percent lower population density per square mile. You could walk for blocks without bumping into a single soul, and public transport is rarely crowded, except during morning and evening rush hour.

As icing on the cake, I was able to speak enough basic German at my *Anmeldung* appointment to get my official letter of registration as a Berlin resident. It felt like a new level of life—and infamous German bureau-cracy—were unlocked.

However, something still loomed over me. Without a residence permit allowing me to legally stay and work in Germany, the threat of getting kicked out of the country weighed heavily on my mind. Desperate, I decided to hire professional help. On my first call with Ina, a relocation consultant, I learned that she was a former dancer and loved helping fellow expats settle in Berlin. Artistic and organized? I was sold.

At first, I felt relieved to get help for my freelance work visa, which would also get me a residence permit. But once Ina emailed me a long checklist of what was required for a successful application, I felt my panic rise again. Beyond collecting documents like my recent bank statements, I also had to prepare a whole slew of other things. I needed two letters of recommendation, three letters of intent to work together from future German clients, and an updated résumé. How the heck was I supposed to manage all that within the next month?

By December of that year, I was totally overwhelmed. Between my consulting work, dealing with my mom's probate case, and trying to get all my shit together for my visa application package, I was on edge. Probate continued to be psychological hell. Just before I traveled back to San Francisco for my first expected court hearing, I learned that the court could not honor my request for a date when I was in the United States. Thankfully, I was able to obtain another court date, one where I could call in from Berlin.

With all the stress in my life, my trip back to San Francisco in mid-December was a blur. I had no energy for most social activities, preferring to hibernate with Jacob. I loved him deeply, but I was still too scared to bring up any questions about us, even though I secretly craved a committed relationship. But we did make plans to meet in Copenhagen to celebrate New Year's Eve together.

I flew back to Berlin feeling anxious about my future. The festive Christmas markets all over the city did manage to cheer me up with holiday lights and spiced wine. However, the stress of probate and my visa application washed over everything.

Leading up to my court date, I holed myself up in my apartment and prepared my documents and a speech for the judge. When the day finally came, I dialed into the hearing and explained why I felt competent enough to petition as the legal administrator of my mom's estate. I thought the judge would be impressed with my preparation. But instead, I felt scoffed at for trying without a lawyer. After I continued to plead my case, the judge finally agreed to let me proceed as the administrator so I could manage my mom's property in Pinole during probate. I'll spare you further legal details, but I realized that probate would take much longer and be way more work than I'd initially anticipated.

The morning after my court hearing, I got on a bus headed to Copenhagen, eager for comfort in Jacob's arms. We spent the next few days snuggled into each other. By the evening of New Year's Eve, when we gathered for dinner with a group of his closest friends, I felt like we were already boyfriend and girlfriend again. Unfortunately, that feeling didn't last long for me.

At a bar after midnight, we got into an argument that made me question where we stood as a couple. I hated that there was so much confusion between us. Suddenly, all my past hurt came flooding back. It wasn't about the present anymore. My fear of abandonment and low self-worth exploded like fireworks in the sky.

The next day, we talked about how it might've been one big misunderstanding with unclear expectations between us. However, I still felt sad and heartbroken. I also felt mad at myself for not being able to speak up for what I really wanted. When we said goodbye to each other at the airport, I didn't know if it might be for the last time.

Once I landed back in Berlin in January of 2018, I hit the ground running on my freelance visa application. At least it provided a distraction from my heartbreak. Thankfully, I wasn't too proud to ask for help. I asked my former clients for letters of recommendation. Then I asked my friends for connections to company founders who could write me letters of intent. By the night before my appointment at the immigration office, I had painstakingly gathered everything I needed, organized in a thick binder.

The morning of my appointment, I woke up at five with huge knots in my stomach. I reviewed my documents obsessively, flipping through each page again and again. Then I shoved the binder into my backpack and grabbed a taxi to the immigration office.

I was glad to find Ina there in the maze of buildings, her brown eyes reassuring me. When we reached the waiting room outside the appointment area, we watched the TV screen like a hawk for my registration number. I kept shaking my legs, unable to keep my anxiety under control. "Stop! You're making me nervous!" she joked, laughing and nudging me playfully.

When my appointment number was finally called, I felt scared, even though Ina would accompany me. We knocked on the door and sat across from a young female immigration agent in a small office. Together, we presented my application package in German. Then we both said *"Vielen Dank"* in unison before we headed back to the waiting room, where we'd stand by for the agent's final decision.

The clock slowly ticked forward. *Would I get to stay in Germany? Or would I be forced to leave?* My anxiety grew with each passing minute. I did not want to be told that I didn't belong. After forty-five minutes, my number finally flashed again on the screen. I jumped up, ready to meet our moment of truth.

When we walked in, the agent handed my application documents back to us, along with an open page on my passport. Ina screamed with excitement, said *"Danke,"* and we left the office so quickly I couldn't grasp what was going on.

"What just happened?" I asked when we got into the hallway.

"Jenn! I've never seen this before in a case like yours! They just gave you a two-year freelance visa on the spot!" she shared.

I couldn't believe my eyes. There, glued into my passport, was my residence permit and my visa to work as a consultant. I jumped up and down, dancing on my way out the doors.

Outside the immigration office, the sky shined radiantly in bursts of bright pink and blue. With happy tears, I turned up to the clouds, knowing that my parents were watching over me. "Thank you, Mommy. Thank you, Baba." As they did decades ago moving to America from China, it was now my turn to start a new life as an immigrant in a foreign land.

Just a few days after I received my visa, another blessing came my way. It was a message from Ina letting me know that one of her clients was moving out of their one-bedroom flat in Prenzlauer Berg. My lease for my temporary apartment would be ending in February, and she knew that I was looking for a new place to live starting in March.

When I visited the Altbau apartment on Bötzowstrasse, I could hardly believe my luck. It had tons of light, was affordable for me at 1,100 euros, spacious enough at 55 square meters (which is approximately 600 square feet), and well located. It even had a long hallway that reminded me of my childhood home, and a balcony where I fantasized about growing flowers. Furthermore, in speaking with the master tenant who I'd be subleasing from, she'd be keeping the furniture like the bed, wardrobe, and couch there, but I could decorate it how I wanted. We could also start with a one-year lease in March with the possibility to extend. I said "yes" to the apartment within hours.

As I had come to see again and again, when something is meant for you, the Universe makes it happen real fast. You just gotta be ready to grab it when it comes.

Moment to Self-Reflect

Reflecting back on my move to Berlin is a trip. When I first immigrated to Germany, I hadn't realized how much I had to overcome in such a short period of time. I was running on manic mode, rolling with the punches and false starts as they came. But now that I'm writing in all the details, I realize that moving to Berlin was a massive undertaking—and a massive blessing—especially amidst my grief.

Moving Away to Find Yourself

Sometimes in life, we're called to leave where we came from and start anew. It can give us the exciting opportunity to chase our dreams elsewhere and uncover our true selves. This could mean a more local move to find yourself, like moving out of your family home or away from roommates, or a big shift, like moving to a new region or country. But it can also come with a lot of uncertainty. Thankfully, despite the unexpected complexities of my big move abroad, immigrating gave me a whole new level of empathy for my parents' journeys. Although I moved under different socioeconomic circumstances, with way more resources and choices than them, the experience of immigration connected us.

A new environment also gave me a fresh start and space to be me, to discover who I was outside of my familial, societal, and cultural conditioning.

When I work with my coaching clients, a topic that often comes up is where they want to live. While some are happy where they are, many want to move and rebuild their lives elsewhere, in more alignment with their authentic selves. Our physical environments have a huge impact on our sense of self.

Reflection Questions:

- In what ways do you feel free to be yourself where you currently live? In what ways do you feel held back?

- On a scale from 1-10, how satisfied are you with where you live? Why did you choose that rating?

- Could you see yourself moving elsewhere? Where? And why?

- If you do want to move, what's stopping you? Can you think of any next steps that you can take—no matter how small—to begin the process?

21

I CHOOSE ME

I WISH THAT I could've celebrated securing my visa and next home more. But the confusion in my heart continued to consume me, along with my grief.

After I felt hurt by our argument from New Year's Eve in Copenhagen, I became increasingly insecure about where I stood with Jacob. But instead of talking to him about it, I did something I'm ashamed to admit: I stalked his social media like I was Sherlock Goddamn Holmes. Unfortunately, social media sleuthing rarely ends with warm, fuzzy feelings. It didn't make me feel better—on the contrary, I felt exponentially worse. I spent days spiraling, feeding further into my fear that he'd run off with someone else. That I'd never be worthy enough to make anyone stay.

Finally, one day in mid-January, I hit a breaking point and discussed it with Jacob directly. Our conversation didn't make me feel better either. My insecurity grew, and with it, the cracks in my trust widened. I was tired of being in a situationship with no clear direction in sight. Although he had booked a flight to Berlin to visit me for my birthday in February, I wondered if I should just give up on us.

To cope with my emotional pain, I resorted to an old method of self-soothing that made me feel good: I activated the dating apps on my phone again, uploaded the most flattering photos of myself, and waited for the notifications of external validation to come pouring in. I went on a few dates and ended up hooking up with someone else. Was it toxic of me to do this? Probably. But it made me feel wanted again.

However, my random hook-up failed to make my feelings of unworthiness go away. Days after, I couldn't sleep. I couldn't focus on work.

The grief of losing my parents returned with a vengeance that January. The reminders of their deaths during probate were relentless, barraging me with guilt. While reviewing my mom's last paycheck to file her final taxes, I saw how little she made at the childcare center before she died. I cried thinking about her struggles and regretted that I never got the chance to repay her for everything she'd done for our family. At the time, I still believed that love was conditional, that it was not freely given but earned.

Whenever I talked to Stan about the resurfacing guilt, he handled it like a monk. "She lived a very full life. And she did it her way. We have to accept that and let go," he'd say. I wish that I could've been as zen as Stan, but the guilt continued to eat away at me.

So I reached out to my former therapist, Susanne, via email to see if she'd be open to meet for a video session. I explained that I was racked with grief about my mom and that I sought clarity on what to do with my situationship. The next week, I was relieved to meet with her online.

Within minutes, I dove straight into it. "I keep thinking about how I fucked up. About how I should've been there earlier on my mom's last day alive at the hospital. About how I could've saved her," I said, sobbing.

Susanne gazed at me compassionately. "But how could you have known? How could anyone have known that it would be her last day?" she asked. After a short pause, she continued. "None of us are fortune tellers. You did what you could at the time."

I let it sink in. "You're right, I guess. But still . . ." I said. Though not entirely convinced that it wasn't my fault, I knew it was something that I had to continue processing on my own.

When Susanne and I switched over to talking about my love life, we discussed attachment styles. By then, I'd already started reading the book *Attached: The New Science of Adult Attachment and How It Can Help You Find—and Keep—Love* by psychiatrist Amir Levine and psychologist Rachel Heller. In the book, they explain how early life experiences, such as the parent-child bond, can impact attachment styles within romantic relationships in adulthood. I realized that instead of having secure attachment where

I could trust others, I was anxiously attached and feared abandonment. Susanne and I discussed how my anxious attachment showed up in my relationships—and how people with anxious attachment often pair with avoidant partners who fear emotional closeness. It was illuminating.

By January 31, the eve of my birthday, something felt different. I could feel it in the air. Each birthday is a chance to review the past and make adjustments for the future. So right before I turned thirty-four, I published a blog post sharing "33 Lessons I've Learned in 33 Years of Living." In reflecting upon what I'd learned, I decided that in the upcoming year, I was going to choose me more, with more self-love. As to what that would look like, I didn't know yet.

I woke up on the morning of my thirty-fourth birthday feeling loved. Birthday wishes trickled in from all over the world, and I was excited to host a dinner party at my apartment on Gartenstrasse. After Jacob landed that afternoon, he greeted me at my apartment with a big hug. My heart burst with joy when I saw him. Even though I was unsure about our future, I felt honored that he'd flown all the way across the world to wish me a happy birthday.

That Thursday evening, we celebrated my birthday with ten of my friends. I felt grateful to have found a place where I could order Cantonese food and was happy to share my heritage with my international group of friends. As I watched everyone grab platefuls of dim sum and chow mein, I felt blessed for the community that I'd already built in Berlin. I was proud to show Jacob my new life. Boyfriend or not, I couldn't deny that he meant a lot to me.

By the next evening, as we had dinner at a restaurant, I already felt glimmers of hope that we might be able to work things out. Our conversation felt more intimate and direct. So direct, in fact, that I ended up admitting to my recent hookup in Berlin. When Jacob expressed that he felt hurt by this, I was surprised. I didn't think it would impact him that much, given that I doubted how serious he was about me. We didn't exchange many more words that evening.

The next morning, I apologized. While cuddling in bed, Jacob told me how much he treasured me, and how he admired that I'd started my own business and moved to Europe. He also shared that he'd realized he could lose me. Afterward, we finally got up, vowing to start over and salvage what we had left of the weekend together. We decided we'd go out that night to KitKat, a fetish nightclub where neither of us had been before. To prepare, we went shopping for the perfect outfits. I bought a short black dress with chain detail in the front, feeling damn sexy.

A few hours later, we entered a massive line at KitKat that extended around the block. While waiting in line, I felt nervous, unsure if we'd get in. Luckily, since we had the proper outfits to satisfy the strict dress code, the bouncers waved us through. As soon as we stepped in, we entered an alternate universe. With multiple levels and seemingly endless rooms, it felt like a hedonistic wonderland. In one of the rooms, there was a dragon that breathed fire. In another room, there was an indoor pool and a sauna. Techno music bumped as beautiful people from all walks of life danced in leather, latex, and lingerie. It was all so much to take in.

Jacob and I entered a world of our own, even amongst the hundreds of half-naked revelers that filled the club. Curling up next to each other on a cushion by the pool, we let down our guard, letting each other into our hearts. He showered me with love all night. I felt like a queen.

I also felt free. Seeing others seem so comfortable with their bodies was liberating to me. For so long, I'd grown up feeling ashamed of my body. Here, people of all shapes and sizes owned their sexuality and were unafraid to express themselves.

By dawn, when we finally left the club, it felt like we'd reached a new level of closeness. And it wasn't just me that seemed to feel a fundamental shift. When Jacob packed his bags at my apartment for his flight that Sunday, he promised he'd come back soon, during Presidents' Day weekend. I was impressed by his dedication. But I wondered: *Where was this going? And what was it that I needed?*

After he left, I spent the next week thinking about my own needs, ultimately arriving at the conclusion that we needed to either commit to a relationship or move on. As much as I loved him and wanted to be with him, I also recognized that I had abundant dating opportunities in Berlin. I had my career in order, a gorgeous new apartment waiting for me in March, and a big heart that was ready for love that lasted. In short, I realized that I was a fuckin' catch.

As it turns out, moving far away from my familial conditioning and hometown gave me a lot of freedom to discover who I really was. It'd only been three months since I moved, but I'd already started to feel like a new person. I had more empathy for my parents' immigration experiences. I had more confidence in my ability to speak German. And I had more self-worth.

When Jacob arrived in Berlin twelve days later, I vowed to myself that I'd show up as the upgraded version of me who was more ready to express my needs.

The Friday he landed, we went out to a bar filled with vintage furniture and charm. As I sipped my glass of Riesling, I decided to tell him what was on my mind.

"Babe. I wanna tell you something," I said, surprising myself with my assertive tone.

"Okay," he said, setting down his beer.

I cleared my throat. "I've been thinking about us. We need to either get back together in a committed relationship, or I need to move on and date other people. I can't do this back and forth anymore. I love you, but it's too painful and confusing."

He gazed at me. "Thank you for saying that. Can I take some time to think about it?"

"Of course," I said. By then, I knew that it was no longer up to me. I spoke up for myself and was ready for whatever would come.

The next evening, we went out to a bustling café and bar in West Berlin.

We had just started digging into our dessert when Jacob took my hand. "Hey. I was thinking about what you said. We can get back together."

I stayed silent for a moment, surprised. After what felt like way too long, I finally responded. "Okay, let's do that."

It wasn't a romantic answer. Because the truth was, as much as I wanted clarity from him, I was shocked to discover that *I* still wasn't clear yet. Outside, I smiled. But inside, I started to freak out. *Could we rebuild our trust? Would the long distance be worth it? Did I even want a relationship so early after my move?*

The rest of the weekend, I tried to wrap my head around the fact that we were boyfriend and girlfriend again. Officially. For the second time. After all that we'd already been through.

When he left Berlin the following Monday, and I had time alone to process my feelings and thoughts, I started thinking of the city as a mirror of myself. It too had once been through devastation and war. But it had rebuilt, vowing never to repeat the cycle of destruction that marred its dark past.

And I realized if Berlin could rebuild and make amends for its history, then I could too—including my relationship with my boyfriend. It was time for a fresh start—one where I chose me, and he chose me too.

Moment to Self-Reflect

Starting over with my boyfriend and giving our love another chance took immense inner work. Looking back, I'm a bit embarrassed that in my past, I resorted to some unhealthy behaviors such as avoidance of direct discussion, passive aggressiveness, social media sleuthing, and hooking up with people for validation. I had let my fear of abandonment and feelings of unworthiness drive me. However, I'm glad that I was finally able to choose to break some of these patterns and choose more healthy love.

Breaking Unhealthy Patterns in Love

Many of us were conditioned to believe that true love is supposed to be easy, fantasizing about fairytale romances that magically happen without much work. Well, news flash: Relationships can require immense inner work, especially when we grew up with childhood trauma that impacted how we think, feel, and act as adults in romantic relationships. Becoming conscious of our relationship patterns—whether through learning about our attachment styles or through other means—is critical to getting the love we deserve.

In my case, I avoided direct communication about what I wanted and expected from my romantic partners out of fear, which lead to silent contempt, resentment, and confusion. However, when I chose to break that pattern and communicate more directly, I became more capable of meeting my partner heart-to-heart.

Furthermore, it's important to recognize that breaking free from unhealthy relationship patterns doesn't just happen overnight. It's totally natural to repeat patterns, especially those that feel familiar to us within our own families of origin. What matters is choosing to respond differently over time. By choosing to act differently, you choose to love yourself more.

Reflection Questions:

- Make a list of patterns that you want to break free from, within your romantic relationships.

- How have these patterns held you back from being able to experience healthy, fulfilling relationships?

- For each pattern listed, what changes could you make to act differently in the future and choose more healthy love?

22

IN THE WRECKAGE

SPRING IS A time of renewal, the returning warmth encouraging bloom and rebirth. As the birds chirped their sweet songs outside, I was excited to start building my new nest in Berlin.

Daylight flooded my one-bedroom apartment on Bötzowstrasse, where I moved into the beginning of March. Though the apartment was already furnished, I overhauled the decor to make it feel more like me. Unlike when I first moved to the city, I felt more ready to commit. Going for a Scandinavian-meets-boho chic look, I went all out at IKEA. I bought new rugs, white side tables, taupe curtains, mid-century lamps, and ample plants. Walking through my new home—from the front, where the spacious living room was, down the long hallway past the kitchen and the bathroom to the bedroom at the back—felt like a zen meditation.

The energy of commitment also reinvigorated my relationship with Jacob. Though we were dating long-distance, we spoke more often than before, and I finally felt like I could relax a little. I say "a little" because my fear of abandonment was still running in the background. However, I was glad that now there wasn't all that guessing about where we stood. We also chose to move forward without rehashing our past. So, I moved forward, at least in the moment.

Meanwhile, something else started to blossom—my desire to create. Professionally, I'd been focusing on my communications consulting work, which was still going well. However, a deep yearning inside called me to write more publicly. I just didn't think I could do it alone, especially since I was feeling creatively stuck after my mom's death. One day, I made a Facebook post asking my network for help. My friend Savannah, who lived in San Francisco, immediately heeded the call for an accountability partner. As it turns out, she also wanted to write. I was totally flattered—and a bit shocked—that she wanted to collaborate with me. After all, she was already a Forbes 30 Under 30 international public speaker, tech marketing consultant, and community manager for the book *Designing Your Life*, of which I was a huge fan. *What could I possibly offer to her?*

Thankfully, within mere weeks of meeting online during our hour-long accountability calls, it became clear that we were meant to work together. We were both Type A native Californians who cussed like hell and who wanted to write more—including our biggest individual aspirations of writing a book. Savannah, a feisty blond with witty humor and sharp intellect, offered valuable insights on visibility and media to our partnership. I provided structure and organization, creating a Google Doc to log our meeting notes. I loved that we helped each other get shit done. She listened compassionately as I talked through outlining my first public grief article. And when I published "First-Aid for Someone Who Has Lost a Parent", she was there to cheer me on.

I did some spring cleaning as well. That April, I flew back to San Francisco to let go of the room that I rented. It'd been my home for eleven years, but it was finally time to move on. Along with a few boxes of mementos, I moved my bed and dresser to my family home. Then I packed some clothes and books for Berlin, giving away most of what remained. As I handed the keys back to my landlord, I felt bittersweet gratitude in my heart.

The rest of 2018 seemed to go quickly. Jacob and I took our rekindled love across the globe, to Hawaii, Copenhagen, London, and Burning Man. And despite still living in separate countries, I felt closer to him than ever before.

Creatively, I was on a roll. With Savannah's encouragement, I started a YouTube channel and uploaded my first video, called "Why I Love Living in Berlin." I also published an article titled "What I Learned Moving to Berlin—10 Lessons from an American Expat" that went viral. It required an enormous amount of energy to consult full-time and create content online.

There were many sleepless nights. However, it felt great in the moment. Every view, like, and positive comment boosted my self-esteem—just as it always had.

By the time New Year's Eve came around again, when I hosted a fabulous party at my apartment with friends, I felt like I was on top of the world. I wish that the high would've lasted. But even phoenixes can fall back down.

I can remember the moment I realized that there was something wrong. Jacob and I were on a beach in Varadero, Cuba, celebrating my thirty-fifth birthday in February 2019. I was standing in the Caribbean sand in a bathing suit, staring out at the clear blue water when I felt a sense of doom hit me. As waves caressed my feet, I felt directionless and hopeless—which made no sense to me at all. I had reached success as a consultant, was growing as a content creator, and had a boyfriend who loved me. *Shouldn't I be happier? What the fuck?!* Feeling ashamed and confused, I decided to keep it a secret from everyone else. I spent the rest of our vacation organizing the footage I'd recorded for YouTube, distracting myself from the doom.

When I got back to Berlin, the feeling of doom persisted, leading me to put even more pressure on myself to perform. *Work should be hard and require relentless self-sacrifice,* I believed. I fired on all cylinders at my Genentech consulting project. I created two educational YouTube videos on Cuba. But no matter how hard I worked, nothing seemed to make me happy, even when my Cuba videos gained tens of thousands of views. When the feelings of hopelessness, insomnia, and irritability took over at the end of February, I finally accepted that I'd burned out—again. The signs were all there. It's no wonder why I felt the doom.

One afternoon, I finally let my secret out, posting on Facebook in the hopes of receiving comfort from friends. Within minutes, empathy poured in from all over, with some friends sharing their own burnout experiences too. Coming out about my struggles made me feel lighter, but I still felt the weight of burnout.

The next month, a magic mushroom trip in San Francisco gave me temporary relief. Hiking amongst the majestic eucalyptus trees in the Presidio, I felt the rapturous beauty of being alive. However, I also felt the pain of life. By then, I'd done psychedelics multiple times, but I'd always focused on the positive. But this time, I allowed myself to think of my parents and all my grief. Suddenly, the entire forest turned black. Terrified of having further dark hallucinations or a bad trip, I quickly turned back to thinking positive thoughts. But the darkness wouldn't go away.

One of the worst things about burnout as a high achiever is that it exhausts you to the point of feeling like a worthless loser—the opposite of being an achiever. And that can put us back on the hamster wheel. That spring and summer, instead of taking more breaks as I should have, I doubled down on trying to control everything. Manic late nights working on consulting and creative projects made me feel better about myself, giving me a false sense of control. Probate also continued to drag on. Every time I vowed to take a break, it was only temporary. I could not stop working, even though my brain knew I needed rest.

I'd suddenly wake up in the middle of the night to work. Eyes wide open, I'd yank the covers off and sneak into the living room, where I'd jump onto my laptop. I could not relax until I'd responded to every email, and I became obsessive about every little detail, wanting to not fuck up. The anxious thoughts in my brain could not turn off.

I did not realize how prevalent my anxious thoughts were until one weekend when I took the psychedelic drug LSD, also known as acid, with some friends who were visiting Berlin. I had taken it recreationally before and loved it, but this time was different. Rather than having fun, I started to freak out and had to leave the club. At home, still on the trip, I kept reviewing my own performance obsessively. *Did I make sure that my friends had a good enough time? Are my clients pleased with my work? Am I doing enough in my relationship?* It felt like I was listening to my anxiety on the loudspeaker. Then I started believing that I might die on the trip. I kept looking at the clock, desperate to get off the acid train. For those of you who are unfamiliar with LSD, a trip can last a long time, anywhere between six to twelve hours.

When my trip finally ended around ten hours in, I felt so much relief! Back to my sober self, I was horrified at how loud my anxious thoughts were.

The next week, as I was talking to another friend who also struggled with control, I had an aha moment. I realized that one of the reasons why I had an anxious madness inside me was because I'd lived in a state of chronic stress for seven years when my parents were sick. Control was a coping mechanism for me during that chaotic period. And when they died, the loss of control I experienced fundamentally changed me. I became obsessed with regaining control. The thing is, even though my mind became aware of this and wanted to change, I could not surrender my grip—until I was physically forced to that July.

I remember that fateful mid-July day clearly. Things started off very positively in the morning. I went to a chiropractor for my back pain from overwork. She practiced network spinal analysis, which uses gentle touches to improve nervous system function, reduce physical tension, and remove energetic blocks. By the end of the session, I already felt more relaxed. As I went outside, I turned toward the sky and said, "My channels are open. I am ready to receive a sign of change." I just didn't expect it to happen that suddenly.

That afternoon, I was in my living room on a video call with my project colleague and friend, Tiffany, when I heard a rustling noise somewhere in the apartment. But when I went to hunt for the culprit, I couldn't find anything out of the ordinary except for the giant moth that had been hanging out in my bedroom. So I shrugged it off and we continued our meeting.

When our call ended, I headed to the kitchen for a glass of water. While I was standing over the sink, I heard rustling noises above me. It sounded like little feet running across the ceiling. As the sounds grew louder, something in my gut told me to run out of the kitchen. Thank God I did. Moments later, the kitchen ceiling split open with a crack two feet long. I stood in the hallway totally stunned. And then, out of the ceiling came a monstrous roar. Terrified, I ran all the way to the living room, fearing for my life. Suddenly, clouds of dust filled the entire flat. I coughed as my skin turned ashy, wondering if it was all just a nightmare. When the crashing noises finally stopped, I mustered up the courage to slink down the hallway and peek into the kitchen.

When I reached the doorway, I gasped in shock. The kitchen looked like a bomb had hit it. Rubble covered the floor. I couldn't even walk through the doorway. It was barricaded with slabs of the collapsed ceiling, twisted metal bars, splintered pieces of wooden beams, and broken electrical wires. The kitchen cabinets were hammered so hard by the collapse that shelves ripped off the wall.

After my eyes took it all in, my ears picked up a whirring sound. I stood there trying to figure it out. *What if something was switched on and could cause an explosion? Was there gas? Live wires? Could my upstairs neighbor's kitchen also fall through?!* Panicked, I threw my passport, laptop, and wallet into a backpack and bolted out of the apartment.

Hands shaking and unsure of the emergency procedures in Germany, I texted a group of my friends. "My ceiling came down and I'm scared. What should I do?" I wrote, attaching a picture of the wreckage.

The responses came in fast. "OMG Jenn! Are you ok? Get out and call emergency 112!" one friend texted. "Do you need me to come over now?" another replied.

I breathed a deep breath in, trying to maintain composure while walking out the building. Then with my broken German, I called the emergency line. Within minutes, multiple ambulances and fire trucks showed up. When the emergency responders got to me, they seemed relieved. As it turns out, they'd thought I'd said that the entire roof of the building had collapsed rather than the ceiling of my kitchen. Whoops, lost in translation. The emergency vehicles faded away to more dire emergencies, and I stood there both embarrassed and scared with one fire truck left.

As I escorted the firefighters to the apartment and realized nothing had blown up yet, I finally stopped holding my breath. At least I'd made it out unharmed. To think, if I had stood in the kitchen any longer. I waited outside the door of my apartment, sweating.

After they assessed the damage, a friendly female firefighter explained in a mix of German and English what had happened. "It looks like the middle part of the ceiling collapsed. In these old buildings, the high ceilings are sometimes lowered with a layer of material."

"But what about the noise?" I asked.

"That was just the fan over the stove. But we turned off all the electricity," she replied.

"So . . . is it safe to go back in?" I asked.

"Yes, it seems the other rooms are safe," she assured.

But when I went back in after they left, my eyes darted around nervously, fearing another collapse. The home had nearly killed me. I didn't feel safe in it anymore, so I moved to a hotel.

Two days after the collapse, a team of contractors finally came to deal with the mess. When they told me the ceiling had collapsed under the pressure of its own weight and shitty construction, I was floored. It was an obvious sign from the Universe that I couldn't ignore. If I didn't stop putting pressure on myself, I'd break too. It was my wake-up call to let go of my need to control.

I packed my belongings into boxes, shoved some stuff in my neighbor Katalin's basement, ended my rental lease, and continued to live out of a hotel. All the while, I was so traumatized by the collapse that I'd wake up in the middle of the night and cry. My already-precarious concept of safety had been royally fucked. It wasn't safe to be me in my family home growing up, and now it wasn't even safe to be home—period.

However, the sudden loss of that home forced me to make space for the new. Standing in the wreckage of what was, I combed apartment listings every day, looking for something even bigger and better. Though Jacob wasn't moving to Berlin until the following year, we started looking for apartments together as he was visiting me. We were determined to find our next home. And within my career, consulting no longer felt soul-aligned for me. I'd originally left my corporate job to create a bigger impact with more freedom as an entrepreneur. However, while I did have more freedom consulting, I was still burning myself out. *When would I start writing a book? If not consulting, what's next?*

I didn't have the answers, but I knew it was time to prototype again.

Nearly two weeks after the collapse, still living in a hotel at the end of July, I became a student again. I had signed up for a Transformational Coaching training course with Animas, an accredited institute, because I knew that I needed a big-ass change. At the time, I didn't actually want to become a coach but hoped that learning how to guide others through deep transformation in their lives would also impact mine. The training would take place over five months in a hotel conference room in Berlin, with one weekend training module per month.

When our instructor kicked off introductions on the first day, there were twenty students in the room. As we introduced ourselves, I came to appreciate the diversity of my peers. Though the class was conducted in English, I could hear many different accents, and our ages also spanned several decades. What united us was our desire to transform.

When it was my turn to introduce myself, I stood up from my seat. "Morning, everyone! I'm Jenn from San Francisco. I'm a marketing communications consultant, but I'm open to seeing how this coaching training can help me create more impact in the world. I think it'll help me become a better listener, writer, partner and, hopefully, mom one day. But I'm not sure beyond that. What I do know is that the Universe also thinks it's time for a transformation. Last week my ceiling collapsed, and now I'm kinda homeless. So yeah."

A couple of people gasped. Some smiled and nodded. I laughed as I sat back down. Sometimes life is a tragicomedy, and you have to approach it with humor to survive.

That weekend in our first training module, we learned the concept of "holding space." Holding space means listening to someone with compassion, without judgment or telling them what to do and how to feel. As other students and I practiced holding space for each other during group exercises, I was blown away by how impactful it was to listen to their problems without trying to fix them.

By that Sunday, I already felt a powerful shift. For so many years, I'd wanted to fix other people's problems, feeling overly responsible—especially in my own family. It gave me a perceived sense of control, but it also led to immense pressure. However, as I was learning, sometimes people don't want to be fixed. Instead, they want to be seen, heard, and empowered to make their own choices. This realization gave me back so much precious mental and emotional energy. It was as if a huge weight had been lifted off my shoulders. It was then that I started letting go of the need to control.

I also realized there was something else to let go of—my Genentech consulting project. While I loved working with my wonderful colleagues and the regular income gave me a sense of control, it was time to let go. It felt scary, but I could no longer ignore the signs. There had been a big moth in my home right before it collapsed. When I told Tiffany, we discussed how moths can be a spiritual symbol of transformation and faith. In some ways, I felt the old version of my career needed to collapse, too, to make room for the new. If I wanted to get serious about writing a book and uncover my next career steps, then I needed a proper break. So I told my main project leads that I'd be ending our contract in August and had faith that it was the right decision.

The beautiful thing about learning to surrender control is that sometimes even better things come to us—and with more ease. A few days after I started coaching training, Jacob and I went to an apartment viewing in Prenzlauer Berg. It was everything I could dream of in a gorgeous, renovated Berliner Altbau. It felt like a palace with a living room, dining room, and two bedrooms. Because it was totally unfurnished—I'm talking not even a sink or stove in the kitchen—it was a blank canvas to fill with our dreams. The extra bedroom was empty, waiting to be filled with furniture and, hopefully, a child one day. We walked across the shiny herringbone hardwood floors, admired the intricate stucco details on the high ceilings, and bathed in the sunlight flooding in from the huge windows on both the north and south sides of the apartment. The marble floors in the two bathrooms made it feel even more regal. As a bonus, the neighborhood was vibrant and family-friendly, with shops, cafés, and restaurants on every block.

We knew that competition was going to be stiff given the housing crisis in Berlin, but we figured it'd be worth a try. Ina and her team helped us with our application package, ensuring we had everything we needed to stand out amongst the hundreds of applicants. To demonstrate our commitment to the home, we told the landlord that we hoped to grow a family in it. It was also a proclamation of commitment between Jacob and me, moving forward to build a future together. Thankfully, the Universe was on our side, rooting us on. A few days after submitting all our documents, the landlord gave us a chance.

The remainder of that summer, I continued to feel divinely guided.

When I turned in my badge and laptop at the Genentech office in South San Francisco in mid-August, all I could feel was blessed. It'd been three and a half years working with the company as a consultant on two global communication projects, and four years working internally as an employee prior to that. My former colleagues gave me the space to be me. My career blossomed because of their support. For that, I will be eternally grateful.

The week after, I headed to Burning Man again. On the drive into the desert, a moth appeared inside my car. Coincidence? I think not. Signs like that kept coming, confirming that I was on the right path. One dusty afternoon, at a camp near mine, I pulled out two handwritten messages from a box. On a small piece of paper, a stranger had written, "About time." And on the second piece of paper that I randomly pulled out, it said, "Finally. You can be yourself." Tears flowed down my face. Tears of joy. And tears of release, letting go of a piece of my old identity that had been serendipitously destroyed by the collapse.

It was finally time to be myself. I had the space now.

I got the keys for our new home in September. Stepping through the door felt like stepping into a dream. The flat looked even more beautiful than I remembered it. The floors even shinier. The sunlight even brighter. I remembered a quote from Marilyn Monroe that got me through past challenges: "Sometimes good things fall apart so better things can fall together."

My last home had physically fallen apart. But in its place came a new home with an old love.

Moment to Self-Reflect

When I look back at my life, the ceiling collapse has got to be one of the most shocking things that's ever happened to me. Now that I've had some years to process it, I can see what a hidden gift it was. It forced me to begin to surrender control and also strengthened my romantic relationship. The Universe has a funny way of doing things. If you ignore the call to change as I did during that second round of burnout, then the signs become louder and louder until they're impossible to ignore.

Letting Go of Control

So many of us try to control things. This might look like taking on too many tasks, struggling to delegate, trying to make things perfect, trying to fix other people's problems, and constantly worrying about outcomes. But control is an illusion, giving us a false sense of security. Underneath the need for control is often something much deeper, such as growing up in unpredictable environments or experiencing trauma where you feel out of control or powerless. In my case, I was trying to regain control after losing my parents. But if I zoom out and look at my whole life, I can see that my desire to control also came from growing up in an unpredictable family home.

Letting go of control is a process, and one that can take some time. Like I mentioned in the previous chapter, patterns often repeat. Do I still struggle with control? Yes. But have I learned to let go more and more? Also yes. While it's still a journey, letting go of control has brought me more inner peace, increased trust in relationships, and alignment in my career. If you struggle with control, perhaps learning to let go can also bring you benefits as well.

Reflection Questions:

- What's your relationship with control? Are there areas of your life where you feel the need to control? If so, which?

- If you struggle to let go of control, where do you think this comes from?

- How have any struggles with control impacted your well-being, relationships, or work?

- How might letting go of control free up your energy for other things that matter to you? What other benefits could letting go bring you?

23

PAST, PRESENT, FUTURE

A HOME IS a place where the past, present, and future can merge. We show up as we are, carrying the boxes of our past, and create space for who we wish to become. And if we move in with someone we love, our lives can merge too, in ways that transform us.

When Jacob and I had to furnish our new apartment in Berlin, it was a massive undertaking that tested our strength. Moving into an unfurnished flat, without even a kitchen sink or stove, brought us a bajillion design decisions to make about size, color, and material of items. About who's responsible for what as we slept on an air mattress and ate off paper plates. As I came to see, merging two strong personalities in one household could lead to some power struggles. I had heard of how moving in together could bring couples tension, but I wondered if I was destined to be alone.

Luckily, coaching training helped me widen my perspective on what was going on. By October 2019, I'd already completed four intensive training modules with Animas Coaching. While every module felt powerful—teaching me about the theory, psychology, and methods behind coaching—there were some things that really stuck with me. When I learned about transactional analysis, a theory developed by psychiatrist Eric Berne to understand how people interact with each other, it blew my mind. Without getting too into the weeds, it's a way to understand how different ego states show up in our communication and behavior. When people unconsciously act in parentlike or childlike ego states, they can trigger one another. To break free from the loop, one must choose to act differently, as a conscious adult. Learning about this helped me become more aware of my actions and reactions. Deciding to take ownership of furnishing different rooms in our new apartment was also helpful. I felt more free to be me. Within days, there was already more peace in our home.

The benefits of coaching extended beyond my relationship. During our training, other students and I got to practice coaching each other. I made so many breakthroughs as a result. I was able to unblock my overwhelm at designing our kitchen and navigate better through the stress of probate. Furthermore, I realized that I truly loved coaching. By then, I'd already gained some practice clients, who came through my network. Every session felt so meaningful. By that November, when I finished training, I realized that I actually wanted to become a coach.

The remainder of 2019 was filled with so much excitement. We got our brand-new IKEA kitchen installed in December, and the rest of our home came together too. I loved cooking in our modern white kitchen with wood countertops and lounging in our minimalist living room with gray and white furniture with antique accents. I felt like a princess walking through the double doors of the living room to our dining room, where we had a long dining table that was perfect for hosting parties or working from home. Our bedroom felt like a sanctuary, with clean Scandinavian design, and the most comfortable mattress I'd ever slept on. The high ceilings also seemed structurally sturdy, with no imminent collapse in sight. I cherished our new home.

The beginning of 2020 kicked off with plenty to celebrate too. In January, Jacob officially moved to Berlin. I got my German freelance visa renewed for three years and joined a creative writing class. Then in February, at thirty-six years old, I completed all the necessary requirements for my coaching diploma and became a certified coach.

That winter truly felt like one big party. I hosted a Roaring 20s-themed party at our home, went to Karneval in Cologne with friends, and finally closed my probate case! Stan and I could finally move forward with preparing to sell the house in Pinole.

I was almost convinced that the high would last. But there was something spreading outside our home, and fast: a deadly new virus making its way around the globe.

The day that Germany seemed to suddenly shut down, I was at the opera with Niels in Berlin. It was March 10, 2020. The singing was incredible, yet amidst the crowd of over 1,000 guests in suits and dresses, there was a nervous air. When the performance ended, the conductor stepped forward onstage. "Unfortunately, this will be our last performance for *Carmen*. All state-owned venues have to close starting tomorrow because of the coronavirus," he announced in German. Afterward, Niels and I left, stunned.

When I got into a taxi, I waved goodbye to him. "I'll see you . . . who knows when?"

Niels stood on the sidewalk and shrugged. "Take care of yourself, Jenn."

As the days passed, we came to understand the gravity of COVID-19, which had by then become a global pandemic. Countries went into lockdown in succession. The once-vibrant sidewalks of Berlin became a ghost town. Hunkered down at home, I watched as patients gasped for air, and as people wailed over coffins on the news. Immediately, I was thrust a decade back to Baba's ICU bed in Chinatown. I could see again the ventilator tube coming from his mouth. I replayed again and again the memory of his chest rising one last time.

Not only did I have to relive the devastation of my family's loss, but I grieved for others too. It was as if their tragedies had become mine. I felt terrible for the Asians who faced discrimination just because the virus had originated in China. *Would I also become a target of xenophobia?*

When the collective horrors seemed too much to bear, I decided I couldn't just sit at home and do nothing. I felt galvanized to put my new coaching skills to use. So, one day in March, I posted in our coaching school's Facebook group, asking whether anyone else was thinking of offering free coaching during the pandemic. The responses came in fast. "Let me know how I can help!" one coach commented. "Would love to be a part of this," commented another. By that afternoon, I was already on a video call with Beatrice, a big-hearted coach based in London, to brainstorm ideas.

Mere weeks later, Beatrice and I became co-founders of Support Haven, a global initiative that offered free online coaching to anyone feeling challenged by the pandemic. By the time we launched, over one hundred amazing coaches from our Animas community had volunteered. We were ready to serve anyone, from healthcare heroes on the front lines to small business owners who'd lost income. It seemed like the perfect way to create impact. However, my manic working behavior came back in full force.

Support Haven consumed me. I worked twelve hours per day on it, acting like it was my full-time job. But that was the problem—it wasn't. By April, I had officially launched my own coaching business and even started drafting the first chapter of this book in my writing class. However, I neglected both. Fueled by Support Haven's cause, I pushed on, working for free. But as the weeks progressed, the fuel turned to fumes. I started crying out of nowhere, snapped at the littlest things, and felt overwhelmed whenever I got an email. The signs for another burnout were all there, but I felt trapped. *How could I stop taking action when people suffered worldwide? Would I let Beatrice down?* However, one day on a video call, we both seemed to be on the edge of a breakdown.

"I need a break. I'm sorry," Beatrice admitted.

"Oh my God, me too. But you can go first," I responded.

She took a well-deserved week off from Support Haven. And after that, I took a week off, telling our team very transparently that it was a mental health break.

Frustrated by my repeat burnout and struggling with the collective trauma of the pandemic, I sought out a regular therapist based in Berlin. I searched online for English-speaking therapists and immediately resonated with Maja's profile.

When Maja and I first met on a video call, I could feel her strong yet warm presence right away. We dove right in.

"So tell me, how's it going?" Maja asked.

"I think I'm burning out again. I've been working twelve hours a day with the light switch in my brain constantly turned on. It doesn't feel sustainable," I explained.

She looked at me, waiting for me to continue as she listened.

"I don't know why I keep working so much. No one is making me do it. I'm putting the pressure on myself, and it started when I saw all the news about the pandemic."

She stayed silent for a few seconds and then spoke. "Maybe it's a trauma response? Trauma from the pandemic and the sense of helplessness many people feel."

Something clicked inside me. "That's it! I feel a sense of helplessness and then needing to do something about it. I feel like if I don't help others, I'm not worthy."

In that first session, we were already able to peel back significant layers. I told her how COVID-19 retriggered my grief of losing Baba. In the next session, we were able to dive even deeper, and I revealed my mom's manic tendencies.

"One time, when my mom was driving on the freeway, she swerved into the center divider to avoid hitting another car. She told me how the car was smashed and how she had to crawl to the backseat to get out. But instead of calling an ambulance or a tow truck, she got back in and drove the car to a repair shop. She was crazy like that," I shared.

Maja looked at me, urging me to go on.

"Then when my grandma was sick, my mom took care of her, burning herself out."

"Jenn, that's really sad. It sounds like, on a subconscious level, maybe she felt anxiety and that was how she coped—by taking care of others but neglecting herself," Maja replied.

Tears welled up in my eyes. I could see how I'd inherited the pattern from my mom. I also reflected upon growing up with childhood neglect.

"I used to entertain myself at home when I was left alone as a kid. I have memories of playing by myself, but not much else," I shared.

Maja explained how me keeping myself busy might've been a way for me to cope with the unbearable pain of separation from my parents.

I nodded, letting it sink in. For so long, I'd wondered why I kept burning myself out. Me trying to constantly do things for others was a desperate cry from Little Jenn for help. I'd been trying to rescue others, including my parents, but *I* was the one who wanted to be saved. With that realization, I knew I needed to make a change.

A few weeks later, Beatrice and I made the decision to ramp down Support Haven. We had done our best for others, and now it was time for us to help ourselves. Luckily, our community of wonderful volunteer coaches understood our decision.

On the day we closed the initiative, at the end of June, I stood on my balcony at home. I sipped a glass of champagne, choosing to be a "human being" rather than "human doing." As the bubbles fizzed down my throat, I decided that before saving anyone else, I needed to save myself first. *The virus may be taking lives, but I'll be damned if it takes mine too.*

During all the pandemic lockdowns and uncertainty, Jacob and I somehow didn't get sick of each other. On the contrary, we fell even deeper in love. Outside, there was chaos. But between us, there was peace. In the monotonous routine of the daily grind, we found in each other adventures of the heart and mind. One day, we decided to try for a baby. Satisfied with where I was in my career, and at thirty-six years old, I finally felt ready. We were lucky. It didn't take long. A few months after we started trying, two lines appeared on my home pregnancy test.

"Babe?" I said to Jacob as I crept into our bedroom.

"Yeah?" he replied, half-asleep.

I sat on the edge of the bed and waved the test in front of him. "Ummm..."

"You're pregnant?!" he asked, bolting up.

"I guess? Yeah?"

He grabbed me and smothered me in what felt like a thousand kisses.

Days later, at my gynecologist's office, I saw a tiny embryo on an ultrasound. It was so exciting! During the early days of my pregnancy, I still had a lot of energy. At the beginning of August, I even attended a virtual *Designing Your Life* coach training, taught by Bill Burnett and Dave Evans, the authors of the book. Not long after that, I received my certification to become a *Designing Your Life* coach. I was on a roll.

However, as my first trimester progressed, I felt like I'd been hit by a truck. Even thinking about food made me want to vomit. Morning sickness—what a misnomer. More like all-day sickness and exhaustion. Crawling out of bed each day, I felt zapped of my energy. But at least I was finally forced to slow down. I needed to preserve my energy for our growing baby. Plus, I needed to deal with the mindfuck of not having my parents around. It killed me to know neither my mom nor dad would be there for the birth. *How could I become a mother without my mom?*

I talked to Maja about it in therapy. "I feel abandoned. I failed to make her stay."

"But how? How could you possibly have made her stay?" Maja asked.

"I dunno. Make her take medicine? Explain why she needed treatment better? I begged her to take medicine, but she refused."

Maja replied, "Maybe you couldn't convince her because she couldn't convince herself? You mentioned that she had trauma from the Cultural Revolution and didn't go back to China for thirty years. Maybe she had to detach from things in order to go on."

That night, I dreamed that I was floating amidst the towering karsts in China. There was an ominous presence as a mist surrounded the entire landscape. I heard a moaning, which got louder until it became a wailing roar. Spirits appeared with pained faces. An old man with a white beard. A woman carrying her child on her back with a cloth wrap. But I was not afraid. I intuitively sensed who they were—my ancestors through many generations.

When I woke up, I realized what my subconscious was trying to tell me: I needed to heal the generational trauma in my family and break the cycle of pain. I needed to understand my parents' own trauma before becoming a mother myself. I needed to do it for my baby. But first, I wanted to celebrate the tiny human growing in my womb.

When I was thirteen weeks pregnant, Jacob and I flew to Slovenia for a babymoon. When we arrived at Lake Bled in early October, a thick mist shrouded the entire lake. Once a bustling resort town teeming with tour buses and boats, it looked like an eerie ghost town during the pandemic. We were the only guests on our entire floor at the hotel.

One day, when the forecast showed it would be sunny, I suggested we go to Vintgar Gorge, a stunning canyon nearby. As soon as we reached the wooden observation walkway built over a glistening turquoise river, I had a huge grin.

"Look! The light is perfect! It's like the sky opened up just for us," I said, motioning toward the spears of sunlight piercing into the gorge.

Jacob grabbed my hand as we continued to walk between the trees and canyon walls.

"Wow. This is one of the most beautiful places I've ever been," I kept gushing.

As we approached an alcove with a tiny stream of water coming down, he paused. "Here. I'll take a video of you walking through the mist. Go back up first," he said.

I turned my back to him and retraced my steps further up the walkway. "Okay, ready?" I asked. But I couldn't see where he was. Confused, I walked forward cautiously. On the other side of the mist, I found my love waiting on one knee.

He pulled a ring from his pocket. "Thank you for all our adventures through the years. You've opened my eyes to so many things, and I want to continue these adventures with you. Will you marry me?"

I whispered through my tears of joy. "Yes. Yes. Yes."

He reached for my hand and slipped on a gold vintage ring with three small diamonds set in circles, representing past, present, and future. I jumped into his arms.

As soon as we got back to Berlin, we confirmed a wedding date at Copenhagen City Hall. Unfortunately, traveling to San Francisco was out of the question. The death toll continued to climb in the United States, the border was closed, and cities were in strict lockdown. It wouldn't be the big festival celebration that we'd dreamed of, but at least it would be intimate.

We emailed invites to Jacob's family and closest friends in Copenhagen, as well as Lily and Niels. But as the RSVPs came in, so did more pandemic regulations, restricting indoor gatherings in Denmark to only ten guests. We had to cancel our original venue for the celebration dinner and split our celebration into two days. On our wedding day, we'd dine with close friends. And the day after, we'd dine with family. Furthermore, Denmark closed its borders to Germany. I was devastated. Stan wouldn't make it, and now I wasn't sure if any of my friends could come either. But by some miracle, Finland was one of the only remaining countries permitted to enter Denmark, and Lily was there. When Lily and Lasse arrived at the Copenhagen airport the day before my wedding, I mobbed them like paparazzi. They'd come despite the odds.

On the morning of lucky Friday the 13th in November 2020, I put on my wedding dress. Simple, white, stretchy, and reaching just past my knees, it was the perfect dress for me at twenty weeks pregnant. Jacob looked handsome in a dark green suit, white dress shirt, and bow tie. Before we headed to City Hall, I called Stan on video chat.

"Congratulations, you two! Looking good!" Stan said. Then he paused, looking directly into the camera lens. "I know you're thinking of them. Mom and Dad would be proud."

I felt a lump in my throat. "I feel them. I miss them, but I feel them," I said.

I could feel my parents walk with me as we entered the giant iron doors of City Hall. I could feel them as we ascended the stairs to the nuptials room. As we waited for our turn to enter, I clasped my white rose bouquet with one hand and my love's big hand in the other. When the clerk motioned for us to come in, we each took a deep breath.

"Do you, Jacob, take Jennifer as your wife?" asked the officiant in a long black robe.

"Yes!" Jacob said with his booming voice.

"Do you, Jennifer, take Jacob as your husband?" asked the officiant.

"Hell yeah!" I shouted with a big grin.

In front of a colorful woven tapestry, we sealed our marriage with a kiss and two signatures. When we proudly walked back out through the iron doors, our family and friends showered us with handfuls of rice. Hungry pigeons flew into the air immediately, surrounding us like feathered confetti.

When we stepped into our private room at the French restaurant we'd booked for afterward, eight of our friends cheered with champagne. We toasted and blasted music on our portable speaker under a large chandelier.

After our first course, Lily clinked her glass and stood up. "Look under your plates," she said.

We all lifted our white porcelain plates and pulled out small, folded pieces of paper from underneath.

I opened mine and saw two Chinese characters. With my hand over my heart, I said out loud in Cantonese, "*Dai gah.*"

Lily smiled. "You got it! What's the meaning? Explain it to these guys," she said, motioning to the seven Danes and one Finn in the room.

"It has two meanings. The first is 'big family.' The second is 'together.' " I paused and gave Lily a big hug. "I love that. Although many of our family members couldn't be here now, you guys are our family too," I said.

A few courses later, while everyone was eating steak, I stood up for my speech.

"When I was thinking about what to say about getting married to this handsome Viking, a line from one of my favorite songs came to mind. It's from Leonard Cohen—a lyric about how even the cracks in things can be beautiful, because they're where the light finds its way in. I think it really represents our relationship. Perfectly imperfect. Those of you who know our love story know that we have an unbreakable bond that has survived the past six years. During this time, there were cracks. There were tears. But we made it. And through the cracks, we found an endless source of light and love. We may live in uncertain times, but I am 100 percent certain of my love for you, Jacob. I am so excited to co-found a family with you. I love you. I'm with you. Together as a team. Always. And thank you everyone for being here today as we show the world our light."

The rest of the weekend felt like a dream come true as we honored our past, celebrated in the present, and embraced the future as husband and wife.

Moment to Self-Reflect

It's crazy how the pandemic fundamentally changed so many lives, including mine. In some ways, it felt like an accelerator, speeding up unrealized dreams. I got pregnant and married within less than a year. I also began to write this book and launched a coaching business. At the same time, the pandemic was a massive collective trauma, impacting a large group of people worldwide. It destroyed a lot collectively, within lives, businesses, and communities—forcing many people to question things and reorient themselves. However, that destructive energy also served a purpose. It took down fragile structures, including parts of ourselves that no longer felt aligned. In my case, after going back to therapy, I finally saw how I needed to let go of the "rescuer" within me, who was obsessed with saving others.

The Rescuer Complex and Allowing Rest

If you grew up with childhood trauma, you might also believe that it's your duty to save others. In my case, I thought that I could save others by co-founding a free coaching initiative. Looking back, I spent most of my life trying to save others—including my parents—but burned myself out. It felt natural to me, especially since I was raised in the Chinese culture, in which helping others is a collective and moral duty. However, I've since learned about the "savior" or "rescuer" complex. It's a pattern in which we feel an irresistible urge to save or help others, as a way to deal with our own unmet needs.

Of course it's great to want to help people. But it's important to recognize when the desire to help others is coming from a healthy place, as opposed to when it's an unhealthy coping mechanism for unresolved trauma. Healthy help could look like helping without expecting anything in return, honoring one's own needs, and not being overly attached to the outcomes. In contrast, unhealthy help could look like expecting validation in return for your help, neglecting your own needs, and feeling unworthy unless you help others.

The "savior" or "rescuer" complex could make us feel more in control of our own lives—at least in the moment. However, it often comes at the cost of ourselves. What we need to remember is that we are human *beings*, not human *doings*. We deserve rest. You're most resourceful when you're well-resourced yourself.

Reflection Questions:

- Have you ever felt the need to "save" or "rescue" others at the expense of yourself? If so, please describe those experiences.

- Growing up, did you see this pattern in your own family, culture, or community? How did that show up?

- If you identify with aspects of the "savior" or "rescuer" complex, what unmet needs (past or present) might be calling for your attention in your life?

- In Chapter 12, I invited you to write down your limiting beliefs about rest. Please revisit those beliefs again and rewrite them into more empowering statements.

  - For example, for my limiting belief "Rest is unproductive and indulgent," I could rewrite it as, "I deserve rest as a human being."

It's unfortunate that I had to burn out again, for the third time, in order to understand this "rescuer" part of myself. However, as my friend and fellow coach Rosie once shared with me: "Next level, same devil." As we level up in growth, a pattern could repeat, giving us an opportunity to go deeper. Burning out again also compelled me to go back to therapy, which, in combination with becoming pregnant, led me to consciously decide to break the cycle of generational trauma in my family.

Generational Trauma

Generational trauma is such a hot topic at the moment—and rightly so. People are becoming aware of the trauma that's been passed down through generations, which shows up in our behavioral, psychological, and emotional patterns. You might've heard somewhere that hurt people hurt people. This can also show up in generational trauma, where family members pass down their hurt to descendants. On my journey, I've come to realize that my parents and ancestors went through significant trauma in their lives, which profoundly impacted me. We'll continue to explore generational trauma in the remainder of this book. However, for now, I'd like to invite you to think about how it might be showing up in your life.

Reflection Questions:

- Are you aware of any significant trauma that your parents or ancestors experienced? If so, how do you see this showing up in your own life?

24

BORN ENOUGH

I'M GLAD WE squeezed our wedding in before the world seemed to shut down again. By December, many establishments in both Denmark and Germany were closed. However, the gift of social isolation was that I had lots of free time to write. Making progress on the first draft of my memoir felt urgent, especially in advance of my son's birth.

Savannah, with whom I was still meeting weekly for our accountability partnership calls, supported me with unwavering encouragement. I also joined an online writing group. Together with other awesome humans, I wrote, allowing the book to take shape organically. I knew that I wanted to write about complicated family love, grief, and self-love. But beyond that, I didn't have an outline and wanted to let the process guide me.

What I didn't expect was that the book would guide me to deeper healing. The more I wrote, the more I uncovered repressed memories. I had to face every part of my past, even the parts I buried for decades in order to survive. My mantra became: *I'm writing and healing.*

Luckily, I had my therapy sessions with Maja to talk things through. Over our video sessions, I revealed how my mom used to hit me—even when I was an adult. I told her how Baba didn't protect me, and how I took my anger out on Stan. Most significantly, I realized how I had thought so many things were totally normal in my family, until I finally wrote the truth of my experience on these pages. By January of 2021, I had already written nearly 30,000 words. However, excavating these words from my psyche came at a cost. I unbottled so much pain.

When I combined that pain with the pregnancy hormones, seemingly endless lockdowns, and the freezing Berlin winter, I felt despair. I'd lie on our couch, looking out at the bare branches clawing against the oppressive gray sky. I had been wanting to get a cat, but even the animal shelter was closed to visitors. However, one evening, there came an unexpected blessing. A friend shared that his mom could no longer take care of their elderly cat, who needed a new home.

A few weeks later, I went over to meet Mec. As I stepped into the apartment, I saw two piercing green eyes. Mec had a gorgeous gray-brown coat with a white chest and white legs. Hiding behind the couch, he seemed so shy that I didn't know if we'd be a match. But as I lured him out with a treat, he rubbed his head against my hand.

"He really likes you!" said my friend's mom.

"Aww, he's a sweetheart. I'll have to think about whether we can take him, though, with a baby coming," I replied.

After I left, I thought about sweet little Mec in his senior years. Then I thought of my mom and dad in their last days alive. I couldn't bear to think of them feeling unwanted or alone. At twelve years old, Mec was in his sixties in human years, around the same age as my parents when they passed.

The next week, I picked up Mec and brought him home. He immediately darted under our couch. However, the next morning when I lured him with tuna, he poked his head out. After licking the plate clean, he walked around the room sniffing everything. By that evening, he was traipsing around the whole house as if he owned the place.

From then on, Mec became my furry sidekick. When I wrote on my laptop at our dining table, he'd sit on the chair next to me. When I lay on the couch exhausted from growing a baby, he'd cuddle with me. And when I wrote the chapter where my mom died, finally forgiving myself for not going to the hospital sooner on her last day alive, he was there. In many ways, he felt like my guardian angel.

In March, I publicly announced I was taking an indefinite maternity leave, at least from my coaching business. By then I'd had multiple paid coaching clients. At thirty-seven, I realized I'd been working nearly nonstop since I was fifteen years old. That's more than twenty years without a proper break! But I have to be honest here—although I took a break from coaching, I kept writing, wanting to finish the first draft of my book.

Unfortunately, at the end of March, something felt off. Mec started to pee outside his litter box and vomited twice a day, so I took him to the vet. When the vet told me there was fluid in Mec's belly and recommended an ultrasound, I was shocked. Back home, I cried, flashing back to my mom's last days when her cancerous belly was full of fluid. We couldn't get an ultrasound appointment for Mec until after my baby's due date, so we gave him lots of love and some medication in the interim. Luckily, he stopped vomiting and seemed like his normal self again—at least for a bit.

Meanwhile, my own health took a sudden turn.

At forty weeks pregnant and five days past my original due date of April 1st, my blood pressure suddenly climbed. When it flashed 160/85 on the monitor at home, I called my gynecologist, who recommended that I go to the hospital immediately.

An hour later, Jacob and I went to Charité Hospital, where I had registered for birth. When it was my turn in the exam area, the nurse strapped a cardiotocograph (CTG) to my belly to measure my baby's heart rate and tightened the blood pressure cuff on my arm. Within minutes, a loud noise clanged from the machine. Not long after, a doctor broke the news. She explained how my blood pressure was so high that it was dangerous for me and the baby. I needed to be induced, but there was no room for me at the hospital. As I started to panic, the doctor called around to other Berlin hospitals.

Thirty minutes later, dashing across the rare spring snow in a taxi, Jacob and I arrived at Sana Klinikum, the only nearby hospital with room to squeeze me in. After two hours of monitoring, the doctor deemed I was stable enough to wait until the next morning for induction. They put me in a maternity room with large windows and an adjustable bed. However, Jacob wasn't allowed to stay at the hospital due to pandemic restrictions. It felt strange to be separated from my husband so close to the birth of our son, but I accepted that nothing was quite normal in the world during that time.

The light from the windows woke me up the next morning. I read through my printed birth plan again, repeating the mantra I'd prepared: *I trust the Universe. I trust the process.* After I waddled to the delivery area, where I had my appointment at 9:30 a.m., the doctor gave me a dose of prostaglandin to induce labor. Not even thirty minutes later, I saw big-ass peaks on the monitor, which showed my baby's heart rate and my uterine contractions. I texted Jacob, who was still at home. "It's starting! Check out these peaks! Probably be some hours before you can come in, though," I texted. He wasn't allowed to join me until labor progressed.

Less than two hours later, the pain became so intense that I doubled over. By then Jacob had arrived. He wasn't allowed in yet, but the midwife suggested I go for a walk outside to assist with the labor. As contractions pummeled my pelvis, I put on my shoes and jacket. Outside the hospital doors, I hung onto my husband for dear life. We strolled along the pavement as tsunami waves of pain took over my body. I felt ashamed. Usually, I have a very high pain tolerance. *Was I just weak?*

Less than an hour later, I kicked my shame to the curb, begging to return to the delivery area. I moaned so loudly that the midwife finally allowed Jacob to come in. The next hours were surreal. Due to my risky birth, I was strapped to the CTG machine and heart monitor in the hospital bed, so I couldn't walk. My contractions felt relentless, with barely any breaks in between. I tried to recall the gentle breathing exercises from my birthing class. But as the pain progressed, I threw all modesty out the window. I flapped my arms as if they were wings, hooting like an owl. If I had to cluck like a chicken, I would've—anything to manage the pain.

Suddenly, I felt a huge gush of water come out of me. And saw a lot of blood too. When the midwife checked, my cervix was barely dilated. Writhing in pain, I begged for an epidural. Not long after, I sat still as the anesthesiologist poked a needle into my spine, excited to finally get some relief. Yet an hour later, I still felt the same excruciating pain.

"You really shouldn't be in that much pain by now. Maybe there's something wrong with the epidural," the midwife said, concerned.

I had read in online forums how some women felt so numb that they couldn't feel any contractions. *What was wrong with me?* As the midwife offered me laughing gas, I laughed at the fact that I'd prepared a lengthy birth plan that included aromatherapy and dim lighting. I laughed at the fact that almost everything on the plan did not go according to plan. While the laughing gas helped, I felt like my unborn child was jackhammering my cervix trying to break free. I feared that at any moment, he would shoot out across the room like a cannonball. At some point, I accepted that I could die during childbirth. At least it would give me peace.

When I was on the verge of a mental breakdown, the midwife offered me a second epidural. When the anesthesiologist came back in, hours after the first epidural attempt, I shouted with glee.

"Praise the Lord! An angel has come!" I gushed, still loopy from the laughing gas.

As the medicine flowed into my body, relief came almost immediately. I felt like a boxer ready to go back in the ring. But I knew I needed to rest first. Outside the window, dusk had turned to night. Jacob sat close to my bed, holding my hand as I succumbed to a nap. However, just an hour later, the midwife woke me up. Gazing at the monitor, she looked concerned.

"We've been discussing your case as a team. Since you're still not dilated enough, labor may be another twenty-four hours or more. You've lost a lot of blood. Your baby appears to be in distress. Combined with your blood pressure, both of you could be at too much risk. We propose a Cesarean section. There's room soon," the midwife explained in a mix of English and German.

I took a few seconds to process their proposal. *Really? A C-section? After sixteen hours of labor?!* Yet I knew what I had to do. I looked at Jacob, who nodded. Shortly after, with hairnets and shoe covers on, we rolled into the sterile operating room down the hall.

As the surgery team worked their magic behind the curtain below my chest, I lay on the operating table with my arms open like Jesus on the cross. I closed my eyes, fighting back the nausea from the anesthesia.

Suddenly, in the quiet stillness before dawn, a loud cry filled the room. On April 8, 2021, a doctor pulled my son out of me and thrust him into the world. When I opened my eyes, I saw two beady brown ones blinking back at me. Atlas, our little world, had come at last.

We named him Atlas for multiple reasons. As an American, Chinese, and Danish family living in Germany, an atlas, which is a book of maps, seemed fitting. And in Greek mythology, Atlas is the bearer of the heavens upon his shoulders. A symbol of endurance, as he'd already shown us so far.

In the hospital room, I gazed at my beautiful baby with wonder, realizing that he was already born enough. He was inherently worthy. Inherently whole.

I just wished I could feel the same for myself.

25

SHADOWS OF RAGE

MY INITIATION INTO motherhood wasn't easy. As my son emerged from the darkness of my womb into the light, I descended into the underworld, where the shadows of my past nearly engulfed me. But first came the sleeplessness.

The days right after giving birth were a blur. Because of the pandemic restrictions, Jacob wasn't allowed to stay with me in the hospital. By the time my baby found my breast and drank his very first meal, mere hours after the birth, his dad had gone home. Then came the physical pain. Although Atlas was born healthy, my blood pressure still spiked, and my insides had been cut open and stitched back up from the C-section. Because of the complications, I had to spend five nights in the hospital, fearful that something else would go wrong. Atlas slept in the wooden crib next to me in the maternity room. At least he slept. I was up every few hours, awakened by the constant medical monitoring and reminders to breastfeed my baby. Every day that he and I made it on this new adventure together felt like a miracle.

Luckily, the hospital care was amazing, with nurses and doctors coming by every few hours to check up on me and my baby. They taught me how to hold him, how to change my first diaper, and how to properly breastfeed. Their compassion filled the hollow absence without my parents. However, the pandemic conditions felt cruel. Visitors—including fathers—were only allowed to visit one hour per day, splitting our family apart.

When I was finally discharged from the hospital, Jacob came to pick us up. The taxi ride home felt surreal. As I gazed at my baby wearing a polka dot onesie next to me in an infant car seat, I could barely believe that he came out of me. Once we got home and opened the door, Mec circled my feet. Then he sniffed Atlas cautiously and butted his head against Atlas's foot, a loving sign of approval. Together in the living room, we stood in front of our golden, full-length mirror and took a picture of our reflection, a family of four reunited at last. Sadly, it wouldn't last for long.

Two weeks after our son's birth, my husband brought Mec to his ultrasound appointment at the vet. Eager for news as I waited at home with Atlas, I checked my phone. When I saw a string of texts from Jacob summarizing the vet's findings, my heart sank.

"Not good news. He has liquid in the belly. Many lymph nodes are swollen," he wrote.

"Oh no," I texted back, bursting into tears.

He continued. "All signs point to cancer. Maybe lymphoma or liver. Vet doesn't think he has long left. Maybe weeks to months."

I collapsed on the kitchen floor, wailing.

When I met with Maja for therapy that week online, I recounted my difficult birth and shared that Mec probably had cancer.

I cleared a lump in my throat. "It feels like history repeating itself. Like I'm causing this. He's skinny like my dad was in the end. Then the cancer with the fluid in the belly. That's like my mom. Can't I just live in peace without something bad happening?"

She held my gaze. "You didn't cause this. How could you? I remember you telling me how you thought he was so skinny when you got him. But you took him in anyway."

"Yeah . . . I couldn't imagine leaving him uncared for. I fucked up by not being there enough for my parents before they died. Maybe somehow Mec is my chance to redeem that," I said.

That evening, I realized how Mec was part of healing my grief—he was a chance to give another family member my loving presence until the very end. I'd sit with Mec in the middle of the night. I'd talk to him as I fed him, hiding his medication inside his food.

Mec continued to sit next to me as my coworking buddy, as did my newborn. Sure, I'd announced to everyone that I was on maternity break, and I was—at least from coaching. In Germany, it's not uncommon for mothers to take a year off work, which includes fourteen weeks of paid leave. However, as a self-employed freelancer, I didn't feel like I could take a long break.

Back to my old workaholic ways, I couldn't resist working on my book. There were many days when Atlas slept in his baby nest in our dining room, and Mec sat next to me as I wrote. By May, I'd finished the first draft of this book, still unaware of how excruciatingly far it was from the finished product. Ah, the sweet naivety of a debut author. I even managed to work on my book proposal, an overview document used to pitch nonfiction books to literary agents and publishers. Together with Felice—an incredible editor, literary agent, and author coach who I hired to guide me through the proposal-writing process—I made huge progress.

In my mind, I could juggle everything, as I had my whole life. However, the colossal challenge of taking care of a newborn shocked me. Atlas slept in a bassinet next to our bed, waking frequently. Days and nights blended with no breaks. Though Jacob was a loving dad who tried to help as much as he could, he was only able to take a few weeks off for paternity leave. Sleep-deprived and without any family around to help, I felt trapped. Every time my baby cried, I felt overwhelmed, desperate to break free.

As the walls started closing in, a monstrous rage swept over me. If I felt pissed off by a comment from Jacob that made me feel unfairly criticized or minimized, I'd scream at the top of my lungs, pounding my fists on tables and doors until my knuckles bruised. "FUCK YOU! I FUCKING HATE THIS!" I'd shout at him. I was a tornado, ready to annihilate anything in my path. I didn't hit anyone in my rage, but I bashed objects as if I would. Sometimes, I'd get right up to my husband's face, shouting as if my hot breath were flames scorching his flesh. I felt possessed. Afterward, I'd feel ashamed and apologize for the rage that reminded me of my mom's.

It wasn't the first time this rage appeared in my life. In my early twenties, I had a few of these episodes when I was blackout drunk. My boyfriend at the time gave my rage-filled alter ego a name: Nej. Nej was Jen spelled backward, and that's how I felt—turned around from my usual self. However, these outbursts were rare, occurring only every few years—typically when I had too much alcohol. Now that they happened almost weekly while I was sober, I was concerned.

In therapy, I learned that underneath the rage there was so much unprocessed pain and anger from my past. I couldn't stand my baby's dependence on me because I'd never been able to fully depend on my own parents. Motherhood blasted the door open on all that was repressed in my own childhood, unleashing a destructive rage I struggled to contain. I couldn't believe the rage that caused me so much pain in my own family of origin was being perpetuated in the family I'd built. On social media, curated images of happy mothers made me feel guilty. I loved my child deeply, yet I resented that he needed me so much. *Was something wrong with me? Where were MY parents when I needed them? And why did they leave me so soon?*

By June of 2021, Germany had opened up again, with COVID-19 restrictions easing up. I finally got to go out again with my close friends Jia and Marwa, enjoying a fabulous dinner together instead of merely chatting on WhatsApp. It felt like a time when I should've been happy. Back in the United States, our longtime tenants had moved out of the Pinole house, and Stan hired contractors for the renovations. We even received an offer on the house from a potential buyer. However, inside my home in Berlin, everything felt like it was falling apart.

On top of my persistent rage episodes, our cat got sicker. Bones stuck out from his chest and back. When he vomited every day, I accepted that we were nearing the end. One morning in June, when he refused to eat his favorite snack of Gouda cheese, I knew. As he put his head down by his water bowl, I crawled down to the floor to lie next to him. "I love you. Thank you," I repeated, rubbing my cheek next to his.

That evening, I brought Mec to the vet for our final appointment. I caressed the top of his head as the vet delivered chemical relief into his veins. Within seconds, Mec was free of his suffering.

Mec came into our lives for a reason. To usher a new life in. And we were there to usher him out. I'd done my best to be there for Mec. And in doing that, I was finally able to forgive myself for not being more present with my parents before they died.

The rest of that summer flew by in waves of highs and lows. Excited to finally have a social life again, I hosted dance picnics in the park with friends and their families. Then in July, Stan and I sold the house in Pinole. It was only then that I realized: The house wasn't just for my parents—it was for me and Stan. While my parents had passed down their trauma, they also passed down resources, taking care of us even after their deaths. I suddenly had money in the bank. Atlas was thriving as a smiley baby with cute chubby arms. But my joy wasn't without despair.

I wrestled with the duality of motherhood. I loved being a mother but also hated some parts of being a mother. I loved breastfeeding but also found it to be a ball and chain. I saw parenthood as an exciting adventure but hated that it retriggered so much childhood trauma. I relished my love for my baby but lamented the freedom I'd lost. Most of all, while I knew I was doing my best to raise a child, I became terrified of my own postpartum rage.

Once a peaceful place during my pregnancy, our home became a hostile prison of contempt. Jacob and I would butt heads whenever I told him that I felt undervalued as a stay-at-home mom who carried an invisible mental and emotional load. He'd expressed that, in his view, I had unrealistic expectations of motherhood and was lucky I didn't have to work a 9-to-5 job. Feeling invalidated and unheard, I'd yell so he could hear it. "Motherhood is even harder than a full-time job! At least during work there's a fucking break!"

There was also tension around topics like control and safety. Many things that were said shouldn't have been that triggering—but they were. In intimate relationships, there are bound to be triggers, especially as childhood wounds bleed into adult beliefs and behaviors.

While I felt immense love and compassion for my husband, all of that went out the window once I was triggered. It didn't help that I felt so drained from raising a baby that I lost my desire for sex. Disconnected from each other and exhausted, we fought.

One day, I dented our kitchen door in a fit of rage. Though it was a tiny dent smaller than a dime, it signified something big. That's when I knew: We needed outside help.

That fall, we hired help. Drowning in the demands of new parenthood, work, and my mental breakdowns, we got a part-time nanny. Ali came as a true blessing from an agency in Berlin. In her late fifties and German, Ali was totally our vibe. She had ample childcare experience, spoke English, was kind, and was hilarious. Her life stories cracked me up.

In September, Ali started coming over twenty hours a week to be with Atlas. Jacob and I both worked from home. The fact that we had a big enough apartment for all this and that we had enough money to pay for childcare felt like a luxury. It wasn't lost on me that my own parents couldn't afford childcare when I was a kid, which contributed to my childhood wounding. It also probably contributed to my mom's rage. Parenthood gave me a whole new level of compassion for my parents' struggles. I had no idea how they managed to raise two kids in a foreign country with limited resources and support.

While having Ali around definitely helped our family survive, tensions were still high at home. I continued to feel unseen. *Couldn't anyone see my commitment to my family and healing my trauma? Would anything I do ever be enough?* In those moments, I just wanted to burn everything to the ground.

Yet every time my husband and I argued, all it took was one look at our sweet, innocent baby to remind us that we also needed to protect our marriage. Committed to keeping our family intact, we started seeing an English-speaking couple's therapist in October. While I was still in individual therapy, we also needed a safe space to work through our dynamics as a couple—one where both of our perspectives could be heard. Those first few online sessions with David, our couple's therapist, were powerful. I learned how important it is for partners to express their individual needs within a family and discuss how to balance careers with the rollercoaster of new parenthood.

I won't pretend it was all rainbows and unicorns once we hired a nanny and a couple's therapist. The constant sleep deprivation during the night was torture for me. By then, Jacob had started sleeping in another room while I slept in our bedroom with Atlas, who woke up every few hours. Our baby never took a bottle nor a pacifier, so breastfeeding was the main way to get him to go back to sleep. Maja explained to me that in a child's first year, they're extremely dependent on their mother. But that level of dependence continued to crush me.

That autumn, the bright light was going to San Francisco in November as a family to introduce our baby to our relatives and friends. I was even able to have a girls' night out with my dear friends Shannon and Hemalee. However, the night wake-ups in the hotel were brutal for me.

Back in Berlin, my exhaustion grew. I kept grinding my teeth at night from the stress, prompting me to get a mouth guard from my dentist. Physically, I was there for my baby. But mentally, I was gone. Whenever I sat down to play with Atlas, who by that December was eight months old, I'd dissociate, surprised to find myself in the exact same position after time had passed. In speaking with Maja, I realized I barely had any memories of my parents playing with me. Logically, I sensed I should've been sad about that, but I struggled to tap into that grief.

Meanwhile, I tried to distract myself through work. In the precious hours that we had our nanny's support, I started querying literary agents, pitching my book to them via email. Unfortunately, all I received was rejections, making me feel unworthy all over again.

The pressure continued to build. It needed release.

All this pent-up energy finally blew up one day in Copenhagen over the Christmas holidays. The moth in our Airbnb was already a sign that a major transformation was coming, but I couldn't have imagined that it would get that bad. It began when Jacob asked to meet up with a friend, which I supported with various scheduling options. But then, when he made a comment that made me feel unappreciated, I blew up. Stomping on the floor, I screamed, "I supported you meeting your friend, and *this* is what I get? This is so unfair! FUCK! YOU!"

Jacob didn't mince words either. During our heated argument, which snowballed out of control, he spewed some hurtful comments about me and my parents, which cut deep into my soul. Then he walked out of the apartment, leaving me alone with Atlas and no word on when he'd return.

For hours I waited. Shaking, I held our baby, worried that my fear of abandonment had come true. My lifelong belief haunted me: *I'm not worthy enough to make people stay.* When my husband came back later that night, I was so relieved. We both went to sleep without saying much. I felt ashamed, shocked, and scared. I did not know if maybe it was the end of us.

The next morning, the cracks between us still felt large. We had both said some things we didn't mean in the heat of the moment. However, we managed to apologize to each other, recognizing that our destructive actions were not how we wanted to raise a family.

It was then that I finally realized: There was no escaping the shadows of my past. I had to dive even deeper into shadow work, making the subconscious conscious, uncovering the hidden parts of myself I repressed to survive. My rage showed me the path into that darkness, guiding me to pain that called for my attention. When I was younger, it wasn't safe for me to express anger or sadness. But now I could see that the repressed pain would destroy me and my family if I didn't bring it to light.

I felt a big shift at the beginning of 2022, as if the epic fight over Christmas shot me into a new era. I recognized that I was no longer a stuck victim of my family trauma, doomed to repeat the cycle of pain. I had a choice to change things moving forward.

Wanting to take agency, and in protest against perfectly curated Instagram feeds, I started talking about my motherhood struggles publicly on social media. In one post, I wrote: "Some days I feel like I'm sinking but there's no life raft." In another, I talked about my rage.

In couple's therapy and individual therapy, I became more conscious of my triggers. I identified that anytime I felt invalidated, criticized, or mischaracterized at home, I felt angry because it reminded me of the emotional wounding from my parents. And if that anger wasn't healthily expressed through talking about it, then I'd explode in rage. Did my husband and I still fight? Yes. Did I still have rage? Also yes. But we learned to recognize our triggers, de-escalate more quickly, and repair with empathy afterward.

There were other changes too, career-wise. I continued to query agents and edit my manuscript while Jacob transitioned to another role within his company that was less demanding. I was delighted to hear that he wanted to focus more on our family. One of the things I love most about him is his commitment to personal evolution.

April was a big month, with multiple major milestones. We celebrated Atlas's first birthday, proud of ourselves for surviving our first year of parenthood—not unscathed, but still intact. I also booked a hotel in Berlin for my first overnight away from my family, for some much-needed me time.

For the first time in a year, I finally got decent sleep. It was heaven. However, my retriggered childhood trauma would continue to raise hell.

Moment to Self-Reflect

When I look back at my first year of motherhood, I'm shocked and relieved that we all survived. No parenting book could've warned me about how crazy it could be. A romantic relationship already invites deep-seated wounds and triggers to come up, but having a kid together, holy shit! It's a whole other level of relational dynamics!

As I came to learn, creating a family can open up all that wasn't dealt with before in one's own family, or in previous generations. I was called to face my pain and do shadow work. Shadow work, a concept by the renowned Swiss psychiatrist Carl Jung, is the process of exploring the unconscious parts of ourselves—often the traits we reject, hide, or fear—to grow into a more whole and authentic self. To get to a more authentic version of myself, I had to become more intimate with my anger and rage.

Anger and Rage

Anger is a healthy emotion that serves a purpose in our lives, often in response to frustration, threat, or injustice. However, many of us were told by our family, culture, or society that anger is bad or wrong. This message could've appeared in many forms. For example, in my family, I didn't feel safe to express anger because I feared triggering my mom's rage. My dad didn't express his anger either. Furthermore, in Chinese culture, people—and especially women—are expected to maintain harmony and not cause a fuss. As a result, I suppressed my anger. You might have too.

However, anger needs a release, such as verbalizing why you're upset, doing exercise, or even screaming into a pillow. Otherwise, anger turns into rage, which is an uncontrollable and extreme outburst of anger. Anger gets a bad rap for being aggressive or violent—but that's rage. I suppressed the anger from my family trauma for most of my life, until it exploded in rage when I became a mother. I feel horrible that my son and husband had to bear witness to it. I wish I could've learned how to express my anger earlier in life.

Anger can also be tied to other feelings, such as sadness, grief, shame, unworthiness, helplessness . . . the list goes on. We'll continue to explore these different dimensions in subsequent chapters, along with ways to channel healthy anger, as my rage continues to show the path to even deeper healing and growth.

For now, I invite you to reflect upon your own relationship with anger.

Reflection Questions:

- When you think about anger, what narratives or beliefs about it come up for you? Where do those narratives or beliefs come from?

- What's your own relationship with anger like? Do you feel it's safe for you to express anger in healthy ways?

- Have you ever had rage episodes before? If so, what might have triggered them?

- What might your triggers be trying to show you?

26

REBIRTH

I IMAGINED THAT once I got more support at home, I'd finally relax—but I didn't. I clung to the need to work, even when I had money from the Pinole house sale and my husband's financial support. As someone who grew up in a chaotic home, my survival mentality was strong. It'd been a core part of my identity for so long.

However, motherhood forced me to revisit who I was. I'd birthed a new life, but old parts of my identity had to die. Rebuilding my sense of self post-birth felt like an enormous task. I floated in an existential void, feeling lost, empty, and disconnected from my purpose and myself. Sure, I'd survived the first year of raising a child, but what the heck was the point of my life?

Who am I, beyond a mother? Who am I, if I'm not working on my career and making money? Who am I, if I'm not fighting for my survival? I pondered. But I didn't have the answers until I finally reconnected with my inner child.

On a beautiful spring day when Atlas was one, I went on a magical nature walk with my friend Lina. A child of immigrants like me, Lina was a Syrian Canadian whom I met in Berlin a year prior. With luscious brown hair and impeccable style worthy of magazine covers, she felt like a long-lost sibling to me, immediately close and familiar. That day in May, we went on an adventure in Tiergarten, a massive green park in the center of the city. While strolling through the lush pink and purple rhododendron gardens, I asked the Universe two questions: "What do I need to let go of?" and "What do I need to invite in?"

As we danced along a lake with electronic music blasting from Lina's portable speaker, the answer came to me in a clear voice in my head. *Jenn, you need to let go of being an adult and invite in being a child.* Simple and profound. I cried, hugging Lina, the heavy weight of adulthood slowly lifting from my shoulders. Because of my childhood trauma, I had adulted too early. I wasn't allowed to be a kid. But one of the gifts of becoming a mother was getting to redo parts of my childhood by raising my son. He was a guide for me to reclaim what I'd lost.

I started to remember all the things I used to love as a kid: rainbow Lisa Frank stickers, my stuffed animal Bear Bear, the color lavender, picking fruit with my parents, and careening down the slide with Stan at Huntington Park.

After our nature walk, I went home feeling lighter, grateful to have rediscovered an innocent and joyful part of myself. I wanted to channel that inner child more but still felt the pressure to work on my book. The responsible adult in me fought hard for my survival, refusing to release her grip on control.

However, the query rejections from agents kept coming, making me question whether I'd ever become a published author. And when I hired Felice to give me an in-depth editorial assessment of the first fifty pages of my manuscript, I learned that I still had a long way to go in developing my craft. My writing wasn't deep enough yet because I still needed to dive deeper into myself. Feeling discouraged by the seemingly insurmountable amount of work that it'd take to get published, I crumbled.

That June, I decided to take an indefinite mental health break. I knew I needed prolonged rest and space to process what still begged to be felt. So I put a hold on my coaching business and any further work on my book. It felt strange to separate from my work, but I wanted to reconnect with my husband and son.

Summer was glorious. Jacob, Atlas, and I watched sunsets in Ibiza and Tulum. Wearing whimsical headpieces, I danced at festivals in Germany and Poland. Then in August, Atlas started going to a *Kita*—a childcare center—just two blocks away from our home. One of the best things about living in Berlin is the incredible support for young families. Children can attend daycare starting at the age of one for free. What a stark contrast from the lack of affordable childcare in America. Us choosing to live in a place where the system supported us felt like a big step in breaking the cycle of generational trauma.

Committed to breaking the cycle of generational trauma further, I decided to dive even deeper into my past. I had reconnected with the joyful aspects of my inner child, but what about the more painful ones?

By fall of 2022, I was meeting weekly with Maja in person at her session space. Along with my couple's therapy sessions with David, I had made significant progress in getting to know my triggers and how they mapped to my upbringing. However, I still felt blocked when accessing the emotional pain from my childhood abandonment.

"My parents did their best. They had no choice other than to leave me while they went to school and work," I said to Maja in a session. Even after their deaths, I still didn't want to betray them by feeling anger toward them.

Maja sat across from me. "You know what I've noticed? You can feel compassion for your parents, but you can't seem to truly feel it for your child self. What about the girl who was left alone for who knows how long?"

My head spun. Shit. She was right. I still didn't feel psychologically safe enough—even as a grown-ass woman at thirty-eight years old who had done plenty of inner work—to face the deeper layers of pain. Therapy, coaching, shrooms, kink, piles of self-help books, thousands of dollars, and countless hours spent on my healing journey—sure, they all helped, but I still couldn't open this last door.

How could I feel grief for my inner child and truly connect with her? I knew that accessing that pain would help me tame the stormy rage within me that threatened to destroy my marriage—that somewhere in the abyss of my existential void, there was a small girl aching to be seen and held.

Intuitively, I sensed that I couldn't access my repressed trauma without further guidance. I needed something beyond talk therapy. That's when Mama Ayahuasca—the divine spirit of an ancient plant medicine—called me, beckoning me with her wisdom. "Let me help you remember," she whispered.

Ayahuasca is a psychedelic plant medicine with roots in South America. A tea boiled with several plants, ayahuasca contains DMT (dimethyl-tryptamine), a psychoactive compound that can induce altered states of consciousness, hallucinations, and out-of-body experiences. Amazonian indigenous tribes have used it for over a thousand years in shamanic and ceremonial practices for spiritual and religious purposes.

I don't remember how I had originally heard of ayahuasca, but I didn't feel ready before. It sounded super intense. People regularly vomit, their bodies purging trauma, toxic matter, and unwanted energies. They recall repressed memories that lurk deep in the shadows, waiting to be brought to the light. Ask me a few years back, and I would've said "hell no" despite my years of experience with psychedelics. But now? Now that I knew I needed to access my repressed memories? Hell yeah! Sign me up!

Except there was a problem. Where could I find an ayahuasca retreat that I could easily reach from Berlin? I couldn't make it across the world to Peru, Brazil, Colombia, or other countries where it's legal. I couldn't leave my family for that long. But I trusted the Universe to bring me an opportunity.

One day in September 2022, while our little family was in Copenhagen, I met up with a friend at a café. He was a psychedelic advocate who was deeply spiritual. Because psychedelics are still illegal in many parts of the world, I'll use pseudonyms and obscure identifying details in this chapter where needed.

"I think I'm finally ready to try ayahuasca. But where do I even begin? How can I find a place to do it?" I asked.

My friend set down his tea on the table between us. "Jenn. Not only do I know of a retreat coming up, but it's here in Denmark. Next month."

My jaw dropped. "Are you freaking kidding me?! Thank you! And thank you, Universe!"

That night, brimming with excitement, I asked Jacob if I could go alone at the end of October to participate in the ceremony. He lovingly agreed and gave me his blessing.

The next weeks leading up to the ayahuasca retreat were full of serendipitous moments preparing me for my soul's journey. They showed me where to look.

The first big clue popped up during an online writing course called "Rewilding the Soul," guided by my friend Alexandra, who was raised in the United Kingdom with Colombian and Moroccan roots. On Zoom, with wavy hair and an angelic face, Alexandra asked us to lie on the ground and sense into the earth. For the whole ten minutes that I laid on the floor in my bedroom, panic pulsed through my body.

Afterward, when we wrote about our experience, I jotted into my notebook: "My bones creak like my hardwood floors do. Why am I so stiff? Why do I ignore my body? If I don't take care of my body, I'll be flat on the ground too. I can't heal my trauma without listening to my body. I've been neglecting my body."

Boom. There it was, one of the deepest truths about myself that I needed to see. Because of my childhood trauma, I disconnected from my body. I recalled how awkward I felt in my body as a kid, flailing my arms during gym class in middle school, always missing the ball. And how I avoided gym class entirely in high school by signing up for JROTC. Military drills felt more comfortable for me than playing sports.

To heal, I needed to reconnect with my body.

The next clues on my journey revealed themselves during a Reiki session in October. Originating in Japan, Reiki is a form of healing energy work where a practitioner uses gentle hand movements to guide the flow of life energy through the body. After another rage episode where I felt the storm within me unleash, I booked my first Reiki session in Berlin. I didn't know what to expect. But it called me.

Luckily, when I arrived at the studio, "Eli", an experienced Reiki Master, calmed my nerves with his gentle voice. During most of the session, I lay down on a massage table with my eyes closed. As he floated around me, I entered a meditative state where I felt immense love for my shadow self, Nej, who was trying to protect me. Then I saw a vision of my childhood home on Polk Street. *This is the place,* I thought. *This is the place to revisit with ayahuasca.* As I sunk into this deep knowing, I felt waves of peace radiate throughout my body.

Afterward, we sat across from each other to discuss the experience.

"You have to look inward. Remember to process your past," Eli said.

I nodded, feeling the resonance of his words.

Then he continued. "You can access things not from this realm. In other dimensions. You have a gift."

I thought about what he meant. "Oh, like the multiverse in that movie *Everything Everywhere All at Once*? I've been thinking about the possibility of multiple dimensions as I prep for my ayahuasca ceremony next week," I said.

His eyes lit up. "Yes. Spirit guides, ancestors, other dimensions. Maybe that's why we're meeting now. I have to tell you, be careful what you let in at the ceremony."

Nodding, I jotted down notes on a piece of paper. Though I felt nervous, I was excited for what was to come.

One week later, I flew to Copenhagen alone. Traveling to the ceremony felt like a pilgrimage. I felt guilty for leaving my boys behind, but I knew that joining the ceremony was the right thing to do. I wanted to become a better mom and partner. I wanted to look deeper within.

I arrived one day before the ceremony. As luck would have it, from my hotel room window I could see City Hall, where Jacob and I had gotten married nearly two years before. When I searched for a place to eat, Atlas Bar, a vegan restaurant, popped up on Google. Then, when I went shopping, I found a blouse with a green and blue print that reminded me of the earth. Immediately, it made me think of Atlas. The brand was called Love & Divine. That's when I knew—my loves were with me in spirit.

On the first day of the retreat, I took a train to the venue outside of Copenhagen. When I arrived at the venue, a gorgeous old building in the middle of nature, I felt nervous. Over twenty of us participants introduced ourselves in English. Other than my friend, I didn't know anyone, but our entire group bonded over our commitment to personal growth.

At dinnertime, everyone gathered in the dining room. As the facilitators spoke, we hung onto every word. Our main ceremony guide was a gifted medicine woman trained in traditional South American medicine ceremonies. We'll call her Yara. In a soothing voice, Yara reviewed the retreat structure. Our first ceremony, that Thursday night, would last over twelve hours and consist of three rounds of ayahuasca. We'd sit up for most of the ceremony in a circle, with music and singing. Then we'd have a day of rest and integration before jumping back into a second ceremony on Saturday night and doing it all over again.

Despite Yara's calming aura, I could feel the trepidation of the ayahuasca virgins like me, our eyes seeking each other out for reassurance, our questions asked in squeaky voices. However, when I saw a giant moth in the room, I knew: It was time for transformation again.

That evening, we sat down to form a circle in a cavernous room with enormous windows. I chose a seat near a corner, on the side furthest away from the door. By then it was dark outside, and candles illuminated our ceremony space. An altar, built with flowers and feathers, decorated the front where Yara sat. Next to her was a talented musician—who we'll call Luz—who was well-versed in medicine ceremonies too. Together with other trauma-informed facilitators, they'd hold a safe space for us. I glanced around the circle in admiration. No longer in sweatpants and jeans, everyone looked majestic in their beautiful robes, colorful dresses, and ethereal pants. I wore an indigo robe embroidered with purple flowers.

After a sacred prayer together, we shared our intentions out loud. "I want to meet my inner child and let her know that she's safe and loved," I said when it was my turn. By the time I drank my first small cup of ayahuasca, I felt ready to dive in.

Within twenty minutes into my first round, I already felt nauseous, pulling an empty plastic container meant for vomit close to me. I closed my eyes, watching neon geometric tendrils snake toward me as I melted into my meditation chair, which rested on the floor. My legs extended in front of me, shivering with sudden cold. Holy shit. Ayahuasca was no joke. As Yara and Luz sang *icaros*, sacred healing songs used by indigenous shamans, I battled my nausea. Every time I thought of something sad like the deaths of my parents, the nausea worsened. Terrified of purging, I tried to suppress my negative thoughts.

However, a few memories did squeeze through. I saw myself at age twenty-six, splitting my elbow open in a Segway accident while tumbling downhill but refusing medical help until the next day when I got stitches. I saw myself driving to the emergency room at twenty-two after ignoring a urinary tract infection that had turned into a kidney infection. I felt the sharp pain in my ankle when I sprained it ice skating in middle school but was too ashamed to tell my parents. I allowed a few tears to roll down, but that was it. Even when people purged loudly around me, I couldn't let go.

I was able to fight the nausea until the second round, which seemed much stronger than the first. After I chugged the thick, dark liquid, a jolt of electricity shot through my body, turning my stomach inside out. I retched and retched. It felt like a never-ending exorcism of primal, dark matter generations old. After I filled Bucky—yes, my vomit bucket acquired a nickname—I closed the lid. No longer nauseous, I could now face my pain. I saw a vision of Baba at my preschool, waiting for me but never giving me a hug. I realized—I don't have a single memory of him ever hugging me. I saw me and Stan washing dishes alone at home, standing on step stools because we were too short to reach the faucet. I realized—we were often alone as kids.

As I trace my childhood backward, I arrive at our Polk Street home, where Little Jenn is. Except the home looks different because I finally remember. I'm not happily playing on the floor. I'm panicked, circling the front door, wandering around the kitchen and bedroom, desperate to find my mom and dad. Little Jenn looks like Atlas, except with shoulder-length hair. I think of my son searching for me, terrified, with no one around. Tears soak my robe. "I could've fucking died. I could've died all alone. What the fuck?!" I mutter, finally allowing myself to feel the anger.

My sobs grow louder, my heart breaking for myself. Little Jenn's helpless. But then, I suddenly realize that I can save her! By being me—conscious adult Mama Jenn! I swing open the front door, scoop up Little Jenn, and give her a hug. "I love you. I'll never leave you. You're not alone," I tell her. At first, she's tense with skepticism. But as our embrace tightens, she starts to smile.

I could've stayed in this moment forever. That's when I realized that the present moment is the most powerful portal for healing. Presence changes everything. When I love my inner child in the present moment, when I hug my son tighter in the now, I'm doing the healing work to create a better future and rectify the past, all at once. Everything everywhere all at once.

Back in the ceremony room, I hugged myself before the third drink of ayahuasca, where I completely surrendered. Inside the trip, I zip up and down strands of DNA, watching the fast-moving source code of the Universe whiz all around me, strings of infinite possibilities passing by. I disintegrate, breaking down into blood and cells, returning to my mother's womb. When I emerge as a baby, I feel the joyous rapture and fierce love of my parents welcoming me.

I'm born again. Happy rebirth day to me.

After a day of rest where we took time to let the first ceremony sink in, we did it all over again on Saturday night. I wore my new, earthy, blue and green blouse and took the same seat again, no longer afraid. By now, I felt a kinship with my newfound friends. They too had lost loved ones, survived trauma, or wanted to unlock the mysteries of their souls. In our communal grief, vulnerability, and puke, we comforted each other.

"I want to reconnect with my body and love it again," I shared in our second ceremony circle. As I stepped up to the altar to receive my first drink, I thought about telling Yara that I wanted only a half dose. That I hated the nausea. But when I got up there, I struggled to advocate for my body, asking her to decide on my dose instead.

About thirty minutes in, I feel dizzy. And then, out of nowhere, I start a conversation with my body.

"Body, what do you need?" I ask.

Surprisingly, she responds in the same voice as me but somehow wiser. "Oh, hi! You can hear me? Finally! Jenn, please go gentle with me. I've worked so hard for you. I want to rest."

"I know. I'm so sorry that I've pushed you all these years. I'm sorry I ignored you. But I'm here now," I say.

"It's okay. You had to do what you needed to survive. I understand," my body says.

"Body, what do you need?" I ask again.

"Water. Get up and get some water. I'm thirsty," my body says.

I obey. The next few hours there's a back-and-forth dialogue with me and my body. We laugh and build trust in each other as I follow her orders, going to the bathroom to pee, drinking glass after glass of water, stretching my legs, and walking around as if I'm her puppet. I see visions where I've ignored her in the past. Where I pass by a mirror and see my shoulders hunched over but don't do anything to fix my posture. Where I stare down at my dark pee in the toilet but don't drink enough water, thinking it's someone else's problem.

I realize that my body has been trying to talk to me this whole time, through chapped lips and stress hives. I realize that by ignoring my body, I didn't give her the love she deserved. To truly love myself and feel worthy, I'd have to love my body and see her worth too.

"I love you, body," I say and hug myself.

"I love you too, Jenn," my body replies.

When I approach Yara during the second round, I say with clarity, "The littlest amount possible. Like an atom's worth. My body told me so."

Yara laughs warmly and respects my request, pouring only a symbolic amount into my cup. She smiles, looking proud of me.

During the second round, I'm present and clear, recognizing that presence is power. I sway in my seat as I hear Luz sing, each musical note carrying love throughout my body. Eyes wide open, I observe others around me. I send well wishes for their journeys, as I anchor myself in a peaceful trance.

By the third round, my body and I agree to drink again, this time half of the first dose. I see visions of feet. Of my son's little feet, of my feet, of my mom and dad's feet. I realize—my parents were once children too. By seeing them as children, I could let go of some of my pain. Then suddenly, a dark cloud appears, and I immediately sense this is the collective trauma of my ancestors, beckoning me to transmute their pain. For a moment, I feel the pressure to go into the pain and fix it. Old me would've instantly. Then I remember Eli's warning: "Be careful what you let in." I'm nauseous again, divided on what to do. But before I can deliberate any further, my body interjects in a slightly gangster tone. "Nah, we don't need all that pain right now. I'm good. I don't wanna be uncomfortable."

I cackle, delighted that we could choose comfort instead. Like lightning, a truth hit me. I don't need to go into the dark cloud to save my ancestors. The inner work that I'm doing in the present has the potential to heal past and future generations. Time is nonlinear. As we heal in the present, it's possible to alter the past and amplify the effect backward and forward. When we heal ourselves, we are healing our ancestors as well as our descendants. My mouth opened so wide in awe that I started drooling, salivating at this profound spiritual download.

Hours later, as day broke and birds chirped outside, we closed out the second ceremony together in spoken prayer and dance, thanking our ancestors, the land, the plants, and the water nourishing life around the world. And on the last day of the retreat, after a shared breakfast, we hugged. We said our goodbyes. Awakened. Transformed. Rebirthed.

That evening, on my flight back home to Berlin, I sat in silent reverence and thanked Jacob and Atlas for loving me. I thanked my parents. I thanked my body. I thanked myself for showing up, for being brave enough to do the inner work.

It felt good to be me again. Not the me defined by my productivity, nor my ability to make money. Not the me who needed to be an adult all the time. Nor the me struggling to survive. But the real me. The soul me.

Moment to Self-Reflect

I freakin' loved writing this chapter. My spiritual rebirth during an ayahuasca retreat was one of the most magnificent experiences of my life. Connecting with my inner child reconnected me with my body and then my soul. However, it wasn't just the plant medicine, it was also my commitment to inner work. All my years of self-reflection had contributed to my awakening. I remembered who I was beyond my conditioning.

I do want to emphasize that, for many people, psychedelic substances aren't the only way to attain this level of inner connection. Meditation, breathwork, yoga, sound baths, and writing are some of the other ways to access altered states of consciousness without substances. I hope that by sharing my realizations about the inner child and the body, you can see for yourself that it's possible to heal even your deepest layers.

Connecting with Your Inner Child

An inner child is a part of ourselves, made up of our childhood experiences and our relationship to that part of ourself. The inner child can be creative, carefree, joyful, and playful. Carl Jung called this the "divine child." But when we've experienced trauma, that inner child can feel vulnerable, small, and in need of protection. This wounded inner child can show up in our subconscious, acting out in our adult lives.

Perhaps you might struggle to connect with your inner child, especially if you've spent years shielding them, building up a wall of protective mechanisms and behaviors. But even if it feels difficult, we can reconnect with our inner child to uncover our true selves and break free of patterns that no longer serve us.

I love holding space for my coaching clients to reconnect with their inner child within sessions. I've also found that encouraging people to write a letter to their inner child can also lead to some profound shifts.

Reflection Exercise: Letter to Your Inner Child

Part 1- Reflections

- Were there any life events from your childhood that felt particularly challenging for you? (For example: a loss, move, parental divorce, or other stressful event.)
- Around what age did that occur? (Sensing into an age can make the connection to your inner child feel more tangible.)

Part 2- Letter to Your Inner Child

- Open your journal to a fresh page. Write at the top, Dear Little (Your Name),
- Write your inner child a letter, with whatever you want to say to them to connect. What loving words of comfort might you want to share with them? What about questions? Allow your words to flow freely, as a stream of consciousness.

Part 3- Letter from Your Inner Child

- Open your journal to another fresh page. Write at the top, Dear Adult (Your Name),
- Write a letter from your inner child back to you. What do they want to tell you? Anything they want to share about their hopes and fears?

Connecting with Your Body

Connecting with your inner child is key to growth and self-love. However, so is connecting with your body. If you feel disconnected from your body, it could've been a protective mechanism. When I was alone in my childhood home as a kid, my bodily needs and emotions betrayed me. Hunger, thirst, fear, sadness. What was the point of feeling those things if no one was there to hear my cries? So I dissociated from my body, severing my connection to the corporal temple that would house my soul for the rest of my life. I could feel anxiety zap around my body, but my connection with my body was limited. It felt like someone else's.

However, as psychiatrist and trauma researcher Dr. Bessel van der Kolk famously explains in his book *The Body Keeps the Score: Brain, Mind, and Body in the Healing of Trauma*, the imprints of unprocessed trauma are stored in our bodies, and healing means addressing it on not just a mental level, but a physical level too.

Reflection Questions:

- Do you have any health issues that you suspect might be tied to stress in your body? If so, what could your body be trying to tell you?

- How could you connect more with your body and listen to its needs?

- What would it be like to love your body more? What would that bring?

27

RETURN HOME TO ME

THE AFTERGLOW OF the ayahuasca ceremony lasted well into my return to Berlin. When I walked through our apartment door at the end of October, my husband looked hotter than ever, his chiseled jawline and strong arms welcoming me. My toddler was extra cute, with his bowl haircut and silly giggle. Cuddling with my family on our giant beanbag felt like a cosmic cuddle with the entire Universe. Everything seemed clearer, including my sense of self. It was as if I'd awoken from a deep slumber, unplugged from the matrix. I remembered who I was—a divine being, inherently worthy and whole, yet also part of a greater oneness.

But my spiritual rebirth wasn't the end. It was the beginning.

It's wonderful to have earth-shattering experiences that awaken us, but they lose their potency if they're not integrated into daily life. So many people chase the high of transformative experiences without implementing the lessons learned from them. True change requires dedication.

I felt much more love for my body than before, but integration meant continuing to listen to it. For so long, I'd been focused on my thoughts, constantly overthinking and ignoring my body. Yet my body was a key part of who I was. Reconnected with my body, I observed that my rage episodes didn't come without warning. Before I'd explode, I'd clench my jaw and my fists. Noticing this pattern was helpful in getting in touch with my anger before it escalated into rage. I also started to drink more water. Before, I'd be so dehydrated that my pee was dark. Now, every time I'd see my clear pee in the toilet, I'd celebrate.

Integrating spirituality was also crucial for me. I had accessed another light-filled dimension where I felt so much peace and love. Was it where we went after we died? Could this place be another layer of reality? I did not know. But I did know that it felt familiar. I'd been in touch with something greater and sensed that spirit could also be found here on earth.

As a human living on this planet, I could admire the divine in nature, appreciating each flower and leaf, just as my mother had taught me. We are one with nature. Connecting with nature is connecting with ourselves. Divinity was also expressed through creation. I continued to write channeled poems about the ocean and trees. I learned about the moon's power. Did you know that the moon's gravitational pull controls the ocean's tides? And that our bodies are 60 percent water? Perhaps the moon's energy could impact us too. I started connecting with the moon through full moon rituals, where I'd write down what I wanted to release. And during the new moon, which symbolizes new beginnings, I'd write down my intentions.

Connecting mind, body, and spirit in my life felt amazing. But it also brought tension. At times, I felt unmoored from normal life, questioning how to operate as a human after touching what felt like God in ceremony. It felt strange to do laundry and file taxes after experiencing something infinite.

I also became sensitive to the idea that my new sense of reality might be dismissed or judged. That sensitivity began to show up in my marriage. Even seemingly trivial comments started to hit a nerve.

When I brought this to therapy with Maja, I learned that I hated feeling like my version of reality was dismissed or judged. We mapped it back to my own family, where my mom would regularly deny my lived experience, even when I was an adult. Once, when I was in my thirties and told her that I wanted to take a singing class, she said, "Ha! You? Singing? You will never be able to sing." It pained me to feel so belittled by my own mom.

Growing up in an unstable family home also that meant that I often questioned my own reality, trying to figure out what was real. So whenever I felt that my husband was making dismissive comments, I wanted to defend myself. While my anger might've sometimes been justified, my rage was not. It felt disproportionate to the triggers. I was ashamed that instead of setting my boundaries and expressing my anger, I'd explode into rage. I hated that the rage overshadowed everything, even after I accessed the divine realm of peace and love.

I had reconnected with my inner child but was frustrated that the rage was still showing up. On the bright side, I was able to tap into the joyful aspects of my inner child. When it was snowing in December, Lina and I wore outrageous polka-dot dresses and created our own fashion photoshoot at a playground. I channeled my inner child when I played hide-and-seek with Atlas, feeling present and engaged. Unfortunately, I also felt overwhelmed by his tantrums. At one and a half years old, he'd cry loudly, shout, and throw his body around when he didn't get his way. On one hand, I wanted to give him the childhood I wish I had—full of attention, nurture, and space for big emotions. On the other hand, I resented that I was not allowed to have tantrums as a kid. They were beaten or berated out of me. In some ways, I saw my rage as adult tantrums—from all the big feelings I'd suppressed for decades.

That Christmas, our little family flew to Copenhagen again. While the holiday season in Denmark always feels cozy, this one felt extra special because Stan and his girlfriend Vee joined us. Originally from China but working in tech in the United States, Vee was a welcome addition to our family. She was smart, quirky, and future-thinking. It was also the first time that Stan met some of Jacob's lovely family, who had become my family too. Over roasted duck, caramelized potatoes, and wrapped gifts, our multi-cultural families merged. After we danced around the Christmas tree singing songs, Stan exclaimed, "It's like a Hallmark movie!"

Seeing my brother in my husband's hometown moved me. I missed my hometown. Sure, San Francisco had deteriorated since I'd moved away, with more homeless living in tents, a rampant fentanyl drug problem, increased crime, and empty downtown storefronts. That, along with my retriggered childhood trauma and the grief of losing my parents, negatively colored my view of the city. However, I would always love my hometown. I also sensed that there was something big missing on my healing journey, and I had to go back to San Francisco to find it.

When we got back to Berlin in January, we booked a family vacation to San Francisco for the following month. Going home didn't just mean my hometown though. Home also meant returning to my body. By then, I'd read psychologist Nicole LePera's book *How to Do the Work: Recognize Your Patterns, Heal from Your Past, and Create Your Self*, which includes a fantastic explanation of the nervous system in relation to trauma. I'd realized that my nervous system was dysregulated from prolonged trauma and wanted to learn how to regulate it so it could move to a calmer state. When my friend Sabrina launched her nervous system coaching business in Berlin, I became one of her clients.

That January, I felt my body relax during sessions in Sabrina's serene practice space. Though I appreciated the check-in discussion at the beginning of our sessions, the real magic for me was when I was on the massage table with my eyes closed. Using a form of biodynamic craniosacral therapy, which leverages light touch, she helped me tap into the inherent wisdom of my body. Through listening to my body, I realized I needed to take up more space and expand, rather than shrink as I was used to. I also realized my rage wasn't just from my own childhood trauma but from the trauma passed down through many generations of women in my family. To heal, I needed to listen to Nej. Most significantly, by the end of January, I remembered what peace felt like in my body, which was foreign to me before.

I turned thirty-nine in February, feeling more myself than ever. I hosted a birthday party at home, where I encouraged everyone to show up in shiny outfits. Wearing a gold crown and silver bodysuit, I read a few pages from my memoir out loud to my friends. I felt so seen.

Then something else happened around my birthday: a discussion about having a second child. But I didn't feel ready yet. Still reeling from the first year of motherhood, I wanted to get to a more stable place—mentally and emotionally. I was also consumed by the inexplicable fear that if I had another child, my family would collapse, and I'd be abandoned.

When I brought this into my sessions with Sabrina, I sensed that my persistent fear of abandonment and catastrophic thinking came from an inner child that didn't feel safe yet. Adult Jenn finally felt worthy and whole. Little Jenn still did not. To help my inner child feel safe in my home and body, I needed to reconcile with my past in San Francisco.

We flew to San Francisco at the end of February 2023 for our two-week family vacation. Though Jacob and I had taken Atlas to the city when he was a baby, this time would be different. I'd return as my awakened self, ready to use the present moment as a portal to transmute the pain from my past. It wasn't just my inner child whom I wanted to be with—it was all my past selves.

From the moment we landed at SFO, I felt guided by a higher purpose. I was ready to revisit the places that I knew and loved—and the places where I'd lost and cried. I wanted to walk through these physical locations, accessing memories both beloved and repressed.

It began with Chinatown. Fortunately, we had found a two-bedroom Airbnb near my family home, where Stan still lived. As we walked down the hill two blocks to Stockton Street, where Baba used to shop for groceries, it immediately felt like a homecoming. I loved seeing the Chinese characters on colorful store awnings, produce stands with mounds of oranges, and roast duck hanging in barbeque shop windows.

From the second day forward, Jacob and I divided our schedules so that each of us could get some precious time to catch up with friends. While I loved taking Atlas around on fun adventures, like going to the Cable Car Museum, he needed constant attention at nearly two years old. I'm convinced the secret to staying sane on family vacations is giving each parent a chance to get a break.

I totally milked those social opportunities in San Francisco. I met up with Savannah at our favorite seafood restaurant on The Embarcadero waterfront, excited to finally see her again in person. Over oysters and chardonnay, we celebrated five years of accountability partnership, which had deepened into one of the greatest friendships I'd ever known.

Sipping my wine, I looked into her eyes and said, "I think I know why we looked so familiar to each other when we first met. It's because we already knew each other from past lifetimes."

Without skipping a beat, Savannah raised her glass with a huge smile. "Oh babe, I already figured that out a long time ago."

Misty-eyed and howling with laughter, we joked about how we must've been in Ancient Egypt together, building the pyramids.

Every meeting with every friend on that trip lit up my soul. It felt like I was already healing different parts of my past by hanging out with them. I sipped cocktails at a rooftop bar with my high school friends Dyanna, Nina, and Sasanna. I ate Korean noodles with Jia, who had moved back to the Bay Area from Berlin. I went to a karaoke bar with Helen and Ted, a couple whom I'd partied with in my twenties. Nicole and Hemalee each came out to spend time with me and Atlas. I also reconnected with Erwin and Mide, two of my favorite former coworkers from Genentech. I'm mentioning all their names because they matter. My community has always lifted me up when I was down. Celebrating with my friends energized me. They gave me the strength and encouragement I needed to revisit the places that hurt.

One day, Jacob and I went for a big day out with Atlas. In the morning, we passed by the beige facade of Chinese Hospital on Jackson Street. It immediately transported me back to Baba's last breaths. At twenty-six years old, I felt numb and dissociated. Now at thirty-nine, I allowed myself to cry, my tears signaling that I was finally safe enough to grieve one of the biggest losses of my life.

Later that day, we visited the care facility on Grove Street, where Baba had lived the last year of his life. Peeking through the glass doors, I saw the hallway I'd walked so many times with my mom and Stan. I remembered how much I was actually there for my dad, and how my family rarely ever let him spend a day alone. More tears came as I forgave myself, hugging my inner twenty-six-year-old.

As Atlas fell asleep in his stroller, Jacob and I walked back across town. The sun shone down on us as we ate at our favorite Greek place in Hayes Valley. Afterward, we continued to stroll but stopped once we got to Polk Street.

There it was—my very first childhood home. I stood next to the ornate steel gate, feeling compassion for my inner child. The gate had interlocking heart shapes, a perfect representation of the love I felt for both Little Jenn and Atlas. Every time I met my child with love, I met myself with love. Taking my new family to the place where my abandonment wound originated felt like a salve for my soul. I'm so glad that I had that healing experience because the next day I'd receive some heartbreaking news.

The next evening, the three of us met up with Stan, and my cousins Judy and Cindy at a Taishanese restaurant in Chinatown. Older than me, they were the daughters of Uncle Four. Over lotus root soup, stir-fried pea shoots, and claypot rice, we excitedly caught up on life. However, just as we were about to leave, I asked my cousins why Baba had moved to Hong Kong. Their responses hit me like a freight train. With solemn faces, they revealed the dark truth that my family had buried for decades.

Judy spoke. "When your dad was around twelve, he went to send off a friend in Hong Kong. His friend's family was moving to Canada, so your dad wanted to say goodbye. At the time, travel between Taishan and Hong Kong was more open. But soon after, with all the changes in China, border controls suddenly changed too. He couldn't return."

"What?!" I asked in disbelief. "So he couldn't go back home to Taishan?"

"No," she replied. "Yeh Yeh was in Hong Kong with him, but they were separated from the rest of the family in Taishan. Your dad didn't see Maa Maa nor my dad for almost thirty years."

Tears streamed down my face as I thought of twelve-year-old Baba, suddenly split from his mom, siblings, and home. "That's so sad. That's so sad," I kept repeating. The torrential downpour outside the restaurant felt like a fitting mirror for my grief.

I'd known about my mom's trauma from the Cultural Revolution, but I'd never heard how the historical shifts of that era impacted my dad's family. *What else did my parents hide from me? Was this why Baba rarely spoke about his youth?* I cried that evening, lamenting that my father died with this unspeakable pain. I had so many questions. Fortunately, Stan and I were about to get the answers.

The next afternoon, my brother and I took the bus to Uncle Four's house. I'd spent so much of my childhood here. In many ways, it felt like home. When I asked Uncle Four about my dad's past, he didn't hold back. We'd never spoken about my paternal family's trauma before, but now that everyone was getting older, it seemed like we should before it was too late.

Uncle Four sat in his recliner as I sat across from him on a stool. In a mix of Taishanese and Cantonese, he told me how my Yeh Yeh—my paternal grandfather—and my dad became displaced. In 1949, after a long civil conflict between the Chinese Communist Party and the Kuomintang (Nationalist Party), the People's Republic of China was established, and the Nationalist government relocated to Taiwan. At the time, the major transitions created fear and uncertainty for many families, including mine. For Yeh Yeh, who had owned land, staying in Taishan no longer felt safe. The fear was palpable—of being taken, of disappearing, of what might happen to someone like him. So he and Baba stayed in Hong Kong, which was still a British colony back then.

When the years passed and hope to return to Taishan dwindled, Yeh Yeh remarried and started a new family in Hong Kong. But it was hard for him and Baba, who had a big falling out and grew more estranged over time. As a teen, Baba had to fend for himself, working random jobs to survive. When Uncle Four revealed this, he broke down and cried.

Captivated and with tears in my eyes, I continued to listen. Uncle Four told me about what his family endured back in Taishan during those turbulent years. Sadly, they became targets during the national upheaval. There was mob mentality during that era. Even villagers turned against one another, driven by survival and fear. Maa Maa, my paternal grandmother, was forced to endure extreme punishment—at one point, kneeling on gravel while she watched other people get executed in front of her. It was a miracle she and the rest of the family survived. But survival was hard. Starving, my family ate tree bark.

The turmoil persisted for years. Uncle Four shared how he had studied to become a doctor—only to have his credentials lost in the chaos. I grieved for him and my entire family, who had their futures derailed. Hearing these stories about my family felt so heavy. I had no idea they'd gone through so much.

Still shocked, I went to my family's apartment the next day. I'd been nervous, afraid of the pain I'd open up in my old home, but at least I felt supported by my husband and son. I needed them and my brother with me as I walked through the long hallway and into each room. A flood of memories and emotions came back, most notably the void without my parents. Tapping into my grief, I decided to finally open my mom's purse. Untouched since her death in 2017, it held the very last items she carried. I had shoved it away in a box, as if preserving her purse was going to preserve her spirit. However, as Atlas hit the keys on my mom's piano in the living room and made a beautiful yet chaotic melody, I knew it was time. Along with Stan, I fished out the items from her purse, examining each one as if we were forensic scientists. There was the spiral-bound book of CT scans from the hospital in Changsha, with cancer screaming across the pages. There was her cell phone, out of battery for the past five years. There was also a plastic water bottle—still half-full—and the prescription medicine that couldn't save her.

I had imagined that I'd be sobbing uncontrollably. But I realized that I had already moved through so much of my grief the past few years. Stan and I decided to throw away the entire purse with its contents, but I did keep one thing—my mother's brown hair clip. I'd bring it back to Berlin, taking a piece of her with me. Every past version of me was proud to be her daughter.

Visiting the places that hurt also had a wonderful side effect I didn't expect—it created more space for joy.

Something shifted in me during the last days of our trip, as if some blocked energy was cleared. My heart exploded when Atlas danced with some elderly ladies at a Chinatown park. My inner toddler danced with him. Then when I visited Fisherman's Wharf with him and Stan, I felt so much gratitude. Standing outside The Cannery, where my mom used to sketch portraits, I cried. I hugged my inner teen, who had subconsciously resented my mom's long work hours but also finally understood how much she'd sacrificed for my family. Afterward, we watched the most perfect sunset at Pier 39 with the sea lions, soaking in the last rays.

By then, the blue skies had returned. One morning, Jacob and I hiked the Lands End Trail, my favorite hike in San Francisco. We had hired a babysitter and wanted to reconnect as a couple in the city where we first fell in love. As we admired the cypress trees at Sutro Baths, where we began our hike by Ocean Beach, we held each other's hands, remembering all the love between us.

I felt myself expand as I stared into the vast ocean and as we climbed the stairs past Baker Beach into the Presidio. As I stepped onto the crisp eucalyptus leaves at my feet, I remembered: *I loved growing up here!* Then, at the National Cemetery where we sat on a bench overlooking rows of white tombstones and the sweeping bay below, I realized: *My parents loved living here too!* My parents—despite being poor for most of their lives—lived an abundant life. America gave them a chance to change their lives—and to change the course of our lineage. They too were breaking the cycle of generational trauma.

Born to them, I was the benefactor of an abundant life. I thought that I'd grown up in scarcity. The truth was that there was also an abundance of the world's beauty, rich culture, and my parents' love. From my backpack, I pulled out a plastic bag with baked buns from Chinatown for lunch. On the pink bag was a red rose and the words, "Thank You!" Feeling overwhelmed with gratitude, I cried tears of joy.

Gratitude extended into the remainder of our trip. I thanked my younger self as I walked by the schools of my youth: Sherman Elementary School, Marina Middle School, and my old Chinese school on Stockton Street. I thanked Jacob as we passed by the Great Star Theater. As a gift from the Universe, someone was working inside the theater and let us in. Sitting amongst the sea of red seats with Atlas, we took a selfie to remind him one day where his mama and papa had first met.

The celebrations continued. I had cake with my friends Rene and Arielle. Then Stan, Vee, and my little family had another dinner at the Taishanese restaurant, this time with my cousins Boning and Yaobin from my mom's side of the family. They were the sons of Uncle Bo and Uncle Wa. Seeing Boning and his wife with their kid reminded me of all the multi-generational meals that my relatives had shared when I was growing up in the city. There was so much love.

On my last day, Stan and I visited our mom and dad at the cemetery. As we burned incense and joss paper for our parents, we thanked them. Seagulls stood on every tombstone around us—nature, divine beings, and the Universe bowing with respect in honor of our parents' lives.

I'd come back to my hometown to meet my younger selves. I left celebrating the woman we'd become.

However, finding out about Baba's past felt like the tip of the iceberg. I wondered how much more lurked within the shadows of secrecy within my family. And I was ready to dig.

Moment to Self-Reflect

Reflecting back on this period brings up so many mixed emotions. I'm glad that we had the opportunity to go back to San Francisco as a family so that I could make peace with my past. However, I still feel immense heartache whenever I think of my dad's childhood and all the hardship that my paternal family went through in China. I'm grateful that I had the capacity to uncover and hear the truth, and I believe that's partially because I'd finally started integrating mind, body, and spirit. From that place of wholeness, I was able to hold brokenness.

Integrating Mind, Body, and Spirit

I believe that integration is one of the most underrated yet powerful aspects of transformation. When I say integration, I primarily mean taking what we've learned and applying it to daily life in the form of meaningful actions and habits that bring us more alignment. As James Clear explains in one of my favorite books, *Atomic Habits: An Easy & Proven Way to Build Good Habits & Break Bad Ones*, tiny changes can lead to massive results over time.

Secondly, I also mean integrating mind, body, and spirit. In the Western world, there's often focus on mind over body and body over spirit. However, somatic healing and spiritual integration are also essential. As I learned, my nervous system had been dysregulated for most of my life, leading to various issues such as hypervigilance, chronic overwhelm, and repeat rage episodes. Believing in something bigger, like the Universe or reincarnation, has brought more peace and meaning into my life. Spirituality could look different for everyone. There are countless religions and spiritual beliefs throughout the world, and there's room for all of them to coexist—just as there's always room for more love.

Reflection Questions:

- Between mind, body, and spirit, which one feels strongest for you right now? Which, if any, feel neglected?
- What small shifts could you make to bring in more balance between mind, body, and spirit?

Places as Present Portals

It can be impactful to revisit places where we lost parts of ourselves in the past and reclaim ourselves in the present. Not only is the present moment a portal for healing, but so are physical places. Going back to feel for my past selves in my hometown was transformative for me. Each time I held compassionate space for the unprocessed emotions from my past as my conscious adult self, I created more safety in my body and with my inner child. I was able to shift from a mindset of scarcity to a mindset of abundance.

However, I do want to mention that it's good to have communal, familial, or professional support for this, as revisiting a place might be difficult or retriggering. Ultimately, you'll be able to sense what feels right for you.

Reflection Questions:

- Are there any physical places that you want to revisit from your past in order to reclaim a part of yourself? If so, where?
- What benefits might you get from revisiting those places?
- Who, or what, might make you feel more supported on your visit(s)?

28

INHERITED PARTS

I COULD NOT stop thinking about Baba's childhood when we got back to Berlin. Learning about the heartbreak that my dad and his family experienced gave me a deeper understanding of who he was. Underneath Baba's gentle and quiet exterior was a lot of pain. Like me, he'd probably repressed so much in order to survive. However, learning about his past also raised questions. *What else happened to my family before I was born? And how does it relate to my rage?*

I did not know yet. But I had to refocus on my own family first, feeling more committed to my husband and son than ever. I didn't want to take them for granted knowing how Baba's family was ripped apart. When I renewed my German visa in March 2023, I applied for a spousal visa, since my husband was a European Union citizen. Old me would've said, "I'm a strong, independent woman! I don't need no man!" But the new me finally allowed myself to rely on someone else. I knew I could depend on Jacob. He was a loving, present, and playful dad. Where I was our child's primary caretaker the first year, it felt like he was the star of Atlas's second year. He made sure that I felt supported, taking over many parenting responsibilities so that it felt balanced between us.

Rewiring my relationship with dependency also shifted my relationship with my son. Instead of resenting his dependency on me, I began to accept it. After all, he'd only be this adorably small once. His going to a wonderful daycare with caring teachers also helped, giving me time and energy back. I bonded with Atlas, celebrating his big personality full of curiosity, excitement, and fearlessness. I held him tighter, even through his tantrums, realizing that they were developmentally appropriate. He wasn't out to get me—he was just being a kid!

However, despite my commitment to our family, I still didn't feel ready for another child yet. I continued to fear that if we had one, my husband would abandon me or live a secret double life with someone else.

In therapy, I learned that the fear might've come from my childhood, in which I'd had to live a double life, afraid to express my true self. There was also a lot of secrecy in my family of origin. *But where else did this fear come from? Was it passed down from other hidden pain in my lineage?*

At the end of March, the Universe guided me closer to my ancestors. In an evolutionary astrology reading with Giorgia, a super-smart astrologer, I learned about my soul's calling to help heal generational trauma in my ancestral lineage. Evolutionary astrology focuses on the soul's growth across lifetimes and offers insights on purpose and lessons in this lifetime. I learned that it's part of my destiny to work with the themes of loss, home, family, roots, culture, belonging, and safety—but in an edgy way where I'd confront taboos. I was blown away. Everything she shared from my birth chart analysis resonated with me.

That spring, my friend Alexandra kicked off another transformative course called "Reclaiming Your Ancestry." In a small group, we explored our relationship with our ancestors and learned how to connect with them through intuitive channels such as meditation, dreamwork, and creative writing. One day, I wrote into my notebook: "I'm a child of our lineage, a carrier of our DNA and pain. A healer amongst us, with great power that you gave me. But how to use it? How to get closer to you? How can I help us? Please give me the language to understand."

What happened next was incredible. I started seeing my ancestors in my dreams. Dai Gu Maa, Baba's eldest sister, appeared one day in a dream, standing by me with a nurturing presence. Po Po appeared in another one, telling me, "Dig further. You're on the right path."

When Alexandra recommended that I read Mark Wolynn's book *It Didn't Start With You: How Inherited Family Trauma Shapes Who We Are and How to End the Cycle*, I ordered it immediately. Mark explains how unresolved trauma that's been passed down through generations could impact us, showing up as unexplained fears or dysfunctional patterns. Even something that happened long ago to a grandparent or great-grandparent could unknowingly impact us.

Through the exercises in the book, I was able to reflect upon my fear of abandonment. I identified that my core fear was that my partner would leave me for someone else. When I journaled about it, I finally realized: There was a huge abandonment wound from Baba's side of the family. He might've felt abandoned after his tragic separation from his family. Maa Maa might've felt abandoned, too, after Yeh Yeh couldn't return to Taishan and started a new family in Hong Kong.

In some ways, my family did live double lives—just as many others did during that time in history. Keeping secrets became a tool for survival. People often felt the need to hide their family histories, personal beliefs, and true feelings—not only to stay safe, but also to protect themselves from their own pain.

I also dug deep into my rage. Although I already knew that it was tied to my own childhood trauma and my mom's rage, I was floored that it likely went further back. During the Cultural Revolution in China, both sides of my family experienced profound loss: of land, property, resources, and the lives they once knew. That's on top of any violence they experienced. Like so many others at the time, they couldn't express their grief or anger openly. They suppressed it for their survival, staying silent to stay safe. But it showed up in my rage.

I wrote to my ancestors in my journal. "I walk with you as you walk away from the land you've known, the people you love, the community who supported you, the home that sheltered you. I feel with you as you feel in your heart the loss, the abandonment, the betrayal, the shame. I hear your stories. I bear witness to your lives. I process what you couldn't at the time. I honor you. I love you."

I'd been so ashamed of my rage. But in a way, it was sacred. It connected me with my ancestors, offering me a sense of belonging. What else could my rage show me? Perhaps it was time to listen to it more deeply and connect with Nej, my shadow self.

After Atlas turned two in April, I finally felt ready to try for another kid. I'd realized that my previous fear of having a second child primarily came from my family conditioning, and emotionally, I felt like I was in a better place. I was also glad to get off hormonal birth control pills and reconnect with my body's natural rhythm.

Unfortunately, Jacob and I still had our difficult moments. I felt triggered when he'd say that I was too negative or obsessed with trauma. Sometimes, I'd try to express my anger, wanting to discuss things in real time. However, I felt urged to let it go. Feeling like I needed to sweep things under the rug pissed me off even more. Inevitably, my resentment would blow over into rage. Once again, I slammed doors and tables, screaming.

Our weekly couple's therapy became a place where I felt safe enough to air my grievances. Unfortunately, that also meant I had saved up so much anger that by the time we met with David in our online sessions, emotions would run high. Whenever Jacob said something that struck a nerve, I'd wonder whether he was projecting his past onto me. Then he'd express that he felt attacked. He wasn't wrong about that. I was ready to fight. Here was the man I loved so much, but when I was angry, he became my enemy.

On some days, I felt hopeful, celebrating that our home felt calmer overall. On others, especially when the rage took over, it felt like we'd made no progress at all. The rage overshadowed everything, leaving little room for introspection and repair. However, that April, I had a huge breakthrough when David suggested I write a letter to Nej. I opened my laptop and started typing a letter to her. However, it wasn't just a letter—it became a whole-ass dialogue between us that looked like a script for a play. I'll share a snippet of it below.

Conscious Jenn: "Hi, Nej. I want to accept you as part of myself. I know that you've been trying to protect me. I've been frustrated with you and all the pain you've caused. But I want to listen to what you have to say. I want to connect with you, love you, and understand you."

Nej: "Thank you, Jenn. Thanks for being open to listening to me. I don't want to be blamed. I don't want to ruin your life. I just want to protect you. Please don't leave me. I'm scared that you don't appreciate me and will abandon me. I'm scared that if you fully heal, there won't be me left. We've been together for so long. I helped you survive."

Conscious Jenn: "I don't want to abandon you, Nej. I know you've done so much for me."

I cried, feeling so much empathy for my shadow self. Through our continued dialogue, which became several pages long, I came to understand that Nej helped me overcome extreme trauma and achieve success in life. That I needed to celebrate her and integrate her.

When I asked her how to do that, Nej asked a surprising question in return. "Mind if I invite Little Jenn to our dialogue?"

Conscious Jenn: "GENIUS! What a great idea!"

Little Jenn: "Hi, everyone. I think I have some explaining to do. Nej, it's me calling upon you, asking you to step in and defend me. I'm so scared of being abandoned. I don't want to be hurt the same way I was in that Polk Street apartment. I don't want to be hurt the same way when Mom would say mean things to me and hit me."

As the three of us continued our dialogue, I realized that Little Jenn trusted Nej to protect her but she didn't trust me, Conscious Jenn, because I'd ignored my inner child for so long. Then Nej would step in, overcompensating in destructive ways. To create safety, we all needed to work together, giving space for each part to feel seen and heard. I also needed to become more conscious of my pain and anger in the present moment whenever I felt triggered and understand its relation to my past. As Nej wisely shared, "Presence is the portal. When Little Jenn is triggered, her feelings are valid and justified, but just in the wrong time frame. It's showing up as the present, but it's the past." By the end of our dialogue, I felt more integration with my parts. We each concluded by saying "I love you" and promised to talk again soon.

Connecting with Nej was such a healing experience for me. It felt like a quantum leap in working with my rage. All this time I'd believed that Nej was unhinged and dangerous. But my shadow self could also be a wise and divine guide. From then on, I started to write dialogue between Nej, me, and Little

Jenn whenever I felt frustrated by my rage. Through one of these dialogues, I was able to uncover some anchors for staying more grounded when I felt triggered. My anchors were: compassion, self-expression, authenticity, agency, and awareness.

One day, I drew Nej in my notebook. With dark hair and a long, flowing robe tied at the waist with a bow, she carried both a sword and a staff. She was an ancient goddess. A strong protector. A powerful warrioress.

However, I realized that I didn't always need protection if I could choose healthy expression instead. Generations before me in my family didn't feel safe enough to express their grief and anger. Neither did I as a child. But I finally felt safe enough to express my emotions now—as the badass sum of my parts, which make me whole.

Moment to Self-Reflect

I'm glad that digging into the shadows of my family's history also led me to dig further into my own shadows. So many things clicked for me. I connected with my ancestors through creative writing and dreams. I connected my own rage and fear of abandonment with my inherited family trauma. I also connected with Nej, my shadow self, who's an essential part of me. Suddenly, I felt so supported with a team to help me break the cycle of generational trauma.

Inherited Trauma and Gifts

Generational trauma can feel nebulous until we learn the stories of our families and the stories we tell ourselves. For so long, I'd believed that most of my limiting beliefs and fears came from my own childhood. But now I can see that they go even further back, beyond my lifetime into ancestral trauma.

I've also come to understand how collective trauma gets passed down through generations. In cases of collective trauma such as war, genocide, revolution, forced migration, political or systemic oppression, natural disasters, or pandemics, the impact isn't just on those who lived through it. Descendants can feel the impact as well. That's why it's important to explore not only our family histories, but also the larger historical forces that shaped them.

While uncovering parts of your family's past may feel heavy for you, it can illuminate truths and bring gifts as well. We don't just inherit trauma from our ancestors—we also inherit gifts. In my family, I inherited my parents' and ancestors' strength, resilience, and ability to rebuild after profound loss.

Understanding what we've inherited from our families can provide clues to ourselves.

Reflection Questions:

- What do you know about your family history?
- What historical events or societal forces may have shaped your family's story?
- Looking at your family history, what struggles or challenges seem to repeat across generations?
- In what ways might some of your fears or anxieties be connected to your ancestral experiences?
- What gifts do you think you inherited from your ancestors?

Working Together with Your Parts

Getting to know our parts can also provide deeper insight into ourselves. Giving space for my shadow self and inner child to feel heard has been a game changer for me, to help me act in more conscious ways. You may see these parts in yourself, or perhaps other parts, such as the inner critic, perfectionist, protector, or people-pleaser. Certain emotions could even be considered parts or characters, as illustrated by the Pixar movie *Inside Out*.

When we don't get in touch with our parts, they can act out subconsciously, leading us to project our unacknowledged feelings or thoughts onto others. For example, someone who's afraid of their own anger could accuse others of being overly angry. Someone who has a strong inner critic can project their own self-judgment onto others by being overly critical. However, there are multiple dimensions to this. Someone who's unaware of their own inner critic might also perceive others as being too critical. Projections are natural in human relating, especially in intimate relationships. They can offer us opportunities to look deeper within ourselves. I admit that I've projected my own stuff onto others before, and I still do. However, becoming more aware of my own projections has been transformative.

If you're interested in learning more, I recommend reading the book *The Archetypes and the Collective Unconscious* by Carl Jung. He also shares about projections, and how they relate to the self, relationships, and the journey toward wholeness. Richard C. Schwartz's book *No Bad Parts: Healing Trauma & Restoring Wholeness with the Internal Family Systems Model* is another great resource. Our parts are not our enemies. They're our friends.

Reflection Questions:

- Are there parts of yourself that you want to understand better? If so, which ones?

- If you invited those parts to meet for a conversation, what would each of them say?

- What parts of you step in when you feel unsafe?

- How could you build trust with your parts so they feel seen and heard?

29

EMBODIED PEACE

INTEGRATING MY PARTS created more safety within me. However, I still didn't feel sustained safety or peace in my body yet. Sure, I'd felt peace in my nervous system coaching sessions, but whenever I'd feel triggered by my husband or son, I still felt a fiery volcano in my body. My shoulders would rise, my jaw would tighten, and my heart would pound. At any moment, I could erupt—and I still did. That's how I knew that I'd need to go deeper into my body.

So in June, when I was thirty-nine, I joined an online course called "Symbolic Initiations" that taught me how to align my mind, body, and spirit in a whole new way. Led by an incredible teacher and somatic healer named Jean-Manuel, the course dove into the main physiological, emotional, and spiritual transitions that we go through in life. From birth to puberty to death, we examined how we grow and unfold over time.

One day, Jean-Manuel invited our class to reflect upon our relationship with health. It shook me to my core. I hadn't realized how much I'd neglected my own health, which was a pattern in my family. Baba smoked, rarely exercised, and died of COPD at seventy-two. My mom constantly overworked, didn't like taking medicine, and died of lymphoma at sixty-eight. Some of my basic health needs were neglected in childhood, and I continued to self-neglect as a result. My heart ached realizing this.

That June, during a dental cleaning, my body communicated its neglect. My gums bled so profusely that the dental assistant struggled to clean my teeth. My breath smelled bad. My gums had started receding. My teeth were covered in plaque. When I made a joke about how I often forgot to brush, she looked concerned.

"This is serious. Your teeth could fall out. The bacteria in your mouth could enter into your body, making you sick. You have to take better care of yourself," she said.

Feeling both grief and shame, I started crying as she continued cleaning. I realized—I don't have any memory of my parents telling me to brush my teeth. Nor did I ever see them brush theirs. They did get me and Stan braces to fix our crooked teeth, but basic hygiene was ignored. It's a miracle that I rarely got cavities.

The dental assistant briefly paused. "Are you okay? Does it hurt?"

"No. It's just . . . uhh . . . I'll talk to my therapist about it," I responded, wiping my tears.

The next day, in therapy with Maja, I realized that health wasn't modeled for me growing up. I came from a family with so much trauma that basic health wasn't the default—it was a luxury. For so long, they'd focused on surviving rather than thriving. *What would it look like to take care of my basic health? Did I even deserve health?*

In Jean-Manuel's class, I learned that our body's symptoms aren't necessarily bad. They're a way of expressing what needs more balance. In listening to our symptoms, we could explore our needs and create more safety for ourselves.

I looked to Jacob as a model for health. He regularly brushed his teeth, exercised multiple times a week, and prioritized his sleep. Not only that, but he was also great at managing our family budget and investing in our shared future. I realized that he was the best partner for me to break the cycle of generational trauma. He embodied so much wisdom. It showed up in his daily actions, like the way he organized things in our home, remained calm through our toddler's meltdowns, and maintained a fit body. Inspired by him, I started to brush my teeth better, use floss, and rinse with mouthwash.

At my checkup a few weeks later, the dental assistant exclaimed, "Wow! Great job! Your gums are healing!" I almost cried happy tears, celebrating how I'd prioritized my physical health. It felt like an inner revolution. An inner reorganization. My nervous system and body were finding new pathways, welcoming the system upgrade.

However, from that place of more embodied health, there was something clawing to come out. It had lived deep within my body, hidden for so long.

My low sex drive could've been a clue. Two years post-childbirth, I still didn't have my sexual appetite back.

Then came my sudden physical aversion to men in public. When I was in an airport security line in Berlin in July 2023, I couldn't stand how close the guy behind me was. I could almost feel his breath on my neck as he kept bumping into me. After putting up with it for a few minutes, wondering why he couldn't give me some fucking space, I turned around. "Excuse me, can you please step back?" I asked. The guy apologized quickly, moved back respectfully, and looked so embarrassed. *Was I just overreacting?*

When I landed in Istanbul to meet Stan and Vee, who were there for vacation, I felt so happy to reunite with them in the seaside metropolis. I loved Istanbul and Turkish culture. However, I hated the uncomfortably long stares I got from men in the streets.

One evening, Stan, Vee, and I went to a popular seafood restaurant with heaps of positive reviews. The fish was fresh, the decor cozy, and the service friendly. However, after we finished our dinner and paid for the bill, the waiter asked for my phone. Thinking that he wanted to take our picture for us, I handed it over. When he went on Google to give the restaurant a five-star review from my phone, I was shocked. *Was that how they ranked so high on Google? How shady!* But not wanting to cause a fuss, we left. Stan and I discussed how uncool it was, but I ended up letting it go. Or at least, I thought I did.

When I got back home to Berlin, something felt very wrong. One morning, while I was standing in our kitchen, I couldn't shake what had happened at the restaurant in Istanbul. Furious, I went on Google and deleted my five-star review. But it wasn't even my review—it was the fucking waiter's! The more I thought about it, the more I felt rage bubbling up. I clenched my jaw. I balled my fists. I screamed in my head. *How dare he cross my boundaries?! I GAVE HIM NO FUCKING CONSENT!*

That's when I had a sudden flashback—to my rape in Madrid. The silent horror of that night in 2012 came writhing out of my body like an invisible entity that'd possessed me for over a decade. I felt a primal rage, wanting to destroy the guy who'd assaulted me. I fantasized about kicking his crotch so hard that his balls would fall off. "I HATE YOU!" I'd shout, standing over his crumpled body, taking my revenge—not just for me, but for every woman who'd ever been violated. But there'd be no revenge. I couldn't even remember his name.

Then came my grief. I wept for my twenty-eight-year-old self who was too scared and frozen to fight back. That afternoon, I told Jacob what I'd resurfaced. It was the first time that we ever spoke about my rape. Recounting the details felt so confusing. I started to question my own version of the truth. *Did I give the wrong signals to Mr. Madrid? Maybe he misunderstood?* Then I realized: *NO! I was asleep! There's no fucking unclear signal there! I DID NOT CONSENT!*

My husband held me in his arms, comforting me. I felt liberated telling him. I was tired of carrying it alone. Not long after, I brought it up in couple's therapy. We talked about how it showed up in my rage and low libido, and how it'd really fucked me up, confirming a belief I'd formed at an early age: *My body is shameful. It's not safe to be in my body.*

But talking about it privately didn't feel enough for me. Emboldened by the viral #MeToo movement against harassment and assault, I wanted to reclaim my body and story. A few days later, I revealed my assault on Instagram with a photo of me in a blue dress and bold text across the photo that said, "I did not consent. My body was not for taking." After unbottling the truth in my public post, I felt a sense of redemption. Twenty-eight-year-old me wasn't abandoned—I was here for her now.

Sadly, just as I'd expected, comments and private messages from other assault survivors came pouring in. I hated that there were so many of us. But I loved that we found solidarity in each other. With mutual empathy, we acknowledged our pain, giving voice to that which had been silenced.

Releasing the unconscious grip that my assault had on me was freeing. I started to welcome more peace in my body. At the end of that July, Jacob, Atlas, and I flew to Sweden for a summer lake vacation. Stepping into the gorgeous design home that we'd rented with our friends, Mathias and Anna and their two kids, I felt my body relax immediately. The floor-to-ceiling windows showcased the magnificent lake in front of us, encircled by tall spruce trees. Over home-cooked meals, marshmallows roasted at the fire pit, and paddleboat rides on the lake, our families formed a tribe. It was hard to leave after our week together in pristine nature where peace was the prize.

Though I welcomed more peace, my body felt drained. What people rarely mention about healing trauma is how much energy it both consumes and releases, and how depleted we can feel as a result. While meditating one day, I saw my mom and hundreds of my ancestors standing before me at a lake. "Rest and peace are the way," they said, staring at me with admiration. I'd been running through life at warp speed in survival mode. It was time to slow down.

I wanted to rest more. I really did. But I still struggled to be in my body, feeling unsexy and sometimes dissociated. I could not relax in my own body. I'd cognitively and spiritually connected with it, but in terms of embodiment, I still had a long way to go.

There was still so much chaos inside. I started to recoil when my husband would lovingly grab my waist. I should've celebrated the physical affection—but my body wouldn't let me. When I brought it into my therapy sessions with Maja, I realized that both my assault and abortion led to some serious sexual trauma. When she mentioned that it sounded like I had PTSD (Post-Traumatic Stress Disorder) symptoms, I felt relieved. It was helpful for me to know that my strong physical and emotional symptoms were flashbacks to a previously traumatic event that made me feel unsafe. I was safe enough to process my sexual trauma now. But sadly, that meant that my PTSD showed up at home, in the form of rage episodes and my unconscious desire to fight. Then came my struggles with Atlas.

When my son started hitting other kids at daycare when he was two years old, I felt ashamed. *Was it my fault? Did I infect him with my rage?* I spent hours online scouring for answers. As I learned, it's totally normal for toddlers to go through a hitting phase. Young children are still developing their language and self-regulation skills, so they might express their strong emotions in physical ways. However, I couldn't stand it when my toddler would hit me at home. I'd calmly tell him to stop, trying to practice gentle parenting. Trying to hold space for his big feelings. But when he wouldn't stop, I'd blow up, yelling at him. "STOP! HITTING! MOMMY!" Then I'd start crying, feeling ashamed of my overreaction.

I felt so frustrated. It was as if I were afraid of my own child—or myself. I never hit my child. But when I was triggered, it took every fiber of my being to hold back. *How was I supposed to embody peace when my kid was hitting me? How could I possibly have done so much work to break the cycle and be subjected to THIS?!* It felt like I was stuck in an impossible situation with no way out.

When I talked to Maja about it, I finally realized that it was triggering because I was having physical and emotional flashbacks to my mom hitting me. I wished that when I was a kid, there was a door between me and my mom. Between her and the wooden sticks she would punish me with. Between the sticks and my flesh as she beat me into submission. I hated the way my mother hit me, that made me hate a part of her, and myself. Especially when she was the person I loved and admired most.

There was so much untapped grief and anger—anger that was supposed to be directed at my mom. I should've defended myself. I should've fought back, but I didn't. It wasn't safe for me to. It was safe for me now. But my rage was directed at the wrong people, creating chaos in my family home.

It wasn't all doom and gloom though. I continued to see how my son was one of the greatest catalysts for my healing. Every time I met him with love, I met Little Jenn with love, reparenting myself. That September, I even co-created an inner child workshop with Lina at a children's café with an indoor playground. Holding space for an intimate group of adults to connect with their inner children felt amazing. Lina and I flowed together as we facilitated fun activities like going down the slide to release limiting beliefs.

However, I continued to struggle with my son's meltdowns. While I celebrated that he felt safe to let all his emotions out, it also made me feel trapped. In my therapy sessions, I came to accept that I likely had Complex PTSD, also known as C-PTSD. Unlike PTSD, which typically occurs after a singular event—like sexual assault in my case—C-PTSD results from long-term, repeated trauma that makes someone feel chronically unsafe, powerless, or trapped. I experienced chronic trauma from childhood neglect and abuse. I also experienced chronic trauma when both my parents fell sick and died.

I had first heard about C-PTSD when I read journalist Stephanie Foo's powerful book, *What My Bones Know: A Memoir of Healing from Complex Trauma*. In her book—which blends storytelling, investigative journalism, and trauma research—she shares her journey with C-PTSD. I immediately loved the book when I first read it in 2022, but for some reason—likely my denial—I didn't recognize that *I* probably had C-PTSD. However, in 2023, when I felt more connected with my body, everything came together and made sense. Sometimes in life, we don't see things until we're ready to see them.

Though no therapist ever officially diagnosed me with C-PTSD, learning about it gave me a useful framework and language to explain what I'd been experiencing. It also gave me so much more self-compassion.

Once again, my rage had guided me to deeper healing. And suddenly, the next step to embodying peace became clear to me.

That October, I realized that for me to truly embody peace, I needed to first believe that peace was possible in my family home. Amidst all the love in my childhood home, there was also a lot of pain and chaos. I couldn't change my past, but I could use the present moment as a portal in my home in Berlin.

So, one afternoon in early October, I performed a sacred psychedelic ceremony to heal my relationship with my family home. Inspired by previous plant medicine ceremonies I'd attended, I created an altar in our living room. I placed a childhood photo of me and Stan with our parents, and a photo of me, Jacob, and Atlas, on a blanket lying on the floor. Then I lit a candle and added flowers to the altar. In my journal, I wrote my intentions: "I believe that the family home is a peaceful place where I can feel safe to be me. I believe in healthy love within my family."

Over the next few hours, I knelt at the altar of my families' past and present, tuning into my intentions. I spoke to my mom and dad. I screamed to them, "I needed you! Where were you?!" I wailed in my grief. I lamented all the things unspoken before my parents died. I let the anger out—the rage for what happened to them that hurt them so badly it made them hurt me too. But I felt so much love too. All the love for my parents and my ancestors. I cried and cried, missing my parents. Missing their love. Missing them missing the birth of their grandson. I walked around, energetically cleansing my home by burning palo santo, releasing any destructive energy. And I forgave. With deep, profound gratitude—for my parents, but also for my husband and son. By the end of the ceremony, I was able to reclaim a sense of safety in my home.

Afterward, I started journaling daily to integrate the ceremony, with my overall intention to believe in healthy love and peace within my family home. Dedicating time for myself to self-reflect each morning felt amazing. I was able to embody more peace, feeling the ripple effect of that within my family. I was able to stay calm and self-regulate when Atlas had big feelings. Also, in my marriage, I felt more safe to discuss triggers and emotions in a healthy way.

From that place of increased safety, I could finally think about sexual intimacy again.

Wanting to reconnect with my husband, I discussed my sexual needs and desires in therapy. However, I was surprised to learn that I still held a lot of resentment from our breakup and the confusing situationship after. I hadn't realized how much this was an intimacy buzzkill for me. I had believed I'd moved on from our past. But clearly I did not. The hurt lived within my body. It acted out in rage. But it was safe to come out now.

I decided to write a letter to Jacob, inspired by my cathartic letters to Nej. I wrote down how I viewed the first few years of our on-and-off dating, and how elements from that time still hurt me. I also asked questions in the letter, hoping to better understand his point of view.

Obviously, I wasn't totally innocent. I had acted in ways that had hurt him too. But writing that letter felt liberating, making all my past selves feel seen. Although I felt nervous about sharing it with Jacob, it felt like the right thing to do.

I couldn't have dreamed of a better reaction. He read the entire letter as we cuddled in bed. Full of love, he acknowledged my feelings and vulnerably shared his perspective from his past selves, answering any of my open questions. I felt so relieved. I'd been fighting him for so long, fighting to defend myself from all the pain from our past. It was time to lower my shield. Most of all, I saw how we continued to choose each other.

A few weeks later, to clear any destructive energy, we performed a closing ceremony, symbolically closing the chapters of our past. At a restaurant, Jacob and I each took a piece of paper and wrote down our answers to two questions: *What do we want to release? What do we want to celebrate?* We then folded the pieces of paper and brought them to one of our favorite clubs. Inside the nightclub, with techno music bumping in the background, we kissed. We danced. We read the notes from our pieces of paper to each other. We celebrated. We released. After we finished sharing our notes, in the most fitting symbolic gesture, we flushed them down the club toilet, letting go of the shit that no longer served us. Our closing ceremony felt so transformative—not only for my marriage, but also for my body.

That November, I was ready to reclaim power in my body, taking it back from the men who had hurt me and my mom who had hit me. In a rage reclamation ceremony guided by my friend and somatic coach Silba, I released the stuck anger, allowing it to flow through and out of me. I rocked back and forth on my knees. I screamed into my pillows. I punched and kicked the air, sweat dripping down my forehead. I cried—but not just for me. For my ancestors who'd survived war and revolution. For all the children who'd ever been separated from their parents. For anyone who'd been oppressed. I felt as if my body was a channel for collective rage.

Afterward, I realized that my body was powerful. That sex was powerful—the ultimate expression of creation in the face of destruction. I'd wanted to embody peace, but I also got back my power. As a beautiful and unexpected gift, releasing the pain created space for pleasure. And I was ready to feel good.

Moment to Self-Reflect

I'm so grateful that my path to peace brought me back to my power. And that my body and rage were such wise guides. As I learned, it's not enough to just *believe* in your worth—you have to also *embody* it. For so long, I felt unworthy until I started healing my trauma, bringing me back to my inherently worthy and authentic self. However, my body was still catching up. My mind had told me that I'd moved on, but my body had not, pointing to the places that still hurt, especially from my sexual trauma. But in that pain, I found a deeper layer of my true self.

Embodiment

Embodiment means being connected to our bodies—sensing, feeling, and experiencing through them, rather than just our minds. It shows up in the ways we move, speak, and act. Embodiment is sometimes in the little things, such as brushing your teeth, taking a nap, or noticing how your heart beats faster during stress. But it means something much bigger. Health. Safety. Peace. Power.

Sometimes when we feel trapped in a current situation, it's because of something that happened in the past. For me, I felt powerless during my assault. I also felt helpless when my mom used to hit me. Those unprocessed emotions and experiences get trapped in the body. That's why it's important to incorporate somatic methods when processing our trauma. Yoga, walking in nature, dancing, shaking our bodies, breathwork, massages, or even punching a pillow are all ways to invite movement and allow processing of emotions in the body.

However, while it's important to focus on the body, it's also critical to connect it to the mind. Embodiment can sometimes feel challenging when we're not cognitively aware of how our beliefs regarding topics such as health, safety, peace, and power impact our lived expression in our bodies. In my case, it took me a while to realize how chaos in my family home impacted my ability to feel safety and peace within my body. Making that connection helped me reclaim my power in a deeply felt way.

Reflection Questions:

- What does peace feel like in your body? How about stress? Or anger?

- What activities or practices make you feel safe and relaxed in your body?

- What's your relationship with health? What about safety?

- How could you reclaim more peace in your body? What about power?

30

LOVE OVER CHAOS

I FELT FIRE burning within me after I reclaimed power in my body. It felt like the flicker of a flame, gently lighting my way back to more pleasure and joy.

It was the fire of candles that lit our dinner table at the end of November, when I was thirty-nine and we hosted our first Thanksgiving feast as a family in our home. We roasted the turkey, which was perfectly juicy, just as Baba had made it before. Atlas dug straight into the sweet potato casserole, devouring the marshmallows as we celebrated with our friends.

It was the fire that burned a letter to my mother, telling her how much I loved her and forgave her, releasing all that'd been unsaid. I delivered the message to her spirit on the other side, watching my words turn to ash.

It was also the heat in my rekindled romance with my husband, where we celebrated the monumental progress we'd made. It felt like a new dawn in our marriage.

Bursting with creativity, I also felt called to work on my memoir again. With Felice's author coaching and manuscript editing support, I'd rework my book from the very first page until the last. The last pages were far from written, and the finish line seemed eons away, but I was finally able to see a path forward. My book baby was gestating and getting ready for birth.

Then it happened again. Just as things started feeling good. Just as there was peace in our home. Just as I thought I'd reached the happy ending I'd always fantasized about on my healing journey. I was a phoenix who rose from the ashes. But I descended back into the flames.

Maybe it was rewriting my book that called me back down to a familiar hell, retriggering my trauma. I was forced to dig even deeper to unearth scenes, memories, and emotions that I still repressed. I started rewriting from Chapter One, reliving one of the worst days of my life. I felt like I was pushing a giant boulder uphill that kept rolling down to crush me.

By December 2023, after I got the first set of edits back from Felice on my first chapters, I almost gave up, discouraged by the sheer volume of changes I still needed to make. The scenes needed more details. The emotions needed more feeling. *What was I even thinking? Was becoming an author too crazy a dream?* I also received rejections from two publishers who had read my book proposal and loved my writing but didn't feel I had a large enough platform to bring the book to the masses.

As salt on my wounds, my family returned to chaos. Winter brought an invasion of germs at daycare, which our kid brought home to us. In between him getting sick, the rest of our family getting sick, and the teachers getting sick, which reduced opening hours, I was struggling. Sleep-deprived and exhausted, I felt my stress skyrocket again. My nerves were frayed. My fuse was short. I felt like I was stuck in a loop.

I'm glad that I still regularly journaled, which kept me sane as I processed the onslaught of chaos. Writing was a spiritual practice for me. Tapping into my intuition for higher guidance, I reflected upon why all this was happening. The answers flowed out of my pen, revealing three big things that my soul was supposed to learn in this lifetime: "1) Expansion within limitations. 2) Stepping into my power to serve humanity, but with care and love for the family and home. 3) I am bound by family but I can also expand through my family, learning lessons from the one we're born into, and the ones we create." Additionally, I received practical guidance: "When peace and love are chosen in my family, then everything else flows."

These were profound realizations. I recognized that my family was in service of my highest growth. That I needed to *choose* peace—even amidst chaos. But I still felt frustrated whenever I was pulled back into the chaos.

When I was alone meditating or writing, it was easy to embody peace and love. However, I didn't live in some crystal cave alone. Whenever I felt triggered by my husband or son, it would send me back to the apartment on Polk Street where I felt trapped. Our interdependency still triggered feelings of helplessness within me.

Our annual Christmas vacation to visit family in Denmark started off cozy and full of love, as it usually did. However, tension grew as the week progressed, replaying a familiar script. Holidays can be such a minefield for triggers and projections. In an effort to focus on what I could change, I wrote during a full moon ritual: "I release the belief that a family traps me. I release my fear of dependency." Basking in the lunar glow, I chose to break free from the loop.

When the clock struck midnight on January 1, 2024, and fireworks danced with stars, I felt both grateful and relieved to have made it through another year.

I love that New Year's often feels like pressing a reset button, kicking off a fresh cycle. I stepped into the new year feeling empowered. Listening to my intuition, I received a clear message that'd become my new mantra: "*Choose love, and love will guide you and illuminate the way.*" It guided me in being more present with Atlas, whom I loved more than ever. It guided me in choosing more peace within my family—even amidst chaos.

Choosing love and peace within my family paid off. That January, we had a beautiful vacation together in sunny Tenerife, in the Canary Islands. As I feasted with my family at the hotel buffet, I felt so much gratitude for our abundant life. I loved watching my son run around on the volcanic, lunar-looking landscape at Mount Teide, as if he were an astronaut. I loved cuddling with him and my husband on our giant bed where we slept together back in Berlin. Many nights, Atlas would fall asleep holding onto the scar on my elbow from my Segway accident. He even had a nickname for my scar:

Scarpie. When he snuggled with Scarpie—my past wound—for comfort, he comforted Little Jenn at the same time.

Love also guided me back to my ancestors. Later in January, I finally booked a trip to go back to my ancestral lands with Stan, wanting to reconnect with my relatives, ancestors, and heritage in Hong Kong and China. The last time we were there was 2017, in the last month that our mom was alive. Watching her slowly die from cancer in China was so traumatic that I wanted to go back and make peace with my past. Eight months prior to my return, in an Akashic Record reading with Alexandra, she'd told me that another pilgrimage to the motherland awaited me. Akashic Records are like the Google database of your soul's past, present, and future, where you can access guidance and insights. Though the reading was mind-blowing, with lots of details including past life memories that I won't share publicly, I didn't feel ready to go back to China then. But I felt ready now. So, I booked the trip for late February, at the tail end of the big Chinese New Year holiday. Jacob was supportive. Stan was available to join. Everything aligned.

At the beginning of February, I turned forty, celebrating with my family in Berlin. I said goodbye to my thirties, thanked them for growing me, and looked forward to the next decade. Professionally, I was on a roll. I was excited about my book again and, through working with Felice, had finally learned how to hone my craft. Receiving her glowing feedback for my writing felt like a huge achievement, propelling me forward with more confidence to finish my book. I also felt blessed to work with my amazing coaching clients.

Leading up to our ancestral pilgrimage, Stan and I prepared by gathering more family research. Not only was my book a container for my healing, but it also was a catalyst for us to find out more about our family history. My brother interviewed Uncle Four again. I didn't expect it to bring so much grief.

I cried upon learning that Baba actually had twelve siblings between his families in Taishan and Hong Kong, but three of his brothers died very young in Taishan. Two before Baba was born and one after. I cried when I learned that my sweet Uncle Six was nearly buried alive in an open grave—saved at the last moment by someone who intervened. I also cried upon learning that Maa Maa, my paternal grandma, suffered so much loss in her childhood. Her mom died soon after Maa Maa's birth, and she also lost her first stepmom from bad cold medicine. Luckily, her second stepmom lived and expanded the family with more kids.

While there were heavy stories, there were also astounding ones from my dad's side of the family. Yeh Yeh, my paternal grandfather, was a serial entrepreneur who had businesses ranging from selling ancestral worship wares to selling handmade jewelry. Going one more generation back, I learned that my great-grandfather once had a farm in Australia but had to leave it behind when World War II began.

For research on my mom's side of the family, I talked again with Uncle Bo, who was going to be our guide in China. I learned through him that my maternal grandparents—Po Po and Gung Gung—had to flee from Japanese soldiers during World War II in China. I was also heartbroken to learn that Po Po had lost contact with her dad, my great-grandfather, when she was very young. He had immigrated to America and worked at a laundry shop in California, making money to send back to his family in China. However, after sending written letters, money, and gifts, he completely disappeared. To this day, no one knows what happened to him. I cried for Po Po, who lost connection with her father. I could see then that the abandonment wound ran deep in my family.

My heart felt heavy, carrying my family's stories. It was as if I felt all of my ancestors' pain. Feeling their unprocessed grief made me feel so connected to them and to my heritage. I felt like I belonged. I read books and articles which helped me understand Chinese history and my ancestors' hardships better. I also read Daniel Foor's book, *Ancestral Medicine: Rituals for Personal and Family Healing*, which helped me understand how to connect even further with my ancestors. Committed to lineage repair work, I was prepared to dig even deeper during my pilgrimage, ready to make the unseen seen and the unfelt felt.

Yet, in mid-February, something in me shifted.

It started when I had an ancestral healing session with Dee, who was a gifted healer originally from China. In our online session, she held space for me to understand the meaning of a recent dream with my mom.

I was back in San Francisco. My mom was healthy. There was no cancer. We were in a white room. I proposed that we go to Union Square, where we spent many magical weekends together when I was a kid. Before we left, my cousin Jimmy stopped by and asked, "Are you ready for the big celebration?"

I proclaimed, "Of course I am!"

I pulled out a duffel bag, unzipping it open. Inside were gorgeous accessories, including a thick, gold necklace.

My mother smiled at me proudly. "Take this energy with you."

My heart burst as I walked over to her and gave her the biggest hug. "I love you. I'm so glad you're still alive."

Reuniting with her was one of the best feelings I ever had. But once I woke up, I felt the ache of her absence.

Now in the healing session, Dee guided me as I closed my eyes in meditation and reentered the room with my mom, curious to know what everything meant. Through our exchange, I learned that the gold necklace was ancient, from Mother Earth, from divine source. But the gold also symbolized generational wealth, love, security, and power that lasted beyond many migrations. My mom handed me an elaborate red and gold gown, which I wore. Then she helped me put on the gold necklace. I realized it was initiation, preparing me to receive my ancestral gifts. Tears streamed down my face as I understood. I felt so much love. Then she apologized for hurting me, telling me how hard her life was with anger that lived in her body. She thanked me for the art gallery celebration of her life, which made her feel seen. I cried, forgiving her. I told her that I'd write about her in my book, that I'd tell the truth of my experience—even the painful parts—so that others could find more love and forgiveness. My mom nodded, telling me that she was there to guide me whenever I needed her. It was transcendent. We had found repair.

A few days later, I felt my mom's presence again during a beautiful ceremony guided by Lina in Berlin. At her apartment, as the sunlight streamed into the living room and medicine music played over the speakers, we sought divine guidance. I asked the Universe to show me what else I needed to see to prepare for my pilgrimage. We closed our eyes, lay down, listened to the music, and meditated as we tuned into our intuition. Sometime during our meditation, a harsh truth hit me: I'd been so attached to my pain, clinging to it like a life raft. Clinging to it as part of my core identity. For so long, I'd run from my pain. Then I became obsessed with it, digging myself into a deeper hole, becoming manic about healing, seeing myself as a project to be fixed. Suffering connected me with my family and the rest of humanity. However, by accessing the divine realm of pure light through meditation and feeling the love of both of our moms in the room, I remembered that there were so many other ways to connect.

Dancing.

Sharing stories.

Eating food.

Laughing.

Then I suddenly realized that Jacob had been right. In the past few years, he'd said that I was too negative at times, too obsessed with trauma. The pain was eating me up. Going from my childhood trauma to ancestral trauma to collective trauma was a wild undertaking. I had chosen to see pain and chaos, letting it consume me, so pain and chaos showed up in our family. How much chaos did I actually invite into my own life? How much chaos did the Universe mirror back to me as I became subconsciously attached to my own internal chaos?

At the end of the ceremony, Lina and I got up to dance around the room as if we were at a festival. It felt like one big somatic release. Happy tears rolled down my cheeks. I was ready to let go of the pain raft and swim to a new raft where I could be creative and live in my fullest expression. Afterward, as I took some time to reflect, I wrote in my journal: "I am not in the past anymore. I am here. I choose to be with Jacob and Atlas now."

When I returned home, I apologized to my husband. For all the times that he chose peace and I chose chaos. The energy between us felt different. I had a choice. I could cling to our past, or I could swim toward our future.

He'd been so supportive all along, being the best dad to Atlas, being the best husband for me. He'd also given me so much freedom to write my book, encouraging me to tell the truth of my experience, even if I mentioned vulnerable aspects of our partnership—even if it dove into taboo topics. I could see it now. I loved him so much. Atlas too, who was one of the greatest gifts of my life. Every time my son said, "I love you" or "I need you," my heart melted. And when he'd ask, "Mama, where are you? I'm scared," whenever he couldn't see me in another room, I'd come running to him, scooping him up in my arms.

With that clarity and that magnitude of love, I kissed my husband and son goodbye and headed to the airport to fly back to my ancestral lands. I was ready to receive my ancestral gifts.

31

ANCESTRAL JOY

THE MOMENT I landed in Hong Kong in late February for our eight-day ancestral pilgrimage, I felt a sense of home. Once my brother landed from San Francisco, we became inseparable. I immediately felt so much love.

Over the next few days, we explored Hong Kong in honor of Baba and Yeh Yeh. We ate *jook* by our hotel in Kowloon, the side of the city where Baba used to live. We burnt incense at Wong Tai Sin Temple, paying respects to our ancestors and Guanyin, the Buddhist goddess of mercy. We also roared with laughter as Stan made fun of me for buying a red traditional Chinese jacket, calling me an *Ah Mo*, Cantonese grandma. But as much fun as we'd had just the two of us, we weren't there to just hang out with each other. We had relatives to see.

Seeing our wonderful uncles, aunties, and cousins in Hong Kong from Baba's side of the family this time felt different. I wasn't dissociated, running from the anticipatory grief of my mom's cancer as I did when I was thirty-three. I was fully present, tuning into each family conversation, hanging on every word as I learned more about my family history from Baba's two half-brothers, whom we called Uncle Seven and Uncle Eight. I was also texting with Uncle Nine and his wife, who joined us virtually from England. Nor did this visit feel like an obligation, something I merely did because my parents had told me to be obedient.

Instead, it felt like one big celebration—one that I chose as my conscious, authentic self. I truly loved spending time with my relatives as we shared stories around the banquet table, eating roast pork and steamed chicken, and speaking Cantonese. I felt deep gratitude as Uncle Eight took us to the crematorium, where we visited Yeh Yeh's final resting place. I thanked my paternal grandpa for everything he'd done for my family. For surviving despite the odds, extending our lineage beyond China to America, Canada, England, and Germany. For his entrepreneurial spirit that he'd passed down to me. Afterward, when my uncles sent me digital copies of photos from my family across generations, I studied each relative's face—each one an extension of myself. The beautiful lanterns lighting up the city during the last days of Chinese New Year reflected how I felt inside—bright and vibrant.

Carrying that light inside me, Stan and I crossed the border into Guangdong Province in Mainland China. We met Uncle Bo and our Auntie in Shenzhen at the train station where they picked us up. I'd been fully prepared to cry, feeling grief in the place where I had my very last meal at a restaurant with my mom. However, revisiting Shenzhen and Uncle Bo's house felt anything but sorrowful. I felt joy in reuniting with my mom's beloved youngest brother, knowing that he also felt joy seeing his sister's daughter and son. My mother had passed. But her love still lived, bringing us together.

Not long after we arrived, the four of us headed to Taishan in Uncle Bo's car. Riding in the backseat with Stan, I marveled at the tall, modern buildings and shiny new cars on the road. Three and a half hours later, we reached Taicheng, a subdistrict in Taishan. For dinner, we ate the crispiest claypot rice with Chinese sausage and smoked duck. It was divine. As we walked around after, I peered into the jewelry shops lining the streets and smiled. In the windows were thick gold necklaces—just as I'd seen in my dream with my mom. They looked so abundant, far from the dire days of famine and war.

The next day, we drove to my dad's ancestral village in Taishan. I had imagined I'd stand inside the ancestral home where Baba grew up, grieving for hours. Grieving for the way that he was suddenly torn apart from his home, unable to see some of his family for thirty years. I also imagined wailing for Maa Maa, who'd lost three young sons. I wanted to process her pain of losing her mom at a young age, and of experiencing so much hardship during her lifetime. But once again, my pilgrimage surprised me.

Although I did shed a few tears for what had happened to my family inside the gray brick ancestral home, I mostly felt happy returning to my paternal ancestral village. I was delighted to reunite with my relatives such as Biu Go, my cousin. As we burnt joss paper and incense at the cemetery where Maa Maa's grave was, I felt honored. Honored to be a descendant of such strong ancestors, who carried the next generation on their backs in cloth wraps. In 2017, I was too distracted by the mosquitoes and my mom's cancer to pay attention. Now, seven years later, I noticed that there were additional burial plots behind Maa Maa's headstone. They were those of my paternal great-grandparents, whom I honored too. I honored all my ancestors before me, who'd lived in Taishan for over 300 years.

In the evening, Uncle Bo drove me, Stan, and Auntie to Chaolian, a subdistrict an hour away in Guangdong. Magenta flowers were in bloom all over, mirroring my blossoming relationship with my motherland—a place I'd previously resented because of all that had happened in my family's past. But where there's a rupture, we can also choose repair. I remembered my mantra: "*Choose love, and love will guide you and illuminate the way.*"

The next day, love took us to my mom's ancestral village, within the Chaolian Subdistrict. I loved hearing from Uncle Bo about how my Gung Gung was a school principal. I appreciated how his love for education was passed down to my mom and then to me. I also loved learning that Gung Gung's dad, my great-grandfather, had studied science and even learned German—like me. Even further back in my lineage, my great-great-great grandfather had several shops in San Francisco Chinatown in the 1800s.

And another ancestor from the Qing Dynasty was sent to the Old Royal Naval College in London to learn military skills. I came to see where many of my own gifts and sense of adventure came from.

When we climbed up a hill to visit the graves of Po Po and Gung Gung, I bowed repeatedly, thanking them. I also paid respects to my great-grand-parents, who lay next to them. As flames burned our offerings, sending resources to my ancestors on the other side, I thanked them for the resources they'd given me. I thanked Po Po for the Honda Accord that she gifted me, which I drove to college and to my first job. She had already passed down her generational wealth to me when she was alive. Not only that, but she had taken such good care of me and Stan when we were kids.

I was not abandoned. I was nurtured.

When we visited my maternal ancestral home, where generations of my family had lived for over 200 years, I felt alive. I felt that the love of all those generations was still alive, even though the home seemed empty now, compared to when fifteen family members had once lived there. Auntie and I picked lettuce in the garden in the back of the home, where several family friends from the village came to grow food. The land provided. The home continued to give.

We took the lettuce back to Shenzhen, where we drove to hours later. That evening, eating a home-cooked meal at Uncle Bo's house felt like the dinners Stan and I used to have with our mom and dad at our family home. The lettuce, grown on the ancient land of my ancestors, tasted extra flavorful. I had come to my senses. I was present. I could taste all the fruits of the labor that my ancestors had toiled through. The labor that almost broke my mom's spirit in the countryside.

Before we headed back to Hong Kong, I asked Uncle Bo where Po Po had studied to become a nurse when she lived in Hong Kong in her teens and early twenties. He told me it was Hong Kong Sanatorium & Hospital. Looking it up on my phone, I couldn't believe that it was right next to a horse track called Happy Valley Racecourse. Baba had loved watching horse races! Wanting to visit where Po Po once worked and where Baba likely watched races, I proposed the idea to Stan. He didn't think that we could catch a horse race though. What were the odds they'd be open on the one remaining day we had left in Hong Kong? Well, the Universe works in beautiful and mysterious ways. When I checked the race schedule, I discovered that YES, it'd be open indeed. Open like a divine portal for us to step into and celebrate our magnificent pilgrimage.

Back in Hong Kong, Stan and I spent the day in Happy Valley, a neighborhood that was so perfectly named, reflecting my overall mood. We visited the location where Po Po used to work. The old hospital was long gone, replaced by a new hospital in a modern skyscraper. It towered over the Happy Valley Racecourse, where Stan and I went afterward. As we walked through the gates, we felt the buzzing energy of thousands of other spectators. As the horses dashed around the oblong green track with jockeys bouncing on their backs, I remembered how much I loved going to the Golden Gate Fields racing track near San Francisco with Baba. I remembered how much he loved betting on the horses with one-dollar tickets, vying for a shot to win big—just as he'd bet his luck on California SuperLotto tickets. Stan and I decided to gamble, betting on horses too. We cheered loudly as they streaked across the track in a blur, but neither of us won.

However, as I took a selfie with my brother in front of the racetrack—as we held up our losing tickets—I realized something so big and beautiful: We *had* won. We had won as the daughter and son of our mom and dad. As the descendants of our beloved ancestors.

I had come on this pilgrimage thinking I was here to transmute my ancestors' pain. But instead, I received the greatest gift of all: Their eternal and infinite love. Their love transcended space and time, as did the joy, talents, and resources that they passed down to us. Their love lived on in all our living relatives, and it'd persist in future generations too.

That love was gold. I'd always been loved. And I finally loved myself. I could feel it in my DNA.

It wasn't just the pilgrimage to my motherland that shifted something in me. It was the realization that I'd come home to myself. My life had been one long pilgrimage back to the real me.

As I boarded my flight home the next day, ready to run into the arms of my husband and son, I felt it deep within my body and soul. I was enough at last—as I was all along.

EPILOGUE

THE OTHER DAY, I felt trapped. I had big work deadlines. My kid was sick again. My husband was in meetings. Everyone was exhausted. I could feel the pressure on myself mounting and my pulse racing. The pattern felt familiar. We'd been in this situation before. And just as I felt like I was going to implode or explode, I realized: *I can choose now.*

I could choose to let go of the immense pressure I put on myself. I could choose to push out my work deadlines. I could choose to nurture my kid back to health, making that the top priority. I could choose to ask my husband if he could shift his schedule around to help. And I could choose not to abandon myself in a locked room, unable to get out.

I'm not a little girl anymore. I'm me now—a powerful, conscious, adult version of me who can choose in the present moment.

I'm not perfect. I still make plenty of mistakes. I still rage. However, I see the patterns faster. I recognize loops. I choose to break cycles.

That's what healing looks like. It's neither an end goal nor a destination to be reached. Rather, healing is a continual, nonlinear journey back to the self. Back to self-awareness. Back to self-acceptance. Back to self-love. Back to self-agency and choice.

Some days can be messy. They can feel chaotic. Emotions might run high. Shit might get real crazy. People might yell. But there's also the ability to bounce back. To recover. To repair.

Staring into old familiar patterns, wounds, and triggers, we can choose to act differently than before. We can express our feelings, thoughts, needs, and boundaries. We can sense into our bodies. We can listen to our intuition. We can ask for help. We can rely on one another. We can build trust within ourselves and in our relationships.

You might've felt helpless before. You might've felt trapped. But you have the keys now. You just have to find the door. And once you look, you'll see that there isn't just one door out—there are many. As you step forward, they appear before you. You can access them. There are possibilities.

You've got this. You can rise. You're enough, as you always were.

With love,
Jenn

ACKNOWLEDGEMENTS

MY GRATITUDE IS INFINITE. This book was born through the support of so many wonderful people.

To my family of origin:

Mommy and Baba. My love for you is all-encompassing and eternal. Thank you for giving me life, raising me, and teaching me so much. The grief of losing you both was enormous, yet it showed me the depth of our transcendent love. Things weren't always easy for us, but I understand now. Thank you for choosing me to be your daughter. It has been a profound blessing.

Stan. Thank you for being the kindest and most hilarious brother I could've asked for. Your support in life, and on this book journey, felt like the biggest gift. Thank you for trusting me to tell this deeply vulnerable story of our family. May truth set us free.

To my uncles, aunties, cousins, and relatives, thank you for your care, your powerful stories of our family history, and your perseverance. We persist and will persist for generations to come.

Thank you to Po Po, my grandparents, great-grandparents, and ancestors, who've been there all along, sending strength, love, wisdom, and resources. We inherit what we can carry.

To my family of creation:

My dear husband Jacob. Thank you for being my partner in life, love, growth, and adventures. Your unwavering support, commitment to our family, big heart, and beautiful mind have transformed me. The home and family we've created is a sanctuary for my soul.

My sweet son Atlas. Thank you for being you—just as you are. You've opened the portal for me to my deepest healing. It is an honor to be your mother, and to love you with a full heart and space for big feelings. Together we break cycles.

To my book family:

Thank you to my incredible author coach and editor Felice Laverne, for your compassionate guidance on this wild writing and publishing journey. You held space for me to write my truth and alchemize my wounds into words.

My accountability partner, writing BFF, and soul fam Savannah Peterson. Thank you for the laughs, tears, cheers, insights, advice, and support on this whole entire book journey. You've been there through it all, almost every week, for years, from page none to page done!

My beta readers and beloved friends Jia Ou-Yang and Nicole DeKelaita. Thank you for your wise perspectives, valuable feedback, empathy, and encouragement. You believed in my story and made me feel so seen.

Gratitude to Caerus Kourt, for working your book design magic on my cover and interior. You designed something that truly captures the spirit of my story.

To my chosen family:

Lily. My BFF since the days of pagers and baggy pants. Thank you for your cherished friendship all these decades, from childhood to motherhood. Growing up with you grew me into the woman I've become. I love you always forever.

Lina. My Brosis. Thank you for inspiring me to live my fullest expression. Times with you feel so joyful, magical, and divine. My inner child is grateful for your inner child. Always.

Niels. Danke for all our deep, soulful conversations and inspiring me to move to Berlin. May we have many dances and dinners together until we grow very old.

Shannon. You showed me how beautiful, vibrant, and full life could be on this earth. Though you've gone to the great beyond, I can still hear your laugh. I miss you, but I feel you. May your brilliant light continue to shine in so many hearts.

Thank you to every precious friend I've mentioned in this book. And to any friend who's ever encouraged me, supported me, and grown me.

To those who held space for me:

To the amazing therapists I've worked with: "Susanne", Maja, and David, thank you for creating a safe space for me to dive deep into my past to break free from old patterns.

To my first coach ever, Lindsay, thank you for guiding me to believe in myself.

Thank you Jana Kobrle and Jenn Katz Brafford, for being such empowering female leaders early in my career. You gave me the encouragement, space, and opportunities to flourish.

Thank you to my therapist friends Anna and Renee, for encouraging me to write about healing trauma through my lived experience and embodied wisdom.

Deep gratitude for every space holder, teacher, and healer I've ever worked with. You're doing divine work.

Thank you also to my spirit guides, higher self, Mother Earth, and the Universe, for providing, guiding, and reminding me that we are one.

And to all of you:

Thank you for doing brave, sacred, and powerful inner work. Together we create the change we wish to see in the world. We are enough.

RESOURCES

Here are the empowering resources I've mentioned in this book, in the order they appear:

Dr. David Burns. *Feeling Good: The New Mood Therapy.*

Michael Pollan. *How to Change Your Mind: What the New Science of Psychedelics Teaches Us About Consciousness, Dying, Addiction, Depression, and Transcendence.*

Tim Ferriss. *The Four-Hour Workweek: Escape 9–5, Live Anywhere, and Join the New Rich.*

Bill Burnett and Dave Evans. *Designing Your Life: How to Build a Well-Lived, Joyful Life.*

Gay Hendricks. *The Big Leap: Conquer Your Hidden Fear and Take Life to the Next Level.*

Sahaj Kaur Kohli. *But What Will People Say?: Navigating Mental Health, Identity, Love, and Family Between Cultures.*

Cheryl Strayed. *Wild: From Lost to Found on the Pacific Crest Trail.*

Amir Levine and Rachel Heller. *Attached: The New Science of Adult Attachment and How It Can Help You Find—and Keep—Love.*

Dr. Bessel van der Kolk. *The Body Keeps the Score: Brain, Mind, and Body in the Healing of Trauma.*

Nicole LePera. *How to Do the Work: Recognize Your Patterns, Heal from Your Past, and Create Your Self.*

James Clear. *Atomic Habits: An Easy & Proven Way to Build Good Habits & Break Bad Ones.*

Mark Wolynn. *It Didn't Start With You: How Inherited Family Trauma Shapes Who We Are and How to End the Cycle.*

Carl Jung. *The Archetypes and the Collective Unconscious.*

Richard C. Schwartz. *No Bad Parts: Healing Trauma & Restoring Wholeness with the Internal Family Systems Model.*

Stephanie Foo. *What My Bones Know: A Memoir of Healing from Complex Trauma.*

Daniel Foor. *Ancestral Medicine: Rituals for Personal and Family Healing.*

For an extended list of curated resources, please visit jennmchoi.com/resources

www.ingramcontent.com/pod-product-compliance
Lightning Source LLC
Chambersburg PA
CBHW021700120626
46545CB00004B/1330